The Drug Supply Chain Security Act *Explained*

Second Edition,
Plus Explanations Of Key FDA
DSCSA Guidances

By Dirk Rodgers

The Supply Chain Security Act Explained
(Second Edition)
Plus Explanations Of Key FDA DSCSA Guidances
By Dirk Rodgers

Published by Dirk Rodgers Consulting, LLC, Naperville, IL
Printed by CreateSpace, An Amazon.com Company
Available from Amazon.com, CreateSpace.com, and other retail outlets

Library of Congress Control Number (LCCN): **2016900493**

ISBN-13: **978-1522904908**
ISBN-10: **1522904905**

RxTrace is a registered trademark of Dirk Rodgers Consulting, LLC, an Ohio corporation.

Cover image: The United State Capital building. Photo taken by the author on November 6, 2013 — just 21 days before the DSCSA became law.

On November 27, 2013 President Barack Obama signed the Drug Quality and Security Act (DQSA)[1] into law, bringing a successful conclusion to efforts by the industry and consumer groups to create a national pharmaceutical serialization and track and trace regulation, one that eliminates the patchwork of state laws in addition to providing new regulations for compounding pharmacies.

This document is an explanation of the **Drug Supply Chain Security Act** (DSCSA) that is contained in Title II of the DQSA with important implications for companies in the U.S. supply chain.

Table of Contents

Disclaimer

This document contains the observations of Dirk Rodgers of Dirk Rodgers Consulting, LLC. It does not constitute legal advice. Dirk Rodgers is not qualified to provide legal advice and makes no warranties regarding the accuracy or fitness of the information contained in this document for any particular purpose. This document is provided "As is". The reader assumes all liability for the use of the information contained in this document. Readers should only make business decisions based on the original text of the U.S. Federal Drug Supply Chain Security Act.

About The Author

 Dirk Rodgers is an independent consultant and founder of **RxTrace.com** where he writes regularly in an exploration of the intersection between the pharmaceutical supply chain, track and trace technology, standards, and regulatory compliance. He has written more than 350 essays on these specific topics. A logical thinker, Dirk is skilled at making complex technical topics understandable to non-technical readers and listeners.

An electrical and computer engineer by education, Dirk has worked as a consultant, software architect, and automation engineer during a career spanning thirty years. In 2002, he joined Cardinal Health, one of the big three U.S. drug distributors, where he studied many approaches to applying serialization and track and trace technology to solve supply chain integrity problems and simultaneously improve supply chain efficiencies. In 2003, he represented Cardinal Health on Accenture's seminal Jumpstart project, an early pharmaceutical supply chain RFID pilot.

Dirk has served on HDMA, NCPDP, EPCglobal, GS1 and GS1 US technical and standards work groups. He served as co-chair of the GS1 EPCglobal Drug Pedigree Messaging (DPMS) work group and the GS1 Network Centric ePedigree (NCeP) work group, among others.

Throughout his career, Dirk's thought leadership has helped to expose hidden complexities and reveal surprising consequences and implications of drug serialization and pedigree laws, while also proposing novel ideas for addressing them.

Contact Dirk at **Dirk.Rodgers@RxTrace.com**.

 http://www.linkedin.com/in/dirkrodgers

 @RxTrace

 https://www.RxTrace.com

Introduction

On November 27, 2013 President Barack Obama signed the Drug Quality and Security Act of 2013 (DQSA)[1,2] into law, bringing a successful conclusion to efforts by the industry and consumer groups to create a national pharmaceutical serialization and track and trace regulation, one that eliminated the patchwork of state laws in addition to providing new regulations for compounding pharmacies.

This document is an explanation of the Drug Supply Chain Security Act (DSCSA) that is contained in Title II of the DQSA with important implications for companies in the U.S. supply chain.

The provisions of the DSCSA have been under development and negotiation for several years[3]. Most recently the industry was represented in those negotiations primarily by the Pharmaceutical Distribution Security Alliance (PDSA)[4], which was composed of representatives from the major industry associations of the U.S. pharmaceutical branded and generic manufacturers, large and small wholesale distributors, chain pharmacies and individual companies[5].

Interest in a Federal approach to pharmaceutical and biologic track and trace was stimulated by the increasing number of State drug pedigree regulations that differed from State to State. Florida was the first U.S. State to enact a pedigree law in 2003.[6] Between 2003 and 2008, nearly 30 states had enacted drug pedigree.[7] The differences between the various State laws eventually led to rising inefficiencies in the operation of the U.S. pharmaceutical supply chain.

The most complex State pedigree regulation — and therefore the most costly with which to comply — was the California pedigree law.[8] This law was the only State law that required pharmaceutical and biologic manufacturers to be involved. It required manufacturers wishing to market their drugs in California to add a unique identifier to each drug package. The need for a unique identifier on each package entering California meant that all drugs in the entire United States would require a serial number because manufacturers could not predict which drug package would eventually make it to California.[9] Furthermore, because manufacturers chose not to use Radio Frequency IDentification (RFID) to carry the mandated serial numbers[10], downstream trading partners would need the manufacturer to capture and pass "aggregation information" at accuracy levels that approach Six Sigma.[11] Aggregation data is the serial number-based shipping container hierarchy used to allow recipients to use "inference" to confidently know which package-level serial numbers they received without opening every container, but instead by only scanning the serial numbers on the shipping containers.[12] The cost of collecting aggregation data at high levels of accuracy was an unexpected expense for most manufacturers.

And so, in February of 2012 the PDSA made public an initial draft of a proposed Congressional bill for comment, known as the "RxTEC" proposal.[13] This proposal was for a nationwide, lot-based track and trace regulation that would preempt all existing and future State serialization and pedigree laws. At that time the goal was to find a sponsor who would introduce the proposed bill with the ultimate target of getting it attached to the Prescription Drug User Fee Act (PDUFA)[14] that was up for renewal that year. Congress must renew the user fee act once every five years to allow the FDA to collect user fees from pharma manufacturers for new drug applications and other services.

A sponsor was found and a bill was successful introduced into the PDUFA 2012 Congressional negotiation process. Congress is always under pressure to enact the PDUFA before the previous version expires in late September of that year. Because of the time pressure, the Congressional Conference Committee was forced to cut off all amendments on a certain day. Unfortunately the pharma track and trace bill was not quite ready to insert as an amendment on that day in June of 2012 so it was cut just prior to PDUFA passage.[15]

The relationships bonded during that experience among the members of the PDSA, Congressional staff of both parties and groups representing consumers ensured that another attempt would be made. In October of 2012 the Senate Health, Education, Labor and Pensions (HELP) Committee and the House Energy and Commerce Committee circulated a draft of a bill that was much like RxTEC but included blanks for people to fill in throughout the document.[16,17,18] The idea was for people to use the draft as a tool to construct a proposal that suited them. These could then be compared during negotiations.

The home stretch toward enactment started in April of 2013, when the Senate Health, Education, Labor and Pensions (HELP) Committee published a new discussion draft with all of the blanks of the previous draft filled in.[19] A few days later, the House of Representatives' Energy and Commerce

Committee published their own draft that had significant differences from the Senate draft.[20] The House bill was introduced and promoted to the full House floor shortly after that.[21] The Senate bill was introduced and promoted to the full Senate floor about a week later.[22] Two weeks later, the U.S. House of Representatives passed their bill.

Unfortunately, the two bills had some significant differences. The House bill would require a purely lot-based system, while the Senate version would implement a lot-based system for 10 years and then elevate to a package-level serial number-based system more like the California law. Even where the two bills were similar, the implementation dates were different. For example, the Senate bill required serial numbers on drug packages in 4 years and the House bill required them in 5 years. To become a law, both houses of Congress must pass the identical text before being signed by the President.

During the 2013 August Congressional recess a group of staff members developed a compromise bill that was introduced and quickly passed the House of Representatives in September.[23,24] Finally, in November the Senate passed[25] the House bill, H.R. 3204, which was then signed by President Obama on November 27, 2013. 1

This document is intended to help people understand this very complex law. It is arranged in the same sequence as the DSCSA. Food, Drug and Cosmetic Act (FD&C) Act numeric references in the DSCSA are replaced with the title of the section, and relative dates are converted to absolute dates. And Dirk Rodgers explains the relationships and significance of each section.

Part 1: The Drug Supply Chain Security Act, Line-By-Line Explanation

This part of the book is a line-by-line explanation of the Drug Supply Chain Security Act.

Overview of the Drug Supply Chain Security Act

The Drug Supply Chain Security Act (DSCSA) is contained within the Drug Quality and Security Act (DQSA). The DQSA was the name of the overall act that was enacted as a single entity, but it is really a packaging of two different acts, represented by the two titles within the overall bill. Title I is the Compounding Quality Act, and Title II is the Drug Supply Chain Security Act, the subject of this paper.

The DSCSA has some similarities to some of the State pedigree laws that preceded it, but it is also a radical departure from those laws because it covers the entire United States and because it is administered by the U.S. Food and Drug Administration (FDA). All drug manufacturers, repackagers, wholesale distributors, third-party logistics providers and dispensers must conform to the law nationwide.

The full DSCSA text is included in the Appendix with the addition of headings for use as references. It includes the following sections:

TITLE II — DRUG SUPPLY CHAIN
SECURITY
Sec. 201. Short title.
Sec. 202. Pharmaceutical distribution
supply chain.

> Sec. 203. Enhanced drug distribution security.
> Sec. 204. National standards for prescription drug wholesale distributors.
> Sec. 205. National standards for third-party logistics providers; uniform national policy.
> Sec. 206. Penalties.
> Sec. 207. Conforming amendment.
> Sec. 208. Savings clause.

These section numbers, 201 through 208, are relative to the DQSA document itself, but within the bill text there are references to new and existing sections in the Federal Food, Drug and Cosmetics Act (FD&C).[26] These include the following new sections:

- Section 581, Definitions
- Section 582, Requirements
- Section 583, National Standards for Prescription Drug Wholesale Distributors
- Section 584, National Standards for Third-Party Logistics Providers
- Section 585, Uniform National Policy

To make things even more confusing, federal bills are designed to update something known as the "United States Code", or U.S.C., which uses different section numbing, so it is common to see text like this:

> "Section 503(d) (21 U.S.C. 353(d)) is amended by adding at the end the following:…"

Here "Section 503(d)" refers to the section of the FD&C that is being amended, and "21 U.S.C. 353(d)" is the matching section of the United State Code that is also being amended.[27] In this example from the DSCSA, both the FD&C and the U.S.C. are being amended by some specific text (not shown).

FD&C section numbers appear here — In this document the section of the FD&C that is most pertinent to the text is printed in the left margin to help the reader jump to the corresponding section of the actual DSCSA contained in the Appendix.

The Sequence of the DSCSA Provisions

The sequence of "The Drug Supply Chain Security Act, Explained" is designed to match that of the DSCSA itself. This may seem a little odd, since the DSCSA starts out with what, at first glance, appears to be just a glossary. In fact, Section 581 "Definitions" is not just a glossary but one of the most important sections of the entire law, which justifies its position as the first section of the DSCSA and of this document.

This section is a list of terms with definitions that apply within the remainder of the DSCSA. The reader is cautioned that most of the definitions of these terms are *not equivalent* to their common or dictionary definitions.[28] In fact, the definitions of terms like "product" and "transaction" include important exemption language that is vital to understanding the application of the law. Do not skip the Definitions section in your study.

Implementation Timelines

The DSCSA is loaded with dates for the activation of various provisions. Some of those dates establish obligations on the FDA to take some action by those dates. Other dates are aimed at various segments of the participants in the U.S. pharma supply chain.

FDA Timeline

In late February of 2014, the FDA published the following timeline that represents their interpretation of their DSCSA deliverables and actions (see Figure 1 below).[29]

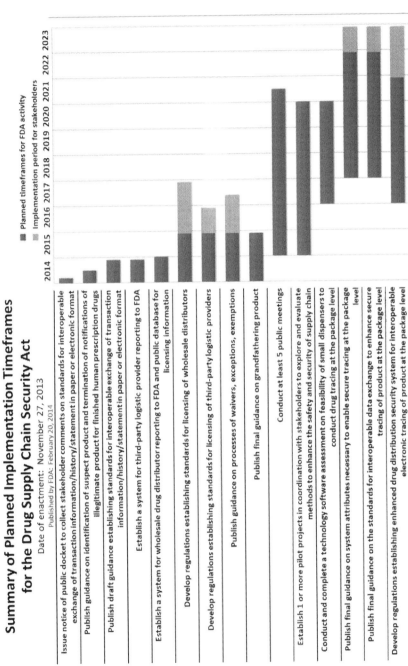

Figure 1. Summary of Planned Implementation Timeframes for the Drug Supply Chain Security Act. Published by the FDA on February 20, 2014.

There is an unfortunate timing situation in the DSCSA that came about as the result of Congress mixing fixed dates with dates that are relative to the enactment of the law. The problem is that as time dragged on while the bill was being debated in Congress, the two types of dates became very close. The fixed date is January 1, 2015, when some members of the supply chain were to begin passing specific data to their trading partners with each change in ownership. The date that is relative to enactment of the law was for the FDA to publish guidance to tell those companies exactly *how* to pass that data.

As it turned out, because the bill was signed into law on November 27, 2013, the FDA had until November 27, of 2014 — one year after enactment — to publish that draft guidance [see Section 582(a)(2), "Initial Standards"]. This left companies only 5 weeks to implement any specific guidance included in that draft. Figure 2 shows this problem on a timeline.

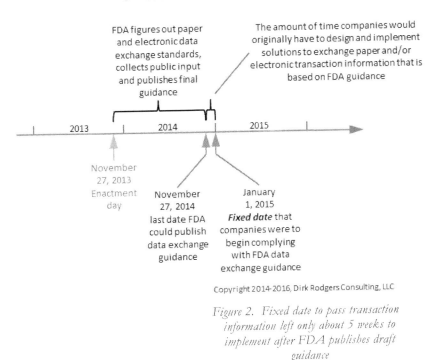

Figure 2. Fixed date to pass transaction information left only about 5 weeks to implement after FDA publishes draft guidance

However, in late December of 2014 the FDA issued guidance that indicated they would not enforce the data exchange requirement on manufacturers, wholesale distributors and repackagers until May 1, 2015, thus opening this gap by an additional four months.

Manufacturer Timeline

Figure 3 summarizes the key DSCSA dates that pharma **manufacturers** should pay close attention to.

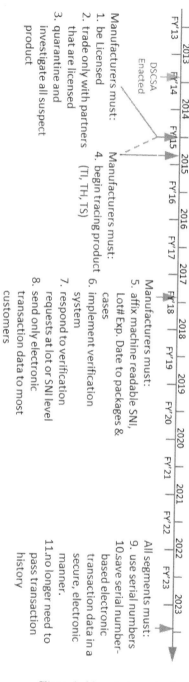

Figure 3. Manufacturer timeline showing key dates

The table below summarizes the key sections of the DSCSA that specify the important dates for manufacturers.

Date	DSCSA Sections	Section Title	Notes
January 1, 2015	582(a)(2)	Initial Standards	
	582(a)(5)	Grand-fathering Product	
	582(b)(1)	Manufacturer: Product Tracing	Enforcement deferred to May 1, 2015
	582(b)(3)	Manufacturer: Authorized Trading Partners	
	582(b)(4)	Manufacturer: Verification	
	503(d)(4)	Authorized Distributors of Record	Relating to the distribution of drug samples
	585	Uniform National Policy	PDMA is eliminated
November 27, 2015	582(a)(3)	Waivers, Exceptions and Exemptions	
November 27, 2017	582(b)(1)	Manufacturer: Product Tracing	
	582(b)(2)	Manufacturer: Product Identifier	
	582(b)(4)(A)	Manufacturer: Suspect Product	
	582(b)(4)(C)	Manufacturer: Requests For	

		Verification	
	582(b)(4)(E)	Manufacturer: Saleable Returned Product	
November 27, 2023	582(g)(1)	EDDS: In General	
	582(k)	Sunset	
	582(m)	Requests For Information	

Wholesale Distributor Timeline

Figure 4 summarizes the key DSCSA dates that pharma wholesale distributors should pay close attention to.

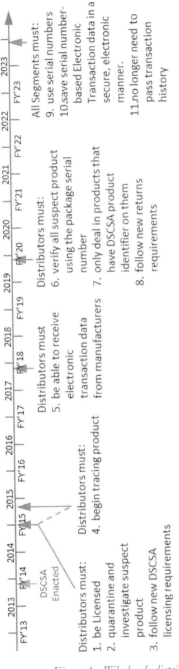

The timeline shows key dates along the years FY'13 through FY'23.

DSCSA Enacted (FY'14)

Distributors must:
1. be Licensed
2. quarantine and investigate suspect product
3. follow new DSCSA licensing requirements

Distributors must:
4. begin tracing product

Distributors must
5. be able to receive electronic transaction data from manufacturers

Distributors must:
6. verify all suspect product using the package serial number
7. only deal in products that have DSCSA product identifier on them
8. follow new returns requirements

All Segments must:
9. use serial numbers
10. save serial number-based Electronic Transaction data in a secure, electronic manner.
11. no longer need to pass transaction history

Figure 4. Wholesale distributor timeline showing key dates

The table below summarizes the key sections of the DSCSA that specify the important dates for **wholesale distributors**.

Date	DSCSA Sections	Section Title	Notes
January 1, 2015	582(a)(2)	Initial Standards	
	582(a)(5)	Grand-fathering Product	
	582(c)(1)	Wholesale Distributor: Product Tracing	Enforcement deferred to May 1, 2015
	582(c)(3)	Wholesale Distributor: Authorized Trading Partners	
	582(c)(4)	Wholesale Distributor: Verification	
	503(d)(4)	Authorized Distributors of Record	Relating to the distribution of drug samples
	583	The New National Standards for Wholesale Distributors	New licensing program
	585	Uniform National Policy	PDMA is eliminated
November 27, 2015	582(a)(3)	Waivers, Exceptions and Exemptions	
November 27, 2017	582(c)(1)	Wholesale Distributor: Product Tracing	Electronic data received from manufacturers

November 27, 2019	582(c)(1)(B)	Wholesale Distributor: Returns	
	582(c)(1)(D)	Wholesale Distributor: Trading Partner Agreements	
	582(c)(2)	Wholesale Distributor: Product Identifier	
	582(c)(4)(A)	Wholesale Distributor: Suspect Product	
	582(c)(4)(D)	Wholesale Distributor: Verification of Saleable Returned Product	
November 27, 2023	582(g)(1)	EDDS: In General	
	582(k)	Sunset	
	582(m)	Requests For Information	

Dispenser Timeline

Figure 5 summarizes the key DSCSA dates that pharma dispensers should pay close attention to.

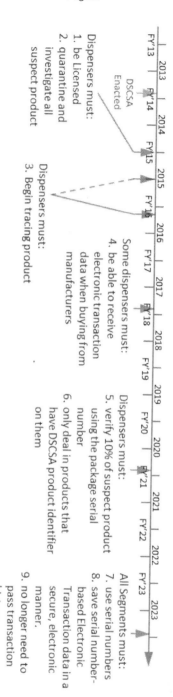

Figure 5. Dispenser timeline showing key dates

The table below summarizes the key sections of the DSCSA that specify the important dates for dispensers.

Date	DSCSA Sections	Section Title	Notes
January 1, 2015	582(a)(2)	Initial Standards	
	582(a)(5)	Grand-fathering Product	
	582(d)(3)	Dispenser: Authorized Trading Partners	
	582(d)(4)	Dispenser: Verification	
	585	Uniform National Policy	PDMA is eliminated
	582(a)(3)	Waivers, Exceptions and Exemptions	
July 1, 2015	582(d)(1)	Dispenser: Product Tracing	Enforcement deferred to March 1, 2016
November 27, 2017	582(d)(1)	Dispenser: Product Tracing	Some may need to receive data from manufacturers electronically
November 27, 2020	582(d)(2)	Dispenser: Product Identifier	
	582(d)(4)(A)	Dispenser: Suspect Product	
November 27, 2023	582(g)(1)	EDDS: In General	
	582(k)	Sunset	
	582(m)	Requests	

		For Information	

Repackager Timeline

Figure 6 summarizes the key DSCSA dates that pharma repackagers should pay close attention to.

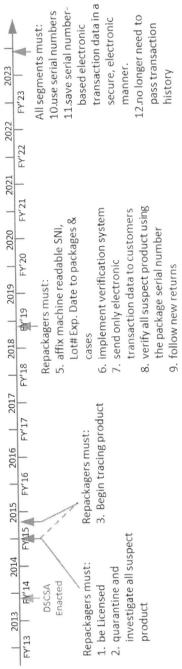

Figure 6. Repackager timeline showing key dates

The table below summarizes the key sections of the DSCSA that specify the important dates for repackagers.

Date	DSCSA Sections	Section Title	Notes
January 1, 2015	582(a)(2)	Initial Standards	
	582(a)(5)	Grand-fathering Product	
	582(e)(1)	Repackager: Product Tracing	Enforcement deferred to May 1, 2015
	582(e)(3)	Repackager: Authorized Trading Partners	
	582(e)(4)	Repackager: Verification	
	585	Uniform National Policy	PDMA is eliminated
	582(a)(3)	Waivers, Exceptions and Exemptions	
November 27, 2017	582(e)(1)	Repackager: Product Tracing	Electronic data received from manufacturers
November 27, 2018	582(e)(2)	Repackager: Product Identifier	
	582(e)(4)(A)	Repackager: Suspect Product	
	582(e)(4)(C)	Repackager: Requests For Verification	
	582(e)(4)(E)	Repackager: Verification	

		of Saleable Returned Product	
November 27, 2023	582(g)(1)	EDDS: In General	
	582(k)	Sunset	
	582(m)	Requests For Information	

Third-Party Logistics Provider Timeline

The table below summarizes the key sections of the DSCSA that specify the important dates for Third-Party Logistics Providers.

Date	DSCSA Sections	Section Title	Notes
November 27, 2014	584(b)	Reporting	Begin annual reporting to FDA
January 1, 2015	584	The New National Standards for Third Party Logistics Providers	

How to Determine if You Must Comply with the DSCSA

At one point or another, all members of the U.S. pharma supply chain will need to be able to determine if a given product in a given transaction must comply with the DSCSA or not. Obviously, manufacturers experienced that need first, but because the DSCSA requires all companies to execute DSCSA-specific actions on drugs that are not exempt, wholesale distributors, repackagers and dispensers also need to determine if a given product is included. Be aware that your determination may differ from others, but every company will likely be held responsible for making their own determination. You may not want to rely on the determination of upstream trading partners in some cases.

Here is a sequence of steps that anyone can follow to help determine if a given product must comply with the DSCSA in a given transaction.

1) If the item in question is included in one of the exempt categories listed in Section 581(13), the definition of "product", then the item is not a product, and therefore transactions involving that product do not need to comply with the DSCSA. If you are unsure if the item falls into one of these categories, contact the FDA for help;

2) If your transaction involving the product is included in one of the exempt categories listed in Section 581(24), the definition of "transaction", then your transaction is not a

DSCSA transaction, and therefore it does not need to comply with the DSCSA. Again, if you are unsure if your transaction fits into one of those categories, contact the FDA for help;

3) If your product and your transaction are covered by the DSCSA, you should then confirm that you are one of the covered entities: manufacturer, wholesale distributor, dispenser or repackager. If you are not one of these entities and you are handling the product in an otherwise legal way, then you are not covered by the DSCSA.

Be careful with this one. Check Section 581(10), the definition of "manufacturer", to determine if you are considered the DSCSA manufacturer. In some cases, you will want to determine whether or not a trading partner is considered the DSCSA manufacturer to determine if you are treated as the manufacturer or a wholesale distributor. In the case of a co-licensed partner of a product, it appears that both companies are treated by the DSCSA as the manufacturer of that product. In that case, both organizations should follow the manufacturer regulations. If you are not sure, check with the FDA.

The definition of dispenser, Section 581(3), excludes those who dispense drugs to animals but appears to include individual practitioners like pharmacists, physicians, nurse practitioners, dentists, and other healthcare professionals who are *"authorized by law to dispense or administer prescription drugs*", in addition to pharmacy companies. If you only dispense the product to animals, then your transactions with this product does not need to comply with the DSCSA.

The definition of repackager, Section 581(16), is fairly straightforward. Any entity that *takes ownership* of drugs in the supply chain that is not a DSCSA manufacturer, a DSCSA repackager or DSCSA dispenser is therefore a DSCSA wholesale distributor. Because the definition of third party logistics provider [Section 581(22)] includes only organizations that do not take ownership of a product, these organizations are not one of the covered parties in the supply chain, although 3PLs must follow the new 3PL licensing requirements.

Foundation Provisions That Apply to All Members of the Supply Chain, Explained

The DSCSA creates a new subchapter, H, within Chapter V of the Food, Drug and Cosmetics Act (FD&C). The new Chapter H, "Pharmaceutical Distribution Supply Chain," holds most of the new regulations contained in the DSCSA. FD&C Section 581 contains the definitions of terms that are critically important through the remaining sections. These exact definitions apply only within the DSCSA itself and for that reason they can be quite narrow and specific to the situation. These definitions should not be confused with dictionary definitions of these terms. In some cases, the dictionary definition would be significantly different from the definitions section of the DSCSA.

581 Definitions, Explained

The definitions below are usually partially paraphrased and occasionally verbatim. For the full definitions, please use the hyperlinks in the left margin to jump to the official text of the DSCSA.

581(1) The definition of **AFFILIATE** is important because it is used to exempt affiliated entities from some provisions of the law. It is also used in the definition of "Manufacturer" below. Companies are affiliated if one controls, or has the power to control, the other, directly or indirectly, or if a third company controls or has the power to control the other two.

581(2)   The definition of **AUTHORIZED** is important because it establishes the foundational requirement of each entity that may participate in the U.S. drug supply chain. Authorization is granted through one of several kinds of licenses, provided by appropriate State and/or Federal agencies. For manufacturers and repackagers, a valid registration with the FDA under Section 510 of the FD&C is sufficient. For wholesale distributors and third-party logistics providers, a valid State license (presumably a State license within each State in which business is conducted) or a federal license as described in the DSCSA is required. For dispensers, a valid license under State law where they operate is required. See also "Licensed".

581(3)   The definition of **DISPENSER** is important because the law uses the term to refer to the collection of organizations that dispense drugs directly to human patients. These include "...*retail pharmacy, hospital pharmacy, a group of chain pharmacies under common ownership and control that do not act as a wholesale distributor, or any other person authorized by law to dispense or administer prescription drugs, and the affiliated warehouses or distribution centers of such entities under common ownership and control that do not act as a wholesale distributor...*". It does NOT include a person who dispenses only products to be used in animals.

This definition *appears* to not only include pharmacy companies but also individual practitioners, including pharmacists, physicians, nurse practitioners, dentists, and other healthcare professionals who are *"authorized by law to dispense or administer prescription drugs"*.

581(4) The definition of **DISPOSITION** is quite a bit different from the dictionary definition so be careful when you read it in this law. It reads, *"...with respect to a product within the possession or control of an entity, means the removal of such product from the pharmaceutical distribution supply chain, which may include disposal or return of the product for disposal or other appropriate handling and other actions, such as retaining a sample of the product for further additional physical examination or laboratory analysis of the product by a manufacturer or regulatory or law enforcement agency."*

In other words, to *disposition* a drug is to remove it from the forward logistical pharmaceutical supply chain. A drug that has previously been "dispositioned" should never again appear in the forward supply chain without becoming a "suspect product".

581(5) The definition of **DISTRIBUTE OR DISTRIBUTION** means the sale, purchase, trade, delivery, handling, storage, or receipt of a product, but the DSCSA explicitly excludes the dispensing of a product to fill a prescription.

581(6) There are no surprises in the definition of **EXCLUSIVE DISTRIBUTOR**. They must purchase a product directly from the manufacturer and they are the sole distributor *"of that manufacturer's product to subsequent..."* supply chain parties.

581(7) The definition of **HOMOGENEOUS CASE** is as expected. It means a sealed case containing only product that has a single NDC and *belonging to a single lot.* It would have been helpful if Congress had also specified that the quantity of units contained in the case conforms to a standard grouping offered by the manufacturer or repackager, but it doesn't.

581(8)   The definition of **ILLEGITIMATE PRODUCT** includes any product where there is *credible evidence* that it is:
  - Counterfeit;
  - Diverted;
  - Stolen;
  - Intentionally adulterated such that it would cause serious adverse health consequences or death to humans;
  - The subject of a fraudulent transaction;
  - Appears otherwise unfit for distribution.

581(9)   The definition of **LICENSED** is as you would expect. For wholesale distributors and third-party logistics providers, having a valid license from the FDA and/or the State(s) in which they are doing business. See also "Authorized" above.

581(10)   The definition of **MANUFACTURER** is important for understanding exactly who needs to comply with the manufacturer regulations. It includes the following:

  1. An approved New Drug Application (NDA)[30]-holder;
  2. An approved Abbreviated New Drug Application (ANDA)[31]-holder;
  3. An approved Biologic License Application (BLA)-holder;
  4. The manufacturer of a product that is not

subject to approval of 1-3 above;

5. A co-licensed partner of the person in 1-4 above as long as they obtain the product directly from the manufacturer as defined here;

6. An affiliate (see definition above) of a person described in 1-5 above that receives the product directly from a person described in 1-5 above.

It appears that this definition does *not* include contract organizations who manufacturer and/or package product on behalf of the true manufacturer (as defined above) under the terms of a contract.

581(11) The definition of **PACKAGE** determines what needs to be serialized elsewhere in the text. In general, a "package" is the smallest individual saleable unit of product for distribution by a manufacturer or repackager that is intended by the manufacturer for ultimate sale to the dispenser. The key here is the phrase "intended by the manufacturer". Wholesaler distributors and others will no longer be able to break down a package of multiple units to sell to a customer who doesn't want to buy the whole package if the manufacturer did not intend for the product to be sold that way. The law further defines what is meant by "individual saleable unit". It is the smallest container of product introduced into commerce by the manufacturer or repackager that is intended by that company for individual sale to a dispenser.

581(12) A **PRESCRIPTION DRUG** is a drug for human use that is subject to FD&C section 503(b)(1). That is, if the law already requires you to mark your product with the symbol "Rx Only", then your product is a prescription drug in the DSCSA.

581(13) The word **PRODUCT** is used in numerous places in the DSCSA. The law defines the term as a prescription drug in a finished dosage form for administration to a patient without substantial further manufacturing. But according to the DSCSA, the following are NOT "products", so they are exempt from the law:

- Blood or blood components intended for transfusion
- Radioactive drugs or radioactive biological products that are already regulated by the Nuclear Regulatory Commission or by a State
- Imaging drugs
- Medical gases
- Appropriately marked homeopathic drugs
- Compounded drugs
- Intravenous products that are intended for the replenishment of fluids and electrolytes or calories
- Intravenous products used to maintain the equilibrium of water and minerals in the body, such as dialysis solutions
- Products intended for irrigation, or sterile water, whether intended for such purposes or for injection.

See the text of the law for the exact wording and interpretation. If you think your product fits one of these exemptions, then it is not a "product" within the DSCSA regulations. That doesn't mean you can ignore the entire law, but it does mean that most of it will not apply to your non-product product since the main provisions of the law deal with supply chain transactions that involve "products".

581(14) A **PRODUCT IDENTIFIER** is a standardized graphic that includes the standardized numerical identifier (SNI), lot number and the expiration date of the product. The FDA published a non-binding guidance document in March of 2010 that defined the SNI as the NDC of the product combined with a unique alphanumeric serial number.[32,33] In that guidance, the FDA identified the GS1 GTIN plus serial number construct as an example of a compliant SNI.

The DSCSA defines the product identifier to be a standardized graphic that is presented on the product package in both human-readable form and within "...a machine-readable data carrier that conforms to the standards developed by a recognized international standards development organization". The term "data carrier" is not defined within the law but, because the product identifier is defined as "...a standardized graphic...", the most logical data carrier is a barcode of some kind.

Within the requirements of FD&C Section 582(a)(9), we will find that the DSCSA narrows this standardized graphic specifically to a two-dimensional (2D) data matrix barcode on packages and a linear or 2D data matrix barcode on cases, but it also allows the FDA to specify other acceptable data carrier technologies through further guidance.

581(15) The term **QUARANTINE** means the storage or identification of a product in a physically separate area, or through other procedures, to prevent further distribution or transfer of products placed there. The separate area must be clearly identified as being specifically for quarantine purposes.

581(16)   The law defines the term **REPACKAGER** as an owner or operator of an establishment that repacks and relabels a product or package for further sale or for distribution without a further transaction. This definition seems to include both commercial repackagers and private, in-house repackaging departments within hospital networks.

581(17)   The term **RETURN** means providing product to the authorized immediate trading partner from which a product was purchased or received, or to a returns processor or reverse logistics provider for handling.

581(18)   A **RETURNS PROCESSOR OR REVERSE LOGISTICS PROVIDER** is an owner or operator of an establishment that "dispositions" or otherwise processes saleable or nonsaleable product received from an "authorized" trading partner such that the product may be processed for credit to the purchaser, manufacturer, or seller or disposed of for no further distribution. This definition makes use of the defined terms "disposition" and "authorized". Remember that the definition of "disposition" is not the definition you would normally expect. Overall the definition of "returns processor or reverse logistics provider" seems to include the processing of product that will never be redistributed as well as product that may be redistributed back into the forward supply chain. Hopefully the FDA will make that clearer.

581(19)   The term **SPECIFIC PATIENT NEED** refers to the transfer of a product from one pharmacy to another only to fill a prescription *for a specifically identified patient*. It does not include the transfer of products from one pharmacy to another just to increase or replenish stocking levels.

581(20) **STANDARDIZED NUMERICAL IDENTIFIER** is defined in the DSCSA as a set of numbers or characters used to uniquely identify each package or homogenous case that is composed of the National Drug Code (NDC)[34] that corresponds to the specific product (including the particular package configuration) combined with the unique alphanumeric serial number of up to 20 characters.

This definition is a good summary of the SNI guidance published by the FDA in March of 2010[35]. This makes the SNI now defined by an act of Congress rather than just by the FDA—at least these essential characteristics.

Some have confused the phrase "a set of numbers or characters" to imply that the SNI is alphanumeric. In fact that is not entirely the case because the SNI includes the NDC, which by FDA definition is all numeric. This leaves only the unique serial number component as possibly containing alphas.

581(21) The term **SUSPECT PRODUCT** takes a special place within the DSCSA because each type of participant in the supply chain must take specific actions whenever they encounter it. Within the DSCSA, the term means a product for which there is reason to believe it is potentially an "illegitimate product" (see definition above), or appears otherwise unfit for distribution such that the product would result in serious adverse health consequences or death to humans. The key words here are "potentially" and "appears". Suspect product may turn out to be fine, or it may turn out to be actually illegitimate or unfit, but until that determination has been made, it is considered "suspect".

581(22) The term **THIRD-PARTY LOGISTICS PROVIDER** (3PL) is defined as an entity that provides or coordinates warehousing, or other logistics services of a product in interstate commerce on behalf of a manufacturer, wholesale distributor, or dispenser of a product, but does not take ownership of the product, nor have responsibility to direct the sale or "disposition" of the product.

581(23) The term **TRADING PARTNER** includes a manufacturer, repackager, wholesale distributor, or dispenser from whom a manufacturer, repackager, wholesale distributor or dispenser accepts direct ownership of a product, or to whom a manufacturer, repackager, wholesale distributor, or dispenser transfers direct ownership of a product. This includes a third-party logistics provider from whom a manufacturer, repackager, wholesale distributor or dispenser accepts direct possession of a product or to whom a manufacturer, repackager, wholesale distributor or dispenser transfers direct possession of a product. Basically this includes all companies that own products in the supply chain, plus 3PLs (who don't actually take ownership of products).

581(24) The definition of the term **TRANSACTION** is very important because it is the concept that the DSCSA uses to regulate the supply chain. In general, if you have not produced a transaction as defined here, then you are not impacted by most of the DSCSA. The law defines a transaction to be the transfer of product between persons *in which a change of ownership occurs*. That's it, except the definition then goes on to enumerate 18 different circumstances that are *exempt* from that definition and are therefore not a transaction. These exemptions are paraphrased here. Please check the original text and make your compliance decisions based on it.

i.   Intracompany distribution of any product between members of an affiliate or within a manufacturer;

ii. The distribution of a product among hospitals or other health care entities that are under common control;

iii. The distribution of a product for emergency medical reasons, except that a drug shortage not caused by a public health emergency shall not constitute an emergency medical reason;

iv. The dispensing of a product to fill a prescription;

v.   The distribution of product samples by a manufacturer or a licensed wholesale distributor;

vi. The distribution of blood or blood components intended for transfusion;

vii. The distribution of minimal quantities of product by a licensed retail pharmacy to a licensed practitioner for office use;

viii. The lawful sale, purchase or trade of a drug or an offer to sell, purchase or trade a drug by a 501(c)(3) charitable organization to a nonprofit affiliate of the organization;

ix. The distribution of a product that is acquired as part of the sale or merger of a pharmacy or pharmacies or a wholesale distributor or wholesale distributors, as long as any records required to be maintained for the product are transferred to the new owner;

x.   The dispensing of an approved product for use

in animals;

xi. Products transferred to or from any facility that is licensed by the Nuclear Regulatory Commission (NRC) or by a State under an agreement with the NRC;

xii. The distribution of a combination product that is regulated by the FDA as a device primary mode of action (PMOA),[36] including "medical convenience kits" as described below

xiii. The distribution of "medical convenience kits", a collection of finished medical devices, which may include a product or biological product, assembled in kit form strictly for the convenience of the purchaser or user, if:

    I. the kit is assembled in an establishment that is registered by the FDA as a *device manufacturer*;

    II. the kit does not contain any controlled substance; and

    III. the kit manufacturer purchased the product contained in the kit directly from the pharmaceutical manufacturer or from a wholesale distributor that purchased it directly from the pharmaceutical manufacturer, and the primary container label of the product contained in the kit is not altered;

    IV. and the product contained in the kit is:

        • An intravenous solution intended for the replenishment of fluids and electrolytes;

        • A product intended to maintain the equilibrium of

water and minerals in the body;

- A product intended for irrigation or reconstitution;
- An anesthetic;
- An anticoagulant;
- A vasopressor; or
- A sympathomimetic;

xiv. The distribution of an intravenous product that, by its formulation, is intended for the replenishment of fluids and electrolytes or calories;

xv. The distribution of an intravenous product used to maintain the equilibrium of water and minerals in the body, such as dialysis solutions;

xvi. The distribution of a product that is intended for irrigation, or sterile water, whether intended for such purposes or for injection;

xvii. The distribution of a medical gas; or

xviii. The distribution or sale of any biologic product that meets the definition of a device.

Some of these exemptions were apparently adopted from the California pedigree law but with modifications. For example, the exemption for combination products contained in the California law was wide open, effectively exempting *all* combination products, but in the DSCSA the exemption only appears to apply to combination products that have a primary mode of action designation by the FDA as a device. [37] The California exemption of radiopharmaceuticals only included drugs after they had been compounded with a radioisotope. The DSCSA exemption includes those too, but it also appears to exempt *any* product sold to a nuclear pharmacy, even those that are not yet radioactive.

The terms *transaction history, transaction information* and *transaction statement* are defined separately, but their importance in the operation of the track and trace system envisioned by the DSCSA is in their combination.

581(26) **TRANSACTION INFORMATION** means:
   A. The proprietary or established name or names of the **product**;
   B. The strength and dosage form of the **product**;
   C. The National Drug Code (NDC) number of the **product**;
   D. The container size;
   E. The number of containers;
   F. The lot number of the product;
   G. The date of the transaction;
   H. The date of the shipment, if more than 24 hours after the date of the transaction;
   I. The business name and address of the person from whom ownership is being transferred; and
   J. The business name and address of the person to whom ownership is being transferred.

By its nature, this set of information would identify a single change of ownership, or, transaction.

581(25) **TRANSACTION HISTORY** means a statement in paper or electronic form, including the transaction information for each prior transaction going back to the manufacturer of the product.

581(27) **TRANSACTION STATEMENT** is a statement, in paper or electronic form, that the entity transferring ownership in a transaction:
   A. is "authorized";

B. received the product from a person that is "authorized"

C. received "transaction information" and a "transaction statement" from the prior owner of the product;

D. did not knowingly ship a "suspect product" or "illegitimate product";

E. had systems and processes in place to comply with DSCSA "verification" requirements;

F. did not knowingly provide false "transaction information"; and

G. did not knowingly alter the "transaction history".

As we will see in later sections, the definitions of transaction history and transaction statement can be modified under some circumstances. In some circumstances the transaction information, transaction history and transaction statement must be in electronic form only, and in other circumstances the transaction history only needs to go back as far as the wholesale distributor that bought the product directly from the manufacturer or repackager. Care must be taken to fully understand exactly what is required for a valid transaction information, transaction history and transaction statement in any given application.

581(28) The terms **VERIFICATION** or **VERIFY** are another set of terms that do not carry the normal dictionary definition within the DSCSA. In this case, these terms mean the act of determining whether the product identifier affixed to, or imprinted upon, a package or homogeneous case corresponds to the SNI or lot number and expiration date assigned to the product by the manufacturer or the repackager. That is, to verify a product, all one needs to do is to confirm that the either the SNI or the lot and expiration date were assigned to that type of product by the manufacturer or repackager.

This definition gets modified slightly 10 years after enactment when verification may only be performed based on the SNI.

581(29) The term **WHOLESALE DISTRIBUTOR** is defined as a person who is engaged in wholesale distribution as defined in FD&C section 503(e)(4) as it is amended by the DSCSA, other than a manufacturer, a manufacturer's co-licensed partner, a third-party logistic provider, or repackager. It is assumed that the exemption of manufacturers, manufacturers' co-licensed partner and repackagers from being considered wholesale distributors only applies for a given product. That is, manufacturers, manufacturer's co-licensed partner and repackagers *of a specific product* are not considered wholesale distributors *of that product*, but this interpretation is subject to debate since the wording provided by Congress does not refer to product specificity. Check with the FDA before you assume your role as a manufacturer of some products eliminates you from the responsibilities of a wholesale distributor of other products that you do not manufacture, repackage and for which you are not a co-licensed partner of the manufacturer.

582 Requirements (General Requirements) Explained

582(a) FD&C Section 582(a) lays out general requirements that all companies must follow whenever engaging in "transactions" involving "product", as defined in the DSCSA.

582(a)(1) Later subsections lay out requirements that are specific to manufacturers, repackagers, wholesale distributors, and dispensers. Companies that fill more than one of these roles as defined by the DSCSA must follow those requirements for each role they fill, except that they are not required to duplicate requirements.

582(a)(2) Initial Standards

The FDA has one year after enactment of the DSCSA to publish a draft guidance document that establishes standards for the interoperable exchange of lot-level transaction information, transaction history, and transaction statements in paper or electronic format. That guidance is critically important for companies in the supply chain because without a widely agreed upon way of exchanging electronic information, they will be unable to fulfill the requirements of the law.

Companies were originally required to start passing transaction information, history, and statements on January 1, 2015 (since deferred to May 1, 2015). That was only about one month after the latest date by which the law requires the FDA to publish their guidance. For that reason, it was very likely that the FDA would identify existing and widely deployed technologies for formatting supply chain information. And because no such technology is universally deployed, paper documents are likely to be used for compliance in many transactions for the first few years.

In establishing these standards for interoperable exchange, the FDA must take into consideration the non-binding Standardized Numeric Identifier (SNI) standard, and any other standard the agency was required to create under section 505D of the FDA Amendments Act (FDAAA) of 2007.[38] The standards must also comply with a form and format developed by a widely recognized international standards development organization. The SNI standard, when used to encode National Drug Code (NDC) numbers, conforms to standards offered by GS1,[39,40] but the SNI is only useful for formatting the combination of an NDC and a unique serial number. The FDA has not yet published any guidance for the format of paper or electronic transaction information, history, or statements.

The DSCSA defines the process the FDA must follow in establishing this draft guidance. It must first gather comments and information from stakeholders and make those comments available to the public for at least 60 days prior to issuing draft guidance.

See Section 582(h)(4), "Standards For Interoperable Data Exchange", for the DSCSA mandate to convert this draft guidance document into final guidance at a later date.

582(a)(3) Waivers, Exceptions and Exemptions

Within 2 years of its enactment, or November 27, 2015, the DSCSA requires the FDA to publish guidance that:

i. establishes a process by which companies in the supply chain may request a waiver from any of the DSCSA track and trace requirements. The FDA may grant a requested waiver if it determines that those requirements would result in an undue economic hardship or for emergency medical reasons, including a public health emergency;

ii. establishes a process by which the FDA determines exceptions and a process for a manufacturer or repackager to follow to request an exception if a product is packaged in a container too small or otherwise unable to accommodate a label with sufficient space to bear the information required for compliance with the DSCSA; and

iii. establishes a process by which the FDA may determine other products or transactions that should be exempt from the track and trace requirements.

The guidance will also include a process for the biennial review and renewal of these waivers and exemptions.

The guidance must provide an effective date that is no less than 6 months prior to the date that manufacturers are required to affix or imprint a product identifier barcode on each package and homogeneous case of product intended to be introduced in a transaction into commerce. Manufacturers are required to do that by November 27, 2017, so the FDA guidance must be published no later than May 27, 2017. Manufacturers and repackagers who need such a waiver or exception should move quickly to apply as soon as this guidance is published to allow time for the FDA to respond before the compliance date.

582(a)(4) Self-Executing Requirements

According to this section, the requirements in FD&C Section 582 are enforceable by the FDA without further regulations or guidance, unless otherwise specified in a particular section. This makes it vitally important for companies to fully understand the DSCSA law and their obligations under it. You are expected to follow the law as written whether the FDA publishes guidance or not.

582(a)(5) Grandfathering Product

There are two types of grandfathering covered in this subsection, tracing and product identifier (in opposite order from the DSCSA text, because this order is chronologic and therefore easier to follow).

For any product that *entered* the pharmaceutical distribution supply chain *before* January 1, 2015, (enforcement deferred until May 1, 2015) but which is still in the supply chain on that date, authorized trading partners are exempt from providing transaction information, but the transaction history required after that date must begin with the owner of the product on that date. Normally, sellers of product after January 1, 2015 (enforcement deferred until May 1, 2015) would have been required to assert receipt of transaction information and transaction statement from the prior owner, but because product that entered the supply chain prior to that date would have probably not come with that information, owners would have been exempt from making that assertion.

Manufacturers and repackagers will eventually be required to affix or imprint a product identifier on their packages, but not until November 27, 2017 and November 27, 2018, respectively. The DSCSA gives the FDA two years to publish final guidance that specifies whether and under what circumstances product that is already in the pharmaceutical distribution supply chain at the time of those effective dates and are not labeled with a product identifier shall be exempted from those requirements.

582(a)(6) Wholesale Distributor Licenses

Until the effective date of the new wholesale distributor licensing regulations contained in FD&C Section 583 (which will be no later than November 27, 2017 and depends on how fast the FDA can publish the new wholesale distributor licensing regulations in final form), the term "licensed" or "authorized" as they relate to a wholesale distributor handling prescription drugs, shall mean a wholesale distributor with a valid license under State law.

582(a)(7) Third-Party Logistics Provider Licenses

Until the effective date of the new third-party logistics provider (3PL) licensing regulations contained in FD&C Section 584 of the DSCSA (which will be no later than November 27, 2016 and depends on how fast the FDA can publish the new 3PL licensing regulations in final form), all 3PLs will be considered "licensed" unless the FDA publishes notice that that a given 3PL has been found by the agency not to utilize good handling and distribution practices.

582(a)(8) Label Changes

Any changes made by manufacturers or repackagers to their package labels solely to incorporate the product identifier may be submitted to the FDA as part of the annual report of an establishment in accordance with section 21 CFR 314.70(d)[41]. With this instruction, Congress has established that the label changes necessary to solely incorporate the product identifier on a product package are considered a "minor change" to the product and therefore the necessary change notification of the FDA may wait until the next annual report. This is good news because it allows manufacturers and repackagers to notify the FDA of these label changes in a more relaxed fashion than might otherwise be the case, but be careful of the word "solely" here. It is anyone's guess exactly where the line is between changes that are "solely" to incorporate a product identifier and those that result in more than that, which may require more prompt notification. Perhaps we will see some guidance or comment from the FDA on this in the future.

582(a)(9) Product Identifiers

Here is where the DSCSA establishes that the product identifiers containing the applicable data affixed or imprinted must be a 2-dimensional (2D) data matrix barcode[42] on packages, and either a linear[43] or a 2D data matrix barcode on homogeneous cases. The DSCSA allows the FDA to specify other technologies, through guidance, in addition to these, or to replace these in the future.

This is a good legislative solution to establishing Automatic Identification, Data Capture (AIDC)[44] data carrier technologies that the industry must begin with because it greatly narrows the initial choices through a mandate, but allows the graceful adoption of new (or just different) technologies in the future.[45] However, there are many linear barcode symbologies and several 2D data matrix symbology variations available for companies to choose among. That could cause fragmentation in the industry, leading to inefficiencies in the supply chain. In the absence of specific guidance from the FDA, consult recommendations[46] made by GS1 Healthcare US[47] and the Healthcare Distribution Management Association (HDMA)[48] to ensure industry alignment for maximum interoperability.

This subsection also establishes that the verification of the product identifier on product may occur by either human-readable or machine readable methods when required. This means that visually reading the NDC, serial number, lot and/or expiration date is sufficient when confirming that they correspond to those that were applied by the manufacturer or repackager of the product. Companies are *not required* by the DSCSA to read the barcodes on packages or homogeneous cases with "machines" (barcode readers). Most companies, other than small volume pharmacies, will find it *more costly* to use human-readable verification than to invest in equipment and systems necessary to read the barcodes, but at least the law does not require it.

Phase 1: 2013 through 2023, Explained

Phase 1 of the DSCSA began on November 27, 2013, and will end 10 years later on November 27, 2023, but few provisions took effect until January 1, 2015. The following sections of this document cover the trading partner-specific subsections of section 582 of the Food, Drug and Cosmetics Act (FD&C). They are broken out by trading partner here because most readers will be particularly interested in the one section that corresponds to their segment of the supply chain.

582(b) **Manufacturer Provisions, Explained**

582(b)(1) **Manufacturer: Product Tracing**

Beginning no later than January 1, 2015, (enforcement was deferred until May 1, 2015) manufacturers were obligated by the DSCSA to make lot-level product tracking a standard part of *every* change of ownership (known as a "transaction") of drugs and biologics (known as "products") in the U.S. supply chain. This subsection explains what they must do to meet that requirement.

Manufacturers must...

- Capture the transaction information, transaction history, and transaction statement for each transaction and maintain this information for at least 6 years after the date of the transaction. Here is where the exact definitions of all of these components become very important. Please take the time to review them now by clicking on the document hyperlinks embedded in the words above.
- Provide the next owner of the product with paper or electronic statements *in a single document* that contains the transaction information, transaction history, and transaction statement for that specific product.

Because a "transaction" is generally any change of ownership [see the full definition in subsection 581(24)], manufacturers are required to capture, construct, provide, and store this information for every shipment of product (except for exempt transactions). But notice that the DSCSA does not provide enough guidance to know exactly how to properly capture, construct, provide and store this mandated paper or electronic document. However, referring back to subsection 582(a)(2), you will recall that it is the FDA's obligation under the DSCSA to establish the standards for doing this. You may also recall that they had one year from the passage of the DSCSA to do that, which means the FDA had until November 27, 2014 to make you aware of the standards that you must begin applying before January 1, 2015 — only about 35 days later. (But in late December 2014 the FDA issued guidance that indicated they would not enforce the product tracing requirements until May 1, 2015, providing a little more time to prepare.)

Not only was that a very tight timeframe, but with the guidance the FDA published, they did not tell us everything we needed to know to be able to begin applying those standards. Fortunately other organizations — such as GS1 Healthcare US[49] and the HDMA[50] — have stepped in to provide additional guidance. One way to monitor all of these pronouncements is to subscribe to RxTrace and read the essays that are published there.

Manufacturers must also be able to react to any request for information by the FDA or any other appropriate State or Federal agency or official in the event of a recall, or for the purpose of investigating suspect product or an illegitimate product. Manufacturers are required to provide any applicable transaction information, transaction history, and transaction statements for the product inquired about. Manufacturers are allowed 1 business day to respond with the appropriate information. In the event of a weekend or holiday, the response time must not exceed 48 hours after receiving the request, although the FDA may define some other reasonable time (which could be longer or, theoretically, shorter, depending on the urgency).

Within 4 years of the passage of the DSCSA — by November 27, 2017 — manufacturers must begin to provide the transaction information, transaction history and transaction statement in *electronic format only, except* when selling directly to a licensed healthcare practitioner who is authorized to prescribe medication under State law, or to other licensed individuals who are under the supervision or direction of such a practitioner who dispenses product in the usual course of professional practice. After this date, very few shipments can be documented with paper statements, but it will be important to retain the ability to produce those paper documents so that these direct-to-practitioner shipments can still be made. These practitioners are exempt from receiving electronic statements and so most will probably not make those investments.

It is by implication that all other types of trading partners in the supply chain must be able to receive this information electronically by this same date. The FDA has established through guidance the required standards necessary to provide this information electronically, but again, manufacturers still need to work with GS1 Healthcare US, the HDMA and their trading partners to ensure that the exact formatting and data exchange methods used are interoperable with all of their downstream trading partners.

582(b)(2) Manufacturer: Product Identifier

Before the deadline of November 27, 2017, manufacturers must begin to affix or imprint a product identifier on each package and homogenous case of a product that is intended to be introduced into the supply chain via the non-exempt transactions. Manufacturers must retain the information about that product identifier and the product for at least 6 years after the transaction that introduces the product into the supply chain. As we already saw in section 582(b)(1) above, manufacturers must also retain for 6 years information about the transaction that introduces the products into the supply chain.

Any product that is required to have a standardized numeric identifier (SNI) is not required to have a unique device identifier (UDI)[51]. This would apply to combination products where there might have been a grey area regarding which type of identifier would be required. This provision ensures that companies would not be subject to duplicate product identification requirements. If there is any question about whether your product requires an SNI or a UDI, contact the FDA Office of Combination Products.[52]

582(b)(3) Manufacturer: Authorized Trading Partners

Beginning on January 1, 2015, manufacturers may only do business with trading partners that are authorized as defined by the DSCSA. It is the manufacturer's responsibility to know that their trading partners are authorized/licensed and where. As part of meeting this requirement, manufacturers should keep track of the State and Federal licenses that each of their trading partners currently hold and when they will expire, so they can adjust their sales and shipment authorizations based on the status of the recipient's licenses.

582(b)(4) Manufacturer: Verification

Beginning on January 1, 2015, manufacturers must have systems in place to enable them to quarantine suspect product and perform investigations into that product, based on the product identifier, to determine if it is legitimate or illegitimate, and then to notify the FDA and their trading partners, as appropriate, of that status. The details are below.

582(b)(4)(A) Manufacturer: Suspect Product

Whenever a determination is made that a product in the possession or control of the manufacturer is suspect product — or upon receiving a request for verification from the FDA that has made a determination that a product within the possession or control of the manufacturer is a suspect product — the manufacturer must quarantine that product until it is cleared or dispositioned. To fully understand this requirement it is important to read and understand the definitions of each of the terms used to describe it.

The manufacturer must promptly conduct an investigation in coordination with trading partners, when applicable, to determine whether the product is an illegitimate product. This investigation shall include validating any applicable transaction history and transaction information held by the manufacturer and it may include "otherwise investigating" to determine whether the product is an illegitimate product.

If the manufacturer finds that the suspect product is not an illegitimate product, they must promptly notify the FDA, if applicable, that the product has been "cleared". At that time it may then be removed from quarantine and may be further distributed.

The manufacturer must keep records of the investigation of suspect products for at least 6 years after the conclusion of the investigation. Prior to November 27, 2017, these investigations may verify the product using the lot and expiration date portions of the product identifier, but after that date they must include the verification of the product *at the package level, including the standardized numerical identifier (SNI)*.

582(b)(4)(B) Manufacturer: Illegitimate Product

Upon determining that a product in the possession or control of a manufacturer is an illegitimate product, the manufacturer must:

- Quarantine the product to separate it from products intended for distribution until it is dispositioned;
- Disposition the illegitimate product (make sure you understand the special definition of "disposition");
- Take reasonable and appropriate steps to assist trading partners to disposition any illegitimate

product in their possession or control;

- Retain a sample of the illegitimate product for further physical examination or laboratory analysis of the product by the manufacturer, the FDA, or other appropriate Federal or State agency or official upon request;
- Notify the FDA and all immediate trading partners that the manufacturer has reason to believe may have received the illegitimate product within 24 hours of making the determination.

Manufacturers must notify the FDA and immediate trading partners that they may have received product which the manufacturer now believes there is a high risk that the product is illegitimate product. These notifications must occur within 24 hours of making the determination or being notified by the FDA or a trading partner of the problem. The manufacturer of the product is obligated to make this notification even if the product was only "purported to be a product manufactured" by them. That is, even if the potentially illegitimate product was manufactured by someone else (even a criminal counterfeiter), as long as the product has the appearance of being made by the manufacturer, they are obligated to make the notification. The term "high risk" here means any specific high risk that could increase the likelihood that illegitimate product may enter the pharmaceutical distribution supply chain and other high risks as identified in guidance published by the FDA.

In response to a notification by the FDA or a trading partner that a determination has been made that a product is an illegitimate product, a manufacturer must identify all illegitimate product in their possession or control that is the subject of that notification, including any product that is subsequently received, and they must perform the activities outlined above under the heading "Manufacturer: Suspect Product".

Upon determining, in consultation with the FDA, that a notification is no longer necessary, a manufacturer must promptly notify the same immediate trading partners notified previously by the manufacturer about this product that the notification has been terminated.

Manufacturers must keep records of the disposition of an illegitimate product for at least 6 years after the conclusion of the disposition.

582(b)(4)(C) Manufacturer: Requests For Verification

Beginning on November 27, 2017, whenever a manufacturer receives a request for verification of a product thought to be manufactured by the manufacturer from an authorized repackager, wholesale distributor or dispenser that is in possession or control of the product, the manufacturer must reply with an indication of whether or not the product identifier provided in the request corresponds to the product identifier affixed or imprinted by the manufacturer. The request may be made using the standardized numerical identifier (SNI) portion of the product identifier on a product package or on a homogeneous case of the product, and if it is, then the manufacturer's reply must be relative to that same level. The reply must be made within 24 hours or some other reasonable time as determined by the FDA, based on the circumstances of the request.

If a manufacturer determines, based on a verification request, that a product identifier that does not correspond to that affixed or imprinted by the manufacturer, the manufacturer must treat that product as "suspect product" and conduct an investigation as described in section 582(b)(4)(A), "Manufacturer: Suspect Product" above. If the manufacturer has reason to believe the product is illegitimate product, the manufacturer must advise the person making the request of that belief at the time of the manufacturer's reply to the request for verification.

582(b)(4)(D) Manufacturer: Electronic Database

A manufacturer may satisfy the requirements of subsection 581(b)(4), "Verification", by developing a secure electronic database or utilizing a secure electronic database developed or operated by another entity. The third-party owner of the database shall establish the requirements and processes to respond to requests and may provide for data access to other members of the pharmaceutical distribution supply chain, as appropriate. However, the development and operation of such a database shall not relieve the manufacturer of the requirement to respond to a request for verification submitted by means other than a secure electronic database.

With the words in this section, Congress appears to be authorizing manufacturers to make use of third-party services that would be designed to help them fulfill these verification requirements. It is worth noting at this point that what Congress defines in the DSCSA as "verification" is very close to what

GS1 Healthcare terms as "Product Identifier Authentication" (PIA)[53]. It is likely that Congress included this section to give an explicit green light to industry efforts to develop standards around PIA for use here in the United States and elsewhere around the globe. However, even if a manufacturer chooses to make use of a PIA service provider, they are also obligated to respond to verification requests that are submitted by other means. The DSCSA does not require trading partners to make use of the electronic service.

582(b)(4)(E) Manufacturer: Saleable Returned Product

Beginning on November 27, 2017, whenever a manufacturer receives returned product that the manufacturer intends to further distribute, they must verify the product identifier, including the standardized numerical identifier (SNI), for each sealed homogeneous case of the product, or, if the product is not in a sealed homogeneous case, verify the product identifier, including the SNI, on each package.

582(b)(4)(F) Manufacturer: Nonsaleable Returned Product

A manufacturer may return a *nonsaleable* product to the manufacturer or repackager, to the wholesale distributor from whom such product was purchased, or to a person acting on behalf of such a person, including a returns processor, *without providing* the transaction history, transaction information and transaction statement for the product.

582(c) Wholesale Distributor Provisions, Explained

Wholesale distributors who engage in the facilitation of the financial transactions of drop shipments and do not physically handle or store the product should review the special drop shipment exemptions found in FD&C Section 582(f), Drop Shipments.

582(c)(1) Wholesale Distributor: Product Tracing

582(c)(1)(A) Beginning no later than January 1, 2015 (enforcement was deferred until May 1, 2015), wholesale distributors were obligated by the DSCSA to make lot-level product tracking a standard part of *every* change of ownership (known as a "transaction") of drugs and biologics (known as "products") in the U.S. supply chain. This subsection explains what they have to do to meet that requirement. To fully understand the meaning of these provisions it is important to study the definitions of the terms that Congress has defined within the DSCSA. That is because these definitions may not be as wide within the DSCSA as their common usage within the industry.

The following provisions apply to Wholesale distributors:

- A wholesale distributor must not accept ownership of a product unless the previous owner provides transaction history, transaction information, and a transaction statement for the product at the time of the transaction or prior to it;

- If a wholesale distributor purchases a product directly from:
  - the manufacturer,
  - the exclusive distributor of the manufacturer, or
  - a repackager that purchased the source product directly from the manufacturer,

then for each transaction in which the wholesale distributor transfers ownership of a product, at the time of the transaction or prior to it, the wholesale distributor must provide to the subsequent purchaser:

  - a transaction statement indicating that the wholesale distributor (or one of its affiliates) purchased the product directly from the manufacturer, exclusive distributor of the manufacturer, or repackager that purchased the product directly from the manufacturer;
  - the transaction history and transaction information, *except that these documents are not required to include:*
    - the lot number of the product;
    - the initial transaction date; or
    - the initial shipment date from the manufacturer.

The DSCSA acknowledges that this is in deviation from its own definition of "transaction information", but it is an exception.

Whenever providing the transaction history, transaction information, and transaction statement as required above, a wholesale distributor shall provide it with the following characteristics:

- If provided to a dispenser, the data must be provided on a *single document* in a paper or electronic format;
- If provided to a wholesale distributor, the data may be provided through any combination of the following:
  - Self-generated paper; This implies that if paper is to be provided the document must be generated by the wholesale distributor. If true, this seems to eliminate the use of packing lists or other paper documents that were generated by an upstream trading partner.
  - Electronic data;
  - Manufacturer-provided information on the product package itself; This last provision seems to imply that for sales from one wholesale distributor to another, the data that already appears on the product label does not need to be in the

paper or electronic documents. This likely includes:

- the NDC,
- lot number,
- expiration date,
- proprietary or established name of the product,
- container size,
- the strength and dosage form.

Check with the FDA for confirmation.

- If a wholesale distributor did *not* purchase a product directly from the manufacturer, the exclusive distributor of the manufacturer, or a repackager that purchased directly from the manufacturer as described in the previous major bullet, then for each transaction or subsequent transaction, the wholesale distributor must provide to the subsequent purchaser a transaction statement, transaction history, and transaction information at the time of the transaction or prior to it, in paper or electronic format that complies with the guidance document issued by the FDA under subsection 582(a)(2), "Initial Standards".

This is the guidance document that Congress has given the FDA until November 27, 2014 to produce, and which wholesale distributors must begin to follow on January 1, 2015— slightly more than one month later (but FDA enforcement was subsequently deferred until

May 1, 2015).

For transactions originating from these wholesale distributors, the transaction history supplied does not need to include the sale from the manufacturer, the exclusive distributor of the manufacturer, or a repackager that purchased directly from the manufacturer. Instead, it shall begin only with the sale from the first wholesale distributor that purchased the product directly. However, the wholesale distributor that *could not* buy direct shall inform the subsequent purchaser that they received a direct purchase statement from the wholesale distributor that did buy directly.

- A wholesale distributor must:
    - Capture the transaction information consistent with the provisions above, transaction history and transaction statement for each transaction described above, and maintain that information for at least 6 years after the date of the transaction. Here is where the exact definitions of all of these components become very important. Please take the time to review them now by clicking on the document hyperlinks embedded in the words above;
    - Maintain the confidentiality of the transaction information (including lot level information), transaction history, and transaction statement for a product in a manner that prohibits

disclosure to any person other than the FDA or other appropriate Federal or State official. This does not block the wholesale distributor from fulfilling their obligation to pass this data to the recipient in a valid transaction and it does not block them from establishing trading partner agreements as explained in Section 582(c)(1)(D) (see Wholesale Distributor: Trading Partner Agreements).

The DSCSA wholesale distributor provisions do not include an *explicit* electronic format requirement comparable to that of the manufacturers [see Section 582(b)(1), "Manufacturer: Product Tracing"]. However, because manufacturers will be required to provide their transaction information, transaction history, and transaction statement to wholesale distributors only in electronic format beginning on November 27, 2017, wholesale distributors who buy directly will need to have fully tested systems in place that are able to receive those electronic documents before that date. This, then, is an *implicit* requirement of the DSCSA. The FDA provided guidance on the electronic formatting, but again, wholesale distributors still need to work with GS1 Healthcare US, the HDMA, and their suppliers to ensure that the exact formatting and data exchange methods used by all companies are interoperable.

582(c)(1)(B) Wholesale Distributor: Returns

Saleable Returns

Even though Section 582(c)(1)(A) prevents a wholesale distributor from engaging in transactions that do not include the exchange of transaction information, transaction history and transaction statements, they are allowed to accept returned *saleable* product from a dispenser or repackager under the terms and conditions of any agreement between the parties until November 27, 2019, without receiving those documents. Furthermore, the wholesale distributor may also distribute that returned product without providing the transaction history during the same period. The wholesale distributor may do this until November 27, 2019. For distributions of saleable returned product after that date, the transaction history of the product must begin with the wholesale distributor that accepted the returned product.

In addition, beginning on November 27, 2019, a wholesale distributor may accept returned product from a dispenser or repackager *only if* the wholesale distributor can associate the returned product with the transaction information and the transaction statement associated with the original sales transaction for that product. For all subsequent distribution transactions, the transaction history of the returned product must begin with the wholesale distributor that accepted and verified the returned product. For all the transactions covered in this paragraph, the transaction information and transaction history need not include transaction dates *"…if it is not reasonably practicable to obtain…"* them.

Nonsaleable Returns
A wholesale distributor may return a *nonsaleable* product to

- the manufacturer or repackager,
- the wholesale distributor from whom the product was purchased, or
- a person acting on behalf of one of the above, including a returns processor,

without providing transaction information, transaction history and a transaction statement.

582(c)(1)(C) Wholesale Distributor: Requests For Information

Wholesale distributors must be prepared to react to any request for information by the FDA or any other appropriate State or Federal agency or official in the event of a recall, or for the purpose of investigating suspect product or an illegitimate product. Wholesale distributors are required to provide any applicable transaction information, transaction history, and transaction statements for the product inquired about. Wholesale distributors are allowed 1 business day to respond with the appropriate information. In the event of a weekend or holiday, the response time must not exceed 48 hours after receiving the request, although the FDA may define some other reasonable time (which could be longer or, theoretically, shorter, depending on the urgency).

582(c)(1)(D) Wholesale Distributor: Trading Partner Agreements

Beginning on November 27, 2019, a wholesale distributor may disclose the transaction information, including lot level information, transaction history, or transaction statement of a product to the subsequent purchaser of the product under a written agreement between the wholesale distributor and the subsequent purchaser. This appears to allow the wholesale distributor to provide this type of information to owners of the product that are farther down the supply chain (subsequent purchaser) than their immediate customer (who would already receive this information), as long as they have an agreement to do so.

582(c)(2) Wholesale Distributor: Product Identifier

Beginning on November 27, 2019, a wholesale distributor may engage in transactions involving a product that is not subject to the grandfathering provisions of Section 582(a)(5) (see Grandfathering Product), only if it is encoded with a product identifier. The two year timespan between the manufacturer's November 27, 2017 requirement to encode their non-exempt product with a DSCSA product identifier and this one, will ensure that most of the product without product identifiers will exit the supply chain by the time wholesale distributors must begin to read and react to them.

582(c)(3) Wholesale Distributor: Authorized Trading Partners

Beginning on January 1, 2015, wholesale distributors may only do business with trading partners that are authorized as defined by the DSCSA. It is the wholesale distributor's responsibility to know that their trading partners are authorized/licensed and where. As part of meeting this requirement, wholesale distributors should keep track of the State and Federal licenses that each of their trading partners currently holds and when the licenses will expire so they can adjust their sales and shipment authorizations based on the status of the recipient's licenses.

582(c)(4) Wholesale Distributor: Verification

Beginning on January 1, 2015, wholesale distributors must have systems in place to enable them to quarantine suspect product and perform investigations into that product, based on the product identifier, to determine if it is legitimate or illegitimate, and then to notify the FDA and their trading partners, as appropriate, of that status. The details are below.

582(c)(4)(A) Wholesale Distributor: Suspect Product

Whenever a determination is made that a product in the possession or control of the wholesale distributor is suspect product — or upon receiving a request for verification from the FDA that has made a determination that a product within the possession or control of the wholesale distributor is a suspect product — the wholesale distributor must quarantine that product until it is cleared or dispositioned. To fully understand this requirement, it is important to read and understand the definitions of each of the terms used to describe it.

The wholesale distributor must promptly conduct an investigation in coordination with trading partners, when applicable, to determine whether the product is an illegitimate product. This investigation shall include validating any applicable transaction history and transaction information held by the wholesale distributor and it may include "otherwise investigating" to determine whether the product is an illegitimate product.

If the wholesale distributor finds that the suspect product is not an illegitimate product, they must promptly notify the FDA, if applicable, that the product has been "cleared". At that time the product may then be removed from quarantine and may be further distributed.

The wholesale distributor must keep records of the investigation of suspect products for at least 6 years after the conclusion of the investigation. Prior to November 27, 2019, these investigations may verify the product using the lot and expiration date portions of the product identifier, but after that date they must include the verification of the product *at the package level, including the standardized numerical identifier (SNI)*.

582(c)(4)(B) Wholesale Distributor: Illegitimate Product

582(c)(4)(B)(i) Upon determining, in coordination with the manufacturer, that a product in the possession or control of a wholesale distributor is an illegitimate product, the wholesale distributor must:

- Quarantine the product to separate it from products intended for distribution until it is dispositioned;
- Disposition the illegitimate product (make sure you understand the special definition of

"disposition");

- Take reasonable and appropriate steps to assist trading partners to disposition any illegitimate product in their possession or control;
- Retain a sample of the illegitimate product for further physical examination or laboratory analysis of the product by the manufacturer, the FDA or other appropriate Federal or State agency or official upon request;

582(c)(4)(B)(ii) In addition, the wholesale Distributor must notify the FDA and all immediate trading partners that the wholesale distributor has reason to believe may have received the illegitimate product within 24 hours of making the determination.

582(c)(4)(B)(iii) In response to a notification by the FDA or a trading partner that a determination has been made that a product is an illegitimate product, a wholesale distributor must identify all illegitimate product in their possession or control that is the subject of that notification, including any product that is subsequently received, and they must perform the activities outlined above under the heading "Wholesale Distributor: Suspect Product".

582(c)(4)(B)(iv) Upon determining, in consultation with the FDA, that a notification is no longer necessary, a wholesale distributor must promptly notify the same immediate trading partners notified previously by the wholesale distributor about this product that the notification has been terminated.

Wholesale distributors must keep records of the disposition of an illegitimate product for at least 6 years after the conclusion of the disposition.

582(c)(4)(C) Wholesale Distributor: Electronic Database

A wholesale distributor may satisfy the requirements of subsection 581(c)(4), "Verification", by developing a secure electronic database or utilizing a secure electronic database developed or operated by another entity. The third-party owner of the database shall establish the requirements and processes to respond to requests and may provide for data access to other members of the pharmaceutical distribution supply chain, as appropriate. However, the development and operation of such a database shall not relieve the wholesale distributor of the requirement to respond to a request for verification submitted by means other than a secure electronic database.

With these words, Congress appears to be authorizing wholesale distributors to make use of third-party services that would be designed to help them fulfill these verification requirements. It is worth noting at this point that what Congress defines in the DSCSA as "verification" is very close to what GS1 Healthcare terms as "Product Identifier Authentication" (PIA)[54]. It is likely that Congress included this section to give an explicit green light to industry efforts to develop standards around PIA for use here in the United States and elsewhere around the globe. However, even if a wholesale distributor were to make use of a PIA service provider, they are also obligated to respond to verification requests that are submitted by other means. The DSCSA does not require trading partners to make use of the electronic service.

582(c)(4)(D) Wholesale Distributor: Verification of Saleable Returned Product

Beginning on November 27, 2019, whenever a wholesale distributor receives returned product that the wholesale distributor intends to further distribute, they must verify the product identifier, including the Standardized Numerical Identifier (SNI), for each sealed homogeneous case of the product, or, if the product is not in a sealed homogeneous case, verify the product identifier, including the SNI, on each package.

582(d) Dispenser Provisions, Explained

582(d)(1) Dispenser: Product Tracing

582(d)(1)(A) Beginning no later than July 1, 2015 – six months later than everyone else (but FDA enforcement was deferred until at least March 1, 2016) – dispensers are obligated by the DSCSA to make lot-level product tracking a standard part of *most* change of ownership (known as a "transaction") of drugs and biologics (known as "products") in the U.S. supply chain. This subsection explains what they have to do to meet that requirement. To fully understand the meaning of these provisions it is important to study the definitions of the terms that Congress has defined within the DSCSA. That is because these definitions may not be as broadly-defined within the DSCSA as their common usage within the industry.

Section 582(d)(1), "Product Tracing", applies to all dispensers except licensed health care practitioners authorized to prescribe or administer medication under State law or other licensed individuals under the supervision or direction of such practitioners who dispense product in the usual course of their professional practice [from Section 582(d)(5), "Exception"].

The following provisions apply to non-exempt dispensers:

- A dispenser must not accept ownership of a product unless the previous owner provides transaction history, transaction information, and a transaction statement for the product at the time of the transaction or prior to it;

- A dispenser must provide the next owner of the product with statements that contain the transaction information, transaction history, and transaction statement for that specific product at the time of the transaction or prior to it, *except* when the next owner is another dispenser and the product is sold to fulfill a specific patient need. If this exemption might apply to you, please familiarize yourself with the definition of "specific patient need" as defined within the DSCSA to be sure. Consult the FDA if you are still not sure. This requirement also *does not apply* when dispensing directly to a patient, or when returning product to the trading partner that supplied it originally.

- A dispenser must capture the transaction information (including lot level information if provided), transaction history and transaction statements as necessary to investigate a suspect product, and maintain that information for at least 6 years after the date of the transaction.

"As necessary" here *appears* to mean that dispensers do not need to capture this information on a routine basis, but *may* only need to do so if there is a suspicion that the product may be illegitimate. In that case, the retention of the information by dispensers for 6 years *may* only apply to the transaction information, transaction history, and transaction statements that are captured as part of the investigation.

The DSCSA dispenser provisions do not include an *explicit* electronic format requirement comparable to that of the manufacturers [see Section 582(b)(1), "Manufacturer: Product Tracing"]. However, because manufacturers will be required to provide their transaction information, transaction history, and transaction statement to customers who are wholesale distributors, repackagers, or dispensers *only in electronic format* beginning on November 27, 2017, dispensers who buy directly from manufacturers will need to have fully tested systems in place that are able to receive those electronic documents before that date. This is true *except* when the dispenser is a licensed health care practitioner who is authorized to prescribe medication [see Section 582(b)(1)(C)(ii) within Manufacturer: Product Tracing for additional clarification].

This, then, is an *implicit* requirement of the DSCSA, at least for dispensers that ever purchase product directly from a manufacturer. See the next section for a possible solution that the DSCSA allows dispensers for dealing with electronic documents.

Furthermore, it is also very likely that wholesale distributors and repackagers will have a strong desire to provide their transaction information, transaction history, and transaction statements to dispensers in electronic format whenever possible. The larger the dispenser business entity, the stronger that desire is likely to be. Check with your suppliers to learn what their plans and expectations are.

The FDA provided guidance on the electronic

formatting in November of 2014, but dispensers still need to work with GS1 Healthcare US, the HDMA, NACDS, and their suppliers to ensure that the exact formatting and data exchange methods used by all companies are interoperable.

582(d)(1)(B) Dispenser: Agreements With Third Parties

The DSCSA allows a dispenser to enter into a written agreement with a third party — which can be an authorized wholesale distributor — under which the third party confidentially maintains the transaction information, transaction history, or transaction statements that are required to be received and maintained under this subsection on behalf of the dispenser. If a dispenser enters into this type of agreement, the dispenser must keep a copy of the written agreement, and this arrangement does not relieve the dispenser from its Product Tracing obligations.

This may be a good solution to the chore of dealing with all these documents, especially when they are electronic. Dispensers that buy products from multiple licensed sources are faced with either deploying their own document retention capability, establishing separate contracts for document retention with each source, or, establishing a single contract with a true third-party service provider that is not aligned with any single trading partner and where all suppliers must send their electronic documents. Watch for the major wholesale distributors to offer this kind of service to their dispensing customers, and perhaps for third-parties to offer single point solutions in the near future.

582(d)(1)(C) Dispenser: Returns

Saleable Returns

Dispensers may return saleable product to the trading partner from which they obtained the product originally without providing transaction information, transaction history, and transaction statements. This is all the DSCSA says about dispenser requirements regarding saleable returns. However, there must be some type of agreement (any type of agreement) that includes terms and conditions for returns, because wholesale distributors are only allowed to accept returned *saleable* product from a dispenser or repackager without receiving transaction information, transaction history, and transaction statements if they are under such an agreement [see Section 582(c)(1)(2)(i), Wholesale Distributor: Saleable Returns]. It is likely that a simple sales agreement could fulfill this requirement as long as it includes terms and conditions that cover product returns. Check with the FDA to confirm this.

Nonsaleable Returns

A dispenser may return a *nonsaleable* product to

- the manufacturer or repackager,
- the wholesale distributor from whom the product was purchased,
- a returns processor, or
- a person acting on behalf of one of the above,

without providing transaction information, transaction history and a transaction statement.

582(d)(1)(D) Dispenser: Requests for Information

Dispensers must be prepared to react to any request for information by the FDA or any other appropriate State or Federal agency or official in the event of a recall, or for the purpose of investigating suspect product or an illegitimate product. Dispensers are required (after March 1, 2016) to provide any applicable transaction information, transaction history, and transaction statements which the dispenser received from the previous owner for the product inquired about. The information provided shall not include the lot number of the product, the initial transaction date, or the initial shipment date from the manufacturer unless this information was included in the transaction information, transaction statement, and transaction history provided by the manufacturer or wholesale distributor.

Dispensers may provide the applicable information in either paper or electronic format.

Dispensers are allowed 2 business days to respond with the applicable information, although the FDA may define some other reasonable time (which could be longer or, theoretically, shorter, depending on the urgency). However, until November 27, 2017, dispensers will be granted:

- additional time, as necessary, only with respect to a request to provide lot level information that was provided to the dispenser in paper format,
- the request time period will be limited to the 6 months preceding the request or other relevant date, and,
- in the event of a recall, the FDA or other appropriate Federal or State official may

request information only if the recall involves a serious adverse health consequence or death to humans.

582(d)(2) Dispenser: Product Identifier

Beginning on November 27, 2020, a dispenser may engage in transactions involving a product only if it is encoded with a product identifier, except products that are subject to the grandfathering provisions of Section 582(a)(5) (see Grandfathering Product). The timespan between the manufacturer's 2017 requirement to encode their non-exempt product with a DSCSA product identifier and this one will ensure that most of the product without product identifiers will exit the supply chain by the time dispensers must begin to receive them.

582(d)(3) Dispenser: Authorized Trading Partners

Beginning on January 1, 2015, dispensers may only do business with trading partners that are authorized as defined by the DSCSA. It is the dispenser's responsibility to know that their trading partners are authorized/licensed and where. As part of meeting this requirement, dispensers should keep track of the State and Federal licenses that each of their trading partners currently hold and when the licenses will expire so they can adjust their purchases based on the status of the supplier's licenses.

582(d)(4) Dispenser: Verification

Beginning on January 1, 2015, dispensers must have systems in place to enable them to quarantine suspect product and perform investigations into that product, based on the product identifier, to determine if it is legitimate or illegitimate, and then to notify the FDA and their trading partners, as appropriate, of that status.
Section 582(d)(4), "Verification", applies to all dispensers except licensed health care practitioners authorized to prescribe or administer medication under State law or other licensed individuals under the supervision or direction of such practitioners who dispense product in the usual course of their professional practice [from Section 582(d)(5), "Exception"].

The details for non-exempt dispensers are below.

582(d)(4)(A) Dispenser: Suspect Product

Whenever a determination is made that a product in the possession or control of the dispenser is suspect product — or upon receiving a request for verification from the FDA that has made a determination that a product within the possession or control of the dispenser is a suspect product — the dispenser must quarantine that product until it is cleared or dispositioned. To fully understand this requirement it is important to read and understand the definitions of each of the terms used to describe it.

The dispenser must promptly conduct an investigation in coordination with trading partners, when applicable, to determine whether the product is an illegitimate product. This investigation shall include validating any applicable transaction history and transaction information held by the dispenser and it may include "otherwise investigating" to determine whether the product is an illegitimate product.

Beginning on November 27, 2020, these investigations must verify whether the lot number of a suspect product corresponds with a real lot number that product. Also beginning on that date, dispensers conducting this type of investigation must verify the product identifier, *including the Standardized Numerical Identifier (SNI)* of at least 3 packages or 10% of the suspect product, whichever is greater, or all packages if there are fewer than 3, to confirm that they correspond with product identifiers of real product.

If the dispenser finds that the suspect product is not an illegitimate product, they must promptly notify the FDA, if applicable, that the product has been "cleared". At that time it may then be removed from quarantine and may be further distributed or dispensed.

The dispenser must keep records of the investigation of suspect products for at least 6 years after the conclusion of the investigation.

582(d)(4)(B) **Dispenser: Illegitimate Product**

Upon determining, in coordination with the manufacturer, that a product in the possession or control of a dispenser is an illegitimate product, the dispenser must:

- Disposition the illegitimate product (make sure

you understand the special definition of "disposition");

- Take reasonable and appropriate steps to assist trading partners to disposition any illegitimate product in their possession or control;
- Retain a sample of the illegitimate product for further physical examination or laboratory analysis of the product by the manufacturer, the FDA or other appropriate Federal or State agency or official upon request;
- Notify the FDA and all immediate trading partners that the dispenser has reason to believe may have received the illegitimate product within 24 hours of making the determination.

In response to a notification by the FDA or a trading partner that a determination has been made that a product is an illegitimate product, a dispenser must identify all illegitimate product in their possession or control that is the subject of that notification, including any product that is subsequently received, and they must perform the activities outlined above under the heading "Dispenser: Suspect Product".

Upon determining, in consultation with the FDA, that a notification is no longer necessary, a dispenser must promptly notify the same immediate trading partners notified previously by the dispenser about this product that the notification has been terminated.

Dispensers must keep records of the disposition of an illegitimate product for at least 6 years after the conclusion of the disposition.

582(d)(4)(C) Dispenser: Electronic Database

A dispenser may satisfy the requirements of subsection 582(d)(4), "Verification", by developing a secure electronic database or utilizing a secure electronic database developed or operated by another entity.

582(e) Repackager Provisions Explained

582(e)(1) Repackager: Product Tracing

582(e)(1)(A) Beginning no later than January 1, 2015 (FDA enforcement was deferred until May 1, 2015), repackagers are obligated by the DSCSA to make lot-level product tracking a standard part of every change of ownership (known as a "transaction") of drugs and biologics (known as "products") in the U.S. supply chain. This subsection explains what they have to do to meet that requirement. To fully understand the meaning of these provisions it is important to study the definitions of the terms that Congress has defined within the DSCSA. These definitions may not be as broadly-defined within the DSCSA as their common usage within the industry.

The following provisions apply to repackagers:

- A repackager must not accept ownership of a product unless the previous owner provides transaction history, transaction information, and a transaction statement for the product at the time of the transaction or prior to it;

- A repackager must provide the next owner of the product with statements that contain the transaction information, transaction history, and transaction statement for that specific product at the time of the transaction or prior to it.
- A repackager must capture the transaction information (including lot level information), transaction history and transaction statements for each transaction described in the bullets above, and maintain that information for at least 6 years after the date of the transaction.

The DSCSA repackager provisions do not include an *explicit* electronic format requirement comparable to that of the manufacturers [see Section 582(b)(1), "Manufacturer: Product Tracing"]. However, because manufacturers will be required to provide their transaction information, transaction history and transaction statement to customers who are wholesale distributors, repackagers or dispensers *only in electronic format* beginning on November 27, 2017, repackagers who buy directly will need to have fully tested systems in place that are able to receive those electronic documents before that date.

This, then, is an *implicit* requirement of the DSCSA, at least for repackagers that ever purchase product directly from a manufacturer.

It is also very likely that wholesale distributors will have a strong desire to provide their transaction information, transaction history and transaction statements to repackagers in electronic format whenever possible. Check with your suppliers to learn what their plans and expectations are.

The FDA provided guidance on the electronic formatting back in November of 2014, but repackagers will still need to work with GS1 Healthcare US, the HDMA, and their suppliers to ensure that the exact formatting and data exchange methods used by all companies are interoperable.

582(e)(1)(B) Repackager: Returns

Nonsaleable Returns
A repackager may return a *nonsaleable* product to

- the manufacturer or repackager,
- the wholesale distributor from whom the product was purchased,
- a returns processor, or
- a person acting on behalf of one of the above,

without providing transaction information, transaction history and a transaction statement.

Saleable or Nonsableable Returns on Behalf of a Third Party
Repackagers may return saleable or nonsaleable product on behalf of a hospital or other health care entity to

- the manufacturer or repackager,

- the wholesale distributor from whom the product was received,

without providing transaction information, transaction history, and transaction statements, as long as the hospital or other health care entity took ownership of that product under the terms and conditions of any agreement between the repackager and that entity.

This is all the DSCSA says about repackager requirements for saleable returns, leaving the appearance that repackagers must supply transaction information, transaction history, and transaction statements to the recipient of any saleable returns of product that they own. However, to avoid this apparent requirement, repackagers should ensure that there is some type of agreement (any type of agreement) that includes terms and conditions for returns with their wholesale distributors because wholesale distributors are only allowed to accept returned *saleable* product from a dispenser or repackager without receiving transaction information, transaction history and transaction statements if they are under such an agreement [see Section 582(c)(1)(2)(i), Wholesale Distributor: Saleable Returns]. It is likely that a simple sales agreement could fulfill this requirement as long as it includes terms and conditions that cover product returns. Check with the FDA to confirm this.

582(e)(1)(C) Repackager: Requests for Information

Repackagers must be prepared to react to any request for information by the FDA or any other appropriate State or Federal agency or official in the event of a recall, or for the purpose of investigating suspect product or an illegitimate product. Repackagers are required to provide any applicable transaction information, transaction history, and transaction statements for the product inquired about.

Repackagers are allowed 1 business day to respond with the appropriate information. In the event of a weekend or holiday, the response time must not exceed 48 hours after receiving the request, although the FDA may define some other reasonable time (which could be longer or, theoretically, shorter, depending on the urgency).

582(e)(2) Repackager: Product Identifier

Before the deadline of November 27, 2018, repackagers must begin to affix or imprint a product identifier on each package and homogenous case of a product that is intended to be introduced into the supply chain via the non-exempt transactions. And repackagers must retain the information about that product identifier and the product for at least 6 years after the transaction that introduces the product into the supply chain. As we already saw in section 582(e)(1), "Product Tracing", above that repackagers must also retain for 6 years information about the transaction that introduces the products into the supply chain.

Any product that is required to have a Standardized Numeric Identifier (SNI) is not required to have a unique device identifier (UDI)[55]. This would apply to combination products where there might have been a grey area regarding which type of identifier would be required. This provision ensures that companies would not be subject to duplicate product identification requirements. If there is any question about whether your product requires an SNI or a UDI, contact the FDA Office of Combination Products.[56]

582(e)(3) Repackager: Authorized Trading Partners

Beginning on January 1, 2015, repackagers may only do business with trading partners that are authorized as defined by the DSCSA. It is the repackager's responsibility to know that their trading partners are authorized/licensed and where. As part of meeting this requirement, repackagers should keep track of the State and Federal licenses that each of their trading partners currently hold and when they will expire so they can adjust their purchases based on the status of the supplier's licenses.

582(e)(4) Repackager: Verification

Beginning on January 1, 2015, repackagers must have systems in place to enable them to quarantine suspect product and perform investigations into that product, based on the product identifier, to determine if it is legitimate or illegitimate, and then to notify the FDA and their trading partners, as appropriate, of that status.

The details for repackagers are below.

582(e)(4)(A) Repackager: Suspect Product

Whenever a determination is made that a product in the possession or control of the repackager is suspect product—or upon receiving a request for verification from the FDA that has made a determination that a product within the possession or control of the repackagers is a suspect product—the repackager must quarantine that product until it is cleared or dispositioned. To fully understand this requirement it is important to read and understand the definitions of each of the terms used to describe it.

The repackager must promptly conduct an investigation in coordination with trading partners, when applicable, to determine whether the product is an illegitimate product. This investigation shall include validating any applicable transaction history and transaction information held by the repackager and it may include "otherwise investigating" to determine whether the product is an illegitimate product.

Prior to November 27, 2018, these investigations may verify the product using the lot and expiration date portions of the product identifier, but after that date they must include the verification of the product *at the package level, including the standardized numerical identifier (SNI)*.

If the repackager finds that the suspect product is not an illegitimate product, they must promptly notify the FDA, if applicable, that the product has been "cleared". At that time it may then be removed from quarantine and may be further distributed.

The repackagers must keep records of the investigation of suspect products for at least 6 years after the conclusion of the investigation.

582(e)(4)(B) Repackager: Illegitimate Product

Upon determining, in coordination with the manufacturer, that a product in the possession or control of a repackager is an illegitimate product, the repackager must:

- Quarantine the product to separate it from products intended for distribution until it is dispositioned;
- Disposition the illegitimate product (make sure you understand the special definition of "disposition");
- Take reasonable and appropriate steps to assist trading partners to disposition any illegitimate product in their possession or control;
- Retain a sample of the illegitimate product for further physical examination or laboratory analysis of the product by the manufacturer, the FDA or other appropriate Federal or State agency or official upon request;
- Notify the FDA and all immediate trading partners that the repackager has reason to believe may have received the illegitimate product within 24 hours of making the determination.

In response to a notification by the FDA or a trading partner that a determination has been made that a product is an illegitimate product, a repackager must identify all illegitimate product in their possession or control that is the subject of that notification, including any product that is subsequently received, and they must perform the activities outlined above under the heading "Repackager: Suspect Product".

Upon determining, in consultation with the FDA, that a notification is no longer necessary, a repackager must promptly notify the same immediate trading partners notified previously by the repackager about this product that the notification has been terminated.

Repackagers must keep records of the disposition of an illegitimate product for at least 6 years after the conclusion of the disposition.

582(e)(4)(C) Repackager: Requests for Verification

Beginning on November 27, 2018, whenever a repackager receives a request for verification of a product thought to be repackaged by the repackager from an authorized manufacturer, wholesale distributor or dispenser that is in possession or control of the product, the repackager must reply with an indication of whether or not the product identifier provided in the request corresponds to the product identifier affixed or imprinted by the repackager. The request may be made using the standardized numerical identifier (SNI) portion of the product identifier on a product package or on a homogeneous case of the product, and if it is, then the repackager's reply must be relative to that same level. The reply must be made within 24 hours or some other reasonable time as determined by the FDA, based on the circumstances of the request.

If a repackager determines, based on a verification request, that a product identifier that does not correspond to that affixed or imprinted by the repackager, the repackager must treat that product as "suspect product" and conduct an investigation as described in section 582(e)(4)(A), "Repackager: Suspect Product" above. If the repackager has reason to believe the product is illegitimate product, the repackager must advise the person making the request of that belief at the time of the repackager's reply to the request for verification.

582(e)(4)(D) Repackager: Electronic Database

A repackager may satisfy the requirements of subsection 581(e)(4), "Verification", by developing a secure electronic database or utilizing a secure electronic database developed or operated by another entity. The third-party owner of the database shall establish the requirements and processes to respond to requests and may provide for data access to other members of the pharmaceutical distribution supply chain, as appropriate. However, the development and operation of such a database shall not relieve the repackager of the requirement to respond to a request for verification submitted by means other than a secure electronic database.

With these words, Congress appears to be authorizing repackagers to make use of third-party services that would be designed to help them fulfill these verification requirements. It is worth noting at this point that what Congress defines in the DSCSA as "verification" is very close to what GS1 Healthcare terms as "Product Identifier Authentication" (PIA)[57]. It is likely that Congress included this section to give an explicit green light to industry efforts to develop standards around PIA for use here in the United States and elsewhere around the globe. However, even if a repackager were to make use of a PIA service provider, they are also obligated to respond to verification requests that are submitted by other means. The DSCSA does not require trading partners to make use of the electronic service.

582(e)(4)(E) Repackager: Verification of Saleable Returned Product

Beginning on November 27, 2018, whenever a repackager receives returned product that the repackager intends to further distribute, they must verify the product identifier for each sealed homogeneous case of the product, or, if the product is not in a sealed homogeneous case, verify the product identifier on each package.

Note that the comparable requirement for a manufacturer includes the requirement for the verification of the product identifiers to include the standardized numerical identifier (SNI) of the homogeneous case and/or package. This language does not appear in the repackager's requirements which may be viewed as an oversight as the original bill was being finalized by Congress. Repackagers should be aware of the difference and watch for any specific rules that the FDA may impose regarding these verifications.

582(f) Drop Shipments

For shipments where a wholesale distributor does not physically handle or store the product, but instead merely provides administrative services, including processing of orders and payments to a manufacturer, repackager or other wholesale distributor, the wholesale distributor is exempt from the requirements of FD&C Section 582 "Requirements" with the following conditions:

- the manufacturer, repackager, or other wholesale distributor that distributes the product to the dispenser by means of a drop shipment on behalf of the wholesale distributor must include the contact information for the wholesale distributor that is performing the administrative services on the transaction information and transaction history provided to the dispenser, and,
- the manufacturer, repackager, or other wholesale distributor must provide the transaction information, transaction history and transaction statements for the products in the shipment directly to the dispenser.

However, the wholesale distributor filling this role is NOT exempt from the notification requirements if product is found to be illegitimate product. See Subsection 582(c)(4)(B), Illegitimate Product, clauses (ii), "Making a Notification", (iii), "Responding to a Notification" and (iv), "Terminating a Notification".

Phase 2: 2023 and Beyond: Enhanced Drug Distribution Security (EDDS), Explained

Section 203 of the DSCSA immediately amends the new Section 582 of the FD&C at the end with additional sections under the overall title, "Enhanced Drug Distribution Security". The first subsection uses the same name.

582(g) Enhanced Drug Distribution Security (EDDS), Explained

582(g)(1) EDDS: In General

This section defines requirements that result in transforming the lot-based paper or electronic pedigree system defined in sections 582(a) through 582(f) into an interoperable, electronic package-level serialization-based tracing system starting on November 27, 2023. This is 10 years after the enactment of the DSCSA.

The following requirements are defined:

582(g)(1)(A)

- The transaction information and the transaction statements as required under the DSCSA shall be exchanged in a secure, interoperable, electronic manner in accordance with the standards established under the guidance issued by the FDA as described in Sections 582(h)(3), "Unit Level Tracing" and 582(h)(4), "Standards for Interoperable Data Exchange", discussed below, including any revision of that guidance issued in accordance with Section 582(h)(5), "Procedure" discussed below.

This paragraph establishes the requirement that the industry must follow guidance and specifications in 10 years that the DSCSA requires the FDA to publish prior to the 10-year anniversary of the enactment. The sections referenced above provide the details of what the FDA is required to do and when they must do it.

582(g)(1)(B)

- The transaction information required under the DSCSA shall include the product identifier at the package level for each package included in the transaction. This is the requirement that will transform the DSCSA into a full serialization-based law. Prior to this 10-year point, manufacturers and repackagers were required to put serial numbers (SNIs) on all of their products, but it is not until this point when the serial numbers must be included in the data that is provided to each new owner. *Prior to this 10-year point, SNIs were absent from the transaction information.*

582(g)(1)(C)

- Systems and processes for verification of product at the package level, including the standardized numerical identifier (SNI), shall be required in accordance with the standards established under the guidance that the FDA published back in November of 2014, defined way back in Section 582(a)(2), "Initial Standards", and those issued sometime after that date as mandated by Sections 582(h), paragraphs (2), "Suspect and Illegitimate Product", (3), "Unit Level Tracing", (4), "Standards for Interoperable Data Exchange", and (5), "Procedure", discussed below. These additional standards may include the use of aggregation[58, 59] and inference[60, 61, 62, 63] for the first time.

This paragraph will likely result in major changes to the way companies must verify product whenever it is required by the earlier sections. For the first 10 years, verification will require companies only to confirm that the product identifier affixed to a given package or homogeneous case matched one that was known to be valid by the manufacturer or repackager. In this enhanced drug distribution security era, the potential requirement for aggregation and inference implies that companies will be expected to confirm that they have received the specific serial numbers on products at the time they take ownership of them. We won't know if that is true until the FDA goes through the long process spelled out in the sections below and publishes their final guidances that are mandated.

582(g)(1)(D)

- Companies are required to deploy any systems and process upgrades necessary to shorten the time to respond with the transaction information and transaction statement for a product upon a request by the FDA or other appropriate Federal or State official in the event of a recall or for the purposes of investigating a suspect product or an illegitimate product. The upgrades must result in a response time that is characterized in the DSCSA as "promptly".

For the first 10 years companies were given between 1 and 2 days to respond to these requests. The term "promptly" is not defined in the DSCSA but if one assumes it means times in the order of minutes, that would mean companies would need to have fully automated systems to perform the necessary data retrieval at least as far back as 6 years and transmission of these electronic documents.

582(g)(1)(E)

- Companies are required to deploy any systems and processes necessary to promptly facilitate gathering the information necessary to produce the transaction information for each transaction going back to the manufacturer, as applicable, at the following times:
  - Whenever a request is made by the FDA or other appropriate Federal or State official on account of a recall or for the purposes of investigating a suspect product or an illegitimate product; or
  - To assist an authorized trading partner with the same kind of request describe in the bullet above when the request and response are made in a secure manner that ensures the protection of confidential commercial information and trade secrets.

582(g)(1)(F)

- Each person accepting a saleable return shall have systems and processes in place to allow acceptance of that product and may accept saleable returns only if they can associate the saleable return product with the transaction information and transaction statement associated with that product from their original shipment.

This expands the requirement that wholesale distributors will be under starting on November 27, 2019 [see Section 582(c)(1)(B)(i)(II), within "Saleable Returns"] to all segments.

582(g)(2) Compliance

582(g)(2)(A) Information Maintenance Agreement

A dispenser may enter into a written agreement with a third party — which could be an authorized wholesale distributor — under which the third party shall confidentially maintain any information and statements required to be maintained under this section. If a dispenser enters into this type of agreement, the dispenser must keep a copy of the written agreement, and this arrangement does not relieve the dispenser from its obligations under this subsection.

This appears to be a reiteration of the very similar text in Section 582(d)(1)(B), "Dispenser: Agreements with Third Parties". It serves to give confidence to dispensers that any third party agreements they established in Phase 1 can be used to fulfill requirements in Phase 2, as long as they meet the Phase 2 requirements, of course.

This may be a good solution to the chore of "promptly" dealing with all of these documents, especially now that they will all be electronic in the EDDS phase. Dispensers that buy products from multiple licensed sources will be faced with either:

- deploying their own electronic document retention capability;
- establishing separate contracts for electronic document retention with each source; or,
- establishing a single contract with a true third-party service provider that is not aligned with any single trading partner and where all suppliers must send their electronic documents.

GS1 is currently working on a new standard, based on their Electronic Product Code Information Services (EPCIS) standard,[64] that will facilitate solutions capable of all three of these approaches. Watch for solutions based on that new standard sometime before 2017.

582(g)(2)(B) Alternative Methods

The DSCSA requires the FDA to conduct an assessment [see Section 582(g)(3) "Assessment" below] in part to uncover potential alternative methods of compliance with any of the requirements contained in Section 582(g)(1), EDDS In General above. This includes:

- establishing compliance timelines for small businesses (including small business dispensers with 25 or fewer full-time employees) in order to ensure that the requirements do not impose undue economic hardship as determined by the FDA,
- establishing a process by which a dispenser may request a waiver from any requirements if the FDA determines that those requirements would result in an undue economic hardship, and,

- establishing a process for the biennial review and renewal of any such waiver.

582(g)(3) Assessment

Within 18 months after the FDA issues their final guidance as required in Section 582(h) "Guidance Documents" below, the FDA is required to enter into a contract with a private, independent consulting firm with the expertise to conduct a technology and software assessment that looks specifically at the feasibility of dispensers with 25 or fewer full-time employees conducting interoperable, electronic tracing of products at the package level. The assessment must be completed no later than May 27, 2021.

As a condition of the contract award, the consulting firm must agree to consult with actual dispensers that have 25 or fewer full-time employees when conducting the assessment.

The assessment must assess the following:

- whether the necessary software and hardware is readily accessible to the dispensers;
- whether the necessary software and hardware is prohibitively expensive to obtain, install, and maintain for the dispensers;
- whether the necessary hardware and software can be integrated into business practices, such as interoperability with wholesale distributors, for these dispensers.

The FDA must:

- publish the statement of work for the assessment for public comment prior to beginning the assessment;
- publish the final assessment for public comment not later than 30 calendar days after receiving the assessment from the consulting firm; and
- hold a public meeting not later than 180 calendar days after receiving the final assessment, at which public stakeholders may present their views on the assessment.

582(g)(4) Procedure

When promulgating any regulations related to the EDDS, the FDA must:

- provide appropriate flexibility by:
  - not requiring the adoption of specific business systems for the maintenance and transmission of data;
  - prescribing alternative methods of compliance for any of the requirements of Section 582(g)(1) "EDDS In General" above, or set forth in regulations implementing such requirements, including:
    - timelines for small businesses to comply with the requirements set forth in the regulations, in order to ensure that such requirements do not impose undue economic

hardship for small businesses [including small business dispensers for whom the criteria set forth in the assessment required by Section 582(g)(3), "Assessment", above is not met], if the FDA determines that such requirements would result in undue economic hardship; and

- the establishment of a process by which a dispenser may request a waiver from any of the requirements set forth in such regulations if the FDA determines that such requirements would result in an undue economic hardship; and

o taking into consideration:

- the results of pilot projects, including pilot projects required by this section and private sector pilot projects, including those involving the use of aggregation and inference;
- the public meetings held and related guidance documents issued under this section;
- the public health benefits of any additional regulations in comparison to the cost of compliance with such

> requirements, including on entities of varying sizes and capabilities;

- the diversity of the pharmaceutical distribution supply chain by providing appropriate flexibility for each sector, including both large and small businesses; and
- the assessment required by Section 582(g)(3) above with respect to small business dispensers, including related public comment and the public meeting, and requirements under this section;

- issue a notice of proposed rulemaking that includes a copy of the proposed regulations;
- provide a period of not less than 60 days for comments on the proposed regulation; and
- publish in the Federal Register the final regulation not less than 2 years prior to the effective date of the regulation.

582(h) Guidance Documents, Explained

The DSCSA requires the FDA to take a number of very specific actions that are spread out across the 10 years that follows enactment.

582(h)(1) In General

To facilitate the successful and efficient adoption of secure, interoperable product tracing at the package level that enhances drug distribution security and further protects the public health, the FDA shall issue the guidance documents as specified by this subsection.

582(h)(2) Suspect and Illegitimate Product

Not later than May 27, 2014, the FDA must issue a guidance document to aid trading partners in the identification of a suspect product and notification termination. The guidance document shall:

- identify specific scenarios that could significantly increase the risk of a suspect product entering the pharmaceutical distribution supply chain;
- provide recommendation on how trading partners may identify such product and make a determination on whether the product is a suspect product as soon as practicable; and
- set forth the process by which manufacturers, repackagers, wholesale distributors, and dispensers shall terminate notifications in

consultation with the FDA regarding illegitimate product as required in the following subsections:

- ○ 582(b)(4)(B) "Manufacturer: Illegitimate Product",
- ○ 582(c)(4)(B) "Wholesale Distributor: Illegitimate Product",
- ○ 582(d)(4)(B) "Dispenser: Illegitimate Product", and,
- ○ 582(e)(4)(B) "Repackager: Illegitimate Product".

If this guidance document is ever revised by the FDA for any reason, the FDA must follow the procedure outlined in 582(h)(5) "Procedure" below.

582(h)(3) Unit Level Tracing

The FDA must issue a final guidance document that outlines and makes recommendations with respect to the system attributes necessary to enable secure tracing at the package level, as required under the requirements established under subsection 582(g), the EDDS. The goal of this guidance document is to enhance drug distribution security at the package level. The FDA must publish this guidance document no more than 18 months after conducting a public meeting on the system attributes that would be necessary to enable secure tracing of product at the package level, including allowing for the use of verification, inference, and aggregation, as necessary.

The guidance document must:

- Define the circumstances under which the

sectors within the pharmaceutical distribution supply chain may, in the most efficient manner practicable, *infer the contents* of a case, pallet, tote, or other aggregate of individual packages or containers of product, from a product identifier associated with the case, pallet, tote, or other aggregate, *without opening* each case, pallet, tote, or other aggregate or otherwise individually scanning each package;

- Identify methods and processes to enhance secure tracing of product at the package level, such as secure processes to facilitate the use of inference, enhanced verification activities, the use of aggregation and inference, processes that utilize the product identifiers to enhance tracing of product at the package level, including the standardized numerical identifier (SNI), or package security features; and

- Ensure the protection of confidential commercial information and trade secrets.

In issuing or revising this guidance document, the FDA must follow the procedure set forth in Section 582(h)(5), "Procedure", below.

582(h)(4) Standards for Interoperable Data Exchange

In Section 582(a)(2), "Initial Standards" under general requirements, the DSCSA required the FDA to issue draft guidance that establishes standards for the interoperable exchange of lot-level transaction information, transaction history and transaction statements in paper or electronic format. That draft guidance must be published by November 27 of 2014. It is not until this current section that that *draft* guidance is converted into a *final* guidance document, which must occur no later than 18 months after FDA conducts a public meeting on the interoperable standards necessary to enhance the security of the pharmaceutical distribution supply chain. The final guidance document must:

- Identify and make recommendations for the standards necessary for adoption to support the secure, interoperable electronic data exchange among the pharmaceutical distribution supply chain. The standards must comply with a form and format developed by a widely recognized international standards development organization;
- Take into consideration the standards established by the FDA when they produced the draft guidance and those that were established under Section 505D of the FD&C, Pharmaceutical Security[65], which was originally mandated by the FDA Amendments Act (FDAAA) of 2007[66]. Section 505D is where the FDA was required to establish the Standardized Numerical Identifier (SNI) standard;
- Facilitate the creation of a uniform process or methodology for product tracing; and
- Ensure the protection of confidential commercial information and trade secrets.

In issuing or revising this guidance document, the FDA must follow the procedure set forth in Section 582(h)(5) below.

582(h)(5) Procedure

In issuing or revising any guidance issued by the FDA to meet the mandates in 582(g), "Enhanced Drug Distribution Security" and 582(h) "Guidance Documents", except the initial draft guidance issued under paragraph 582(a)(2)(A) "Initial Standards", the FDA must:

- Publish a notice in the Federal Register for at least 30 days announcing that the draft or revised draft guidance is available;
- Post the draft guidance document on the FDA's website and also make it available in hard copy;
- Provide an opportunity for comment and review and take into consideration any comments received;
- Revise the draft guidance, as appropriate;
- Publish a notice in the *Federal Register* for at least 30 days announcing that the final guidance or final revised guidance is available;
- Post the final guidance document on the FDA website and also make it available in hard copy; and
- Provide for an effective date of not earlier than 1 year after the guidance becomes final.

582(i) Public Meetings, Explained

The FDA must hold at least 5 public meetings to enhance the safety and security of the pharmaceutical distribution supply chain and provide for comment. *The FDA is explicitly barred from holding the first public meeting prior to November 27, 2014.* In carrying out the public meetings the FDA must:

- Prioritize the topics necessary to inform the issuance of the guidance described in Sections 582(h) paragraphs (3), "Unit Level Tracing", and (4), "Standards For Interoperable Data Exchange"; and
- Take all reasonable and practicable measures to ensure the protection of confidential commercial information and trade secrets.

Each of the following topics must be addressed in at least one of the public meetings:

(A) An assessment of the steps taken under subsection 582(b), "Manufacturer Provisions", through 582(e), "Repackager Provisions", to build capacity for a unit-level system, including the impact of the requirements of those sections on:
- The ability of the health care system collectively to maintain patient access to medicines;
- The scalability of the requirements, including as they relate to product lines; and

- The capability of different sectors and subsectors, including both large and small businesses, to affix and utilize the product identifier.

(B) The system attributes necessary to support the requirements set forth under subsection 582(g), "Enhanced Drug Distribution Security", including the standards necessary for adoption in order to support the secure, interoperable, electronic data exchange among sectors within the pharmaceutical distribution supply chain.

(C) Best practices in each of the different sectors within the pharmaceutical distribution supply chain to implement the requirements of this section.

(D) The costs and benefits of the implementation of this section, including the impact on each pharmaceutical distribution supply chain sector and public health.

(E) Whether electronic tracing requirements, including tracing of product at the package level, are feasible, cost effective, and needed to protect the public health.

(F) The systems and processes needed to utilize the product identifiers to enhance tracing of product at the package level, including allowing for verification, aggregation, and inference, as necessary.

(G) The technical capabilities and legal authorities, if any, needed to establish an interoperable electronic system that provides for tracing of product at the package level.

(H) The impact that such additional requirements would have on patient safety, the drug supply, cost and regulatory burden, and timely patient access to prescription drugs.

(I) Other topics, as determined by the FDA.

582(j) Pilot Projects, Explained

582(j)(1) The FDA must establish 1 or more pilot projects, in coordination with authorized manufacturers, repackagers, wholesale distributors, and dispensers, to explore and evaluate methods to enhance the safety and security of the pharmaceutical distribution supply chain. Such projects shall build upon efforts, in existence as of the date of enactment of the DSCSA (November 27, 2013), with the same goal. The FDA must take into consideration any pilot projects conducted prior to that date, including any pilot projects that use aggregation and inference, and inform the draft and final guidance under subsection 582(h), paragraphs (3), "Unit Level Tracing", and (4), "Standards For Interoperable Data Exchange".

582(j)(2) Content

The FDA shall ensure that the pilot projects conducted and considered under this subsection reflect the diversity of the pharmaceutical distribution supply chain and that the pilot projects, when taken as a whole, include participants representative of every sector, including both large and small businesses.

The pilot projects must be designed to:

- utilize the product identifier for tracing of a product, which *may* include verification of the product identifier of a product, including the use of aggregation and inference;

- improve the technical capabilities of each sector and subsector to comply with systems and processes needed to utilize the product identifiers to enhance tracing of a product;
- identify system attributes that are necessary to implement the requirements established under this section; and
- complete other activities as determined by the FDA.

582(k) Sunset, Explained

Section 582(g), "Enhanced Drug Distribution Security", contains the new features of the drug track and trace system that the DSCSA imposes at the 10--year anniversary of its enactment. This section identifies the features that will "turn-off" at that anniversary. The following requirements shall have *no force or effect* after November 27, 2023 (10 years after enactment):

- The provision and receipt of transaction history under the entire Section 582 "Requirements". The elimination of this requirement at the 10 year point transforms the operation of this system from a "pedigree-like" system to a "one-up, one-down" record-keeping system.
- The requirement for any member of the supply chain to accept saleable returned product only if they can associate that product with the transaction information and transaction statement associated with the original sale of that product. This means that, as long as the returned product is not suspect product, members of the supply chain can accept any conforming product and then distribute it further or dispense it without checking to see if they originally sold that product.

  The requirements for saleable returns that will have no force or effect after this point include:
    - For manufacturers: Section 582(b)(4)(E), "Saleable Returned Product";

- For wholesale distributors: Section 582(c)(1)(B)(i), "Saleable Returns";
- For dispensers: Section 582(d)(1)(C)(i), "Saleable Returns"; and
- For repackagers: Section 582(e)(4)(E), "Verification of Saleable Returned Product".

- The wholesale distributor requirements *as applied to lot level information only*, dealing with their ability or inability to share transaction data with specific parties. The subparagraphs that will have no force or effect after this point include:
  - 852(c)(1)(A)(v)(II), maintain the confidentiality of the transaction information, and transaction statements; and
  - 582(c)(1)(D), "Trading Partner Agreements".

582(l) **Rule Of Construction, Explained**

The requirements set forth in Enhanced Drug Distribution Security subsections:

- 582(g)(4), "EDDS Procedure";
- 582(i), "Public Meetings"; and
- 582(j), "Pilot Projects",

shall not be construed as a condition, prohibition, or precedent for precluding or delaying the provisions becoming effective pursuant to subsection 582(g), "Enhanced Drug Distribution Security". This seems to imply that the effective date of the EDDS provisions will not be delayed if insufficient public meetings or pilot projects occur, or even if the FDA has not published the required standards and guidance documents on time as specified. It is in the best interest of the industry to help the FDA successfully complete those activities before the November 27, 2023 date so that they have the maximum guidance for meeting their obligations under the law, since the EDDS provisions will not be delayed.

582(m) Requests For Information, Explained

Starting on November 27, 2023, the timeline for responses to requests for information from the FDA, or other appropriate Federal or State official, as applicable, under subsections:

- 582(b)(1)(B), "Manufacturer: Requests For Information";
- 582(c)(1)(C), "Wholesale distributor: Requests For Information"; and
- 582(e)(1)(C), "Repackager: Requests For Information",

shall be not later than 24 hours after receiving the request from the FDA or other appropriate Federal or State official, as applicable, or in such other reasonable time as determined by the FDA based on the circumstances of the request. Prior to the 10-year anniversary of enactment, this response time was 48 hours. The time that dispensers have to respond to requests (2 business days) is not affected by this clause and so it does not change [see Section 582(d)(1)(D), "Dispensers: Requests For Information"].

204 (a) The New National Standards for Wholesale Distributors, Explained

Prior to the enactment of the DSCSA, pharmaceutical wholesale distributors were licensed and regulated solely by each state. The FDA had no jurisdiction over the operation of the drug supply chain. This made sense when the sales territory of the typical wholesale distributor of drugs was fully within the borders of a single state. But beginning in the 1980's, the wholesale distribution segment of the pharma supply chain in the United States consolidated to the point where three companies dominate the business and cover the entire United States. Smaller companies serve customers in multiple states. The enactment of the DSCSA is Congress' way of acknowledging that the distribution of drugs is a national business and that it should be licensed and regulated that way.

These amendments took effect on January 1, 2015.

204 Section 204 of the DSCSA establishes new national standards for wholesale distributors of drugs regardless of size or territory. From now on, if you are in the business of distributing drugs anywhere in the United States, you must follow these standards.

503(e)(1) Requirement

On the other hand, the 50 U.S. States have an existing revenue stream from licensing all of the wholesale distributors that operate in their State, whether large or small, and eliminating that stream and the local regulations would be disruptive to those State governments. Therefore, Congress retained the licensing program of the states. But if a State does not have an established licensing program, companies distributing drugs in that State must hold a license issued by the FDA, once the FDA establishes their licensing program.

The State- and FDA-issued licenses must meet the standards, terms, and conditions that will be established by the FDA under the new section 583, "National Standards for Prescription Drug Wholesale Distributors".

503(e)(2) Reporting and Database

Beginning on January 1, 2015, any person who owns or operates an establishment that engages in wholesale distribution of drugs shall:

- Report to the FDA on an annual basis as scheduled by the FDA:
  - The States in which the person is licensed and the State license number for those states;
  - The name, address, and contact information of each facility from which the person conducts business, including

all trade names used.

- Report to the FDA any significant disciplinary actions, such as the revocation or suspension of a license, taken by a State or Federal Government during the reporting period against the wholesale distributor.

No later than January 1, 2015, the FDA must establish a database of authorized wholesale distributors. This database shall:

- Identify each authorized wholesale distributor by name, contact information, and each State where that wholesale distributor is appropriately licensed to engage in wholesale distribution;
- Be available to the public on the FDA website; and
- Be updated regularly on a schedule determined by the FDA.

The FDA shall establish a format and procedure for appropriate State officials to access the information held in the database in a prompt and secure manner.

The FDA must not disclose any information that is a trade secret or confidential information subject to section 552(b)(4) of title 5, USC, or section 1905 of title 18, USC.

This database may now be found on the FDA's website at: http://www.fda.gov/Drugs/DrugSafety/DrugIntegrityandSupplyChainSecurity/DrugSupplyChainSecurityAct/ucm423749.htm

503(e)(3) Costs

If a State does not establish a licensing program for **wholesale distributors** of drugs, the FDA must license those who engage in that business in that State and may collect a reasonable fee. The fee is to reimburse the FDA for costs associated with establishing and administering the licensure program and conducting periodic inspections. The FDA shall adjust fee rates as needed on an annual basis to generate only the amount of revenue needed to perform this service. Fees authorized by this paragraph shall be collected and available for obligation only to the extent and in the amount provided in advance in appropriations Acts. Such fees are authorized to remain available until expended. The money necessary may be transferred from the FDA salaries and expenses appropriation account that does not have a fiscal year limitation to the appropriation account for salaries and expenses that does have a fiscal year limitation.

Nothing in the DSCSA shall prohibit States from collecting fees from **wholesale distributors** in connection with State licensing of those companies. The States' revenue streams are maintained.

503(e)(4) Wholesale Distribution

For the purposes of this subsection and subsection 503(d), the term "wholesale distribution" means the distribution of a drug subject to subsection 503(b), "Prescription by physician" etc., to a person other than a consumer or patient, or receipt of a drug subject to subsection 503(b) by a person other than the consumer or patient, but does not include the following:

(A) Intracompany distribution of any drug between members of an affiliate or within a manufacturer;

(B) The distribution of a drug, or an offer to distribute a drug among hospitals or other health care entities which are under common control;

(C) The distribution of a drug or an offer to distribute a drug for emergency medical reasons, including a public health emergency declaration under section 319 of the Public Health Service Act, except that, for purposes of this paragraph, a drug shortage not caused by a public health emergency shall not constitute an emergency medical reason;

(D) The dispensing of a drug pursuant to a prescription executed in accordance with subsection 503(b)(1);

(E) The distribution of minimal quantities of drug by a licensed retail pharmacy to a licensed practitioner for office use;

(F) The distribution of a drug or an offer to distribute a drug by a charitable organization to a nonprofit affiliate of the organization to the extent otherwise permitted by law;

(G) The purchase or other acquisition by a dispenser, hospital, or other health care entity of a drug for use by such dispenser, hospital or other health care entity;

(H) The distribution of a drug by the manufacturer

of that drug;

(I) The receipt or transfer of a drug by an authorized third-party logistics provider provided that such third-party logistics provider does not take ownership of the drug;

(J) A common carrier that transports a drug, provided that the common carrier does not take ownership of the drug;

(K) The distribution of a drug, or an offer to distribute a drug by an authorized repackager that has taken ownership or possession of the drug and repacks it in accordance with section 582(e), "Repackager Requirements";

(L) salable drug returns when conducted by a dispenser;

(M) the distribution of a collection of finished medical devices, which may include a product or biological product, assembled in kit form strictly for the convenience of the purchaser or user (referred to in this subparagraph as a 'medical convenience kit') if:

    i. the medical convenience kit is assembled in an establishment that is registered with the Food and Drug Administration as a device manufacturer in accordance with section 510(b)(2);

    ii. the medical convenience kit does not contain a controlled substance that appears in a schedule contained in the Comprehensive Drug Abuse Prevention and Control Act of 1970;

    iii. in the case of a medical convenience kit that includes a product, the person that manufacturers the kit:

    I. purchased such product directly from the pharmaceutical manufacturer or from a wholesale distributor that purchased the product directly from the pharmaceutical manufacturer; and

    II. does not alter the primary container or label of the product as purchased from the manufacturer or wholesale distributor; and

iv. in the case of a medical convenience kit that includes a product, the product is:

    I. an intravenous solution intended for the replenishment of fluids and electrolytes;

    II. a product intended to maintain the equilibrium of water and minerals in the body;

    III. a product intended for irrigation or reconstitution;

    IV. an anesthetic;

    V. an anticoagulant;

    VI. a vasopressor; or

    VII. a sympathomimetic;

(N) the distribution of an intravenous drug that, by its formulation, is intended for the replenishment of fluids and electrolytes (such as sodium, chloride, and potassium) or calories (such as dextrose and amino acids);

(O) the distribution of an intravenous drug used to maintain the equilibrium of water and minerals in the body, such as dialysis solutions;

(P) the distribution of a drug that is intended for irrigation, or sterile water, whether intended for such purposes or for injection;

(Q) the distribution of medical gas, as defined in section 575;

(R) facilitating the distribution of a product by providing solely administrative services, including processing of orders and payments; or

(S) the transfer of a product by a hospital or other health care entity, or by a wholesale distributor or manufacturer operating at the direction of the hospital or other health care entity, to a repackager described in section 581(16)(B) and registered under section 510 for the purpose of repackaging the drug for use by that hospital, or other health care entity and other health care entities that are under common control, if ownership of the drug remains with the hospital or other health care entity at all times.

503(e)(5) Third-Party Logistics Providers, Explained

503(e)(5)

Each entity that meets the definition of a third-party logistics provider under section 581(22) shall obtain a license as a third-party logistics provider as described in section 584(a), "Requirements", and is not required to obtain a license as a wholesale distributor if the entity never assumes an ownership interest in the product it handles.

503(e)(6) Affiliate

For the purposes of this subsection, the term "affiliate" means a business entity that has a relationship with a second business entity if, directly or indirectly:

(A) one business entity controls, or has the power to control, the other business entity; or

(B) a third party controls, or has the power to control, both of the business entities.

583 National Standards for Prescription Drug Wholesale Distributors, Explained

The DSCSA creates the new Section 583 to provide direction to the FDA about how Congress wishes to regulate wholesale distributors of prescription drugs.

583(a) In General

Before November 27, 2015, the FDA must publish standards for the licensing of persons under section 503(e)(1), including the revocation, reissuance, and renewal of licenses.

583(b) Content

To ensure uniformity of the standards created by this section, the standards established shall apply to all State and Federal licenses described under section 503(e)(1), "Requirement", and shall include standards for the following:

(1) The storage and handling of prescription drugs, including facility requirements.

(2) The establishment and maintenance of records of the distributions of such drugs.

(3) The furnishing of a bond or other equivalent means of security, as follows:

(A)

    (i) For the issuance or renewal of a wholesale distributor license, an applicant that is not a government owned and operated wholesale distributor shall submit a surety bond of $100,000 or other equivalent means of security acceptable to the State.

    (ii) For purposes of clause (i) above, the State or other applicable authority may accept a surety bond in the amount of $25,000 if the annual gross receipts of the previous tax year for the wholesaler is $10,000,000 or less.

(B) If a wholesale distributor can provide evidence that it possesses the required bond in a State, the requirement for a bond in another State shall be waived.

(4) Mandatory background checks and fingerprinting of facility managers or designated representatives.

(5) The establishment and implementation of qualifications for key personnel.

(6) The mandatory physical inspection of any facility to be used in wholesale distribution within a reasonable time frame from the initial

application of the facility and to be conducted by the licensing authority or by the State, consistent with subsection 583(c), "Inspections", directly below.

(7) In accordance with subsection 583(d), "Prohibited Persons", the prohibition of certain persons from receiving or maintaining licensure for wholesale distribution.

583(c) Inspections

To satisfy the inspection requirement under subsection 583(b)(6) directly above, the Federal or State licensing authority may conduct the inspection or may accept an inspection by the State in which the facility is located, or by a third-party accreditation or inspection service approved by the FDA or the State licensing the wholesale distributor.

583(d) Prohibited Persons

The standards shall include requirements to prohibit a person from receiving or maintaining licensure for wholesale distribution if the person:

(1) has been convicted of any felony for conduct relating to wholesale distribution, any felony violation of subsection 301(i) or 301(k), or any felony violation of section 1365 of title 18, USC, relating to product tampering; or

(2) has engaged in a pattern of violating the requirements of this section, or State

requirements for licensure, that presents a threat of serious adverse health consequences or death to humans.

583(e) Requirements

In promulgating any regulation to meet this section, the FDA shall:

(1) issue a notice of proposed rulemaking that includes a copy of the proposed regulation;

(2) provide a period of not less than 60 days for comments on the proposed regulation; and

(3) provide that the final regulation take effect on the date that is 2 years after the date that the final regulation is published.

204(b) Authorized Distributors of Record, Explained

The term "Authorized Distributor of Record", or "ADR", has been the subject of some controversy[67] over the last 15 years. The term was first defined by the Prescription Drug Marketing Act in 1988, using exactly the same words that are inserted into Section 503(d)(4), "Authorized Distributors of Record", by the DSCSA below. The controversy arose because the PDMA did not include a definition of the phrase "ongoing relationship". In 1999 the FDA defined that phrase in the final rule for implementation of the PDMA.[68] The term "ADR" is apparently defined in the section below to remove any ambiguity where the term is used outside of the section where the PDMA defined it, related to the distribution of drug samples. The term was already in use in Section 503(d) but was not defined there until now.

204(c)   Effective January 1, 2015, Section 503(d) (21 U.S.C. 353(d)), "Distribution of Drug Samples", is amended by adding at the end the following:

503(d)(4) Authorized Distributors of Record

In this subsection, the term 'authorized distributors of record' means those distributors with whom a manufacturer has established an ongoing relationship to distribute such manufacturer's products.".

205 The New National Standards for Third-Party Logistics Providers, Explained

Until the enactment of the DSCSA, pharmaceutical third-party logistics providers were licensed and regulated as wholesale distributors only in some states. The FDA had no jurisdiction over the operation of the drug supply chain, including these entities. With the passage of the DSCSA, third-party logistics providers will now need to be licensed, either by the states in which they do business, or by the FDA.

584(a) Requirements

No third-party logistics provider in any State may conduct activities in any State unless each of their facilities:

(1)

    (A) is licensed by the State from which the drug is distributed by the third-party logistics provider, in accordance with the regulations promulgated under subsection 584(d); or

    (B) if the State from which the drug distributed by the third-party logistics provider has not established a licensure requirement, is licensed by the FDA, in accordance with the regulations promulgated under subsection 584(d), "Regulations"; and

(2) if the drug is distributed interstate, is licensed by the State into which the drug is distributed by the third-party logistics provider if that State licenses third-party logistics providers that distribute drugs into the State and the third-party logistics provider is not licensed by the FDA as described in paragraph (1)(B) above.

584(b) Reporting

Beginning on November 27, 2014, a facility of a third-party logistics provider shall report to the FDA, on an annual basis on a schedule determined by the FDA:

(1) the State by which the facility is licensed and the appropriate identification number of such license; and

(2) the name and address of the facility and all trade names under which such facility conducts business.

584(c) Costs

584(c)(1) Authorized fees

If a State does not establish a licensing program for a third-party logistics provider, the FDA must license these providers and may collect a reasonable fee in the amount necessary to reimburse the FDA for costs associated with establishing and administering the licensure program and conducting the necessary periodic inspections. The FDA may adjust the fee rates as needed on an annual basis to generate only the amount of revenue needed to perform this service. The fees will be collected and available for obligation only to the extent and in the amount provided in advance in an appropriations Act. The fees are authorized by Congress to remain available until expended. The money necessary may be transferred from the FDA salaries and expenses appropriation account that does not have a fiscal year limitation to the appropriation account for salaries and expenses that does have a fiscal year limitation.

584(c)(2) State Licensing Fees

As long as a State establishes a program to license third-party logistics providers that operate within their State, that State may collect licensing fees. However, if a State does not establish a licensing program, they will be prohibited from collecting a licensing fee from third-party logistics providers.

584(d) **Regulations**

584(d)(1) **In General**

Before November 27, 2015, the FDA shall issue regulations regarding the standards for Federal and State licensing of third-party logistics providers, including the revocation and reissuance of licenses.

584(d)(2) **Content**

Such regulations shall:

(A) establish a process by which a third-party accreditation program approved by the FDA shall, upon request by a third-party logistics provider, issue a license to each third-party logistics provider that meets the requirements set forth in this section;

(B) establish a process by which the FDA shall issue a license to each third-party logistics provider that meets the requirements set forth in this section if the FDA is not able to approve a third-party accreditation program because no such program meets the FDA's requirements necessary for approval;

(C) require that the entity complies with storage practices, as determined by the FDA, including:

    i. maintaining access to warehouse space of suitable size to facilitate safe operations, including a suitable area to quarantine suspect product;

   ii.   maintaining adequate security; and

   iii. having written policies and procedures to:

       I.   address receipt, security, storage, inventory, shipment, and distribution of a product;

       II.   identify, record, and report confirmed losses or thefts in the United States;

       III. correct errors and inaccuracies in inventories;

       IV. provide support for manufacturer recalls;

       V.   prepare for, protect against, and address any reasonably foreseeable crisis that affects security or operation at the facility, such as a strike, fire, or flood;

       VI. ensure that any expired product is segregated from other products and returned to the manufacturer or repackager or destroyed;

       VII. maintain the capability to trace the receipt and outbound distribution of a product, and supplies and records of inventory; and

       VIII. quarantine or destroy a suspect product if directed to do so by the respective manufacturer, wholesale distributor, dispenser, or an authorized government agency;

(D) provide for periodic inspection of the facility warehouse space by the licensing authority, as determined by the FDA, to ensure compliance with this section;

(E) prohibit a facility from having as a manager or designated representative anyone convicted of any felony violation of subsection 301(i) or 301(k) or any violation of section 1365 of title 18, USC relating to product tampering;

(F) provide for mandatory background checks of a facility manager or a designated representative of the manager;

(G) require a third-party logistics provider to provide the applicable licensing authority, upon a request by the authority, a list of all product manufacturers, wholesale distributors, and dispensers for whom the third-party logistics provider provides services at the facility; and

(H) include procedures under which any third-party logistics provider license:

    i.   expires on the date that is 3 years after issuance of the license; and

    ii. may be renewed for additional 3-year periods.

584(d)(3) Procedure

In promulgating the regulations under this subsection, the FDA shall:

(A) issue a notice of proposed rulemaking that includes a copy of the proposed regulation;

(B) provide a period of not less than 60 days for

comments on the proposed regulation; and

(C) provide that the final regulation takes effect upon the expiration of 1 year after the date that the final regulation is issued.

584(e) Validity

A third-party logistics provider license shall remain valid as long as the00203PL remains licensed consistent with this section. If the FDA finds that the third-party accreditation program demonstrates that all applicable requirements for licensure are met, they will issue a license to a third-party logistics provider receiving accreditation.

585 Uniform National Policy: The Preemption Provisions, Explained

This is the section that establishes the supremacy of the DSCSA over all similar State laws and sunsets the Federal Prescription Drug Marketing Act of 1988 on January 1, 2015.

585(a) Product Tracing and Other Requirements

Beginning on November 27, 2013 — the date of enactment of the DSCSA — no State or political subdivision of a State may establish or continue in effect any requirements for tracing products through the distribution system (including any requirements with respect to statements of distribution history, transaction history, transaction information, or transaction statement of a product as such product changes ownership in the supply chain, or verification, investigation, disposition, notification, or recordkeeping relating to such systems, including paper or electronic pedigree systems or for tracking and tracing drugs throughout the distribution system) which are inconsistent with, more stringent than, or in addition to, any requirements applicable under section 503(e), as amended by the DSCSA, or this subchapter (or regulations issued thereunder), or which are inconsistent with:

(1) any waiver, exception, or exemption as allowed by sections 581 "Definitions" or 582 "Requirements"; or

(2) any restrictions specified in section 582 "Requirements".

585(b) Wholesale Distributor and Third-Party Logistics Provider Standards

585(b)(1) In General

Beginning on November 27, 2013, no State or political subdivision of a State may establish or continue any standards, requirements, or regulations with respect to wholesale prescription drug distributor or third-party logistics provider licensure that are inconsistent with, less stringent than, directly related to, or covered by the standards and requirements applicable under section 503(e), as amended by the DSCSA, in the case of a wholesale distributor, or section 584, "The New National Standards for Third-Party Logistics Providers", in the case of a third-party logistics provider.

585(b)(2) State Regulation of Third-Party Logistics Providers

No State shall regulate third-party logistics

providers as wholesale distributors.

585(b)(3) Administration Fees

Notwithstanding paragraph (1) above, a State may administer fee collections for effectuating the wholesale drug distributor and third-party logistics provider licensure requirements under sections 503(e), 583, "National Standards for Prescription Drug Wholesale Distributors", and 584, "The New National Standards for Third-Party Logistics Providers".

585(b)(4) Enforcement, Suspension, and Revocation

Notwithstanding paragraph (1) above, a State:

(A) may take administrative action, including fines, to enforce a requirement promulgated by the State in accordance with section 503(e) or this subchapter;

(B) may provide for the suspension or revocation of licenses issued by the State for violations of the laws of that State;

(C) upon conviction of violations of Federal, State, or local drug laws or regulations, may provide for fines, imprisonment, or civil penalties; and

(D) may regulate activities of licensed entities in a manner that is consistent with product tracing requirements under section 582 "Requirements".

585(c) Exception

Nothing in this section shall be construed to preempt State requirements related to the distribution of prescription drugs if such requirements are not related to product tracing as described in subsection 585(a) "Product Tracing And Other Requirements" or wholesale distributor and third-party logistics provider licensure as described in subsection 585(b) "Wholesale Distributor And Third-Party Logistics Provider Standards" applicable under section 503(e) or this subchapter (or regulations issued thereunder).

206 Penalties, Explained

The existing prohibited acts section of the FD&C is modified by this part of the DSCSA to include the failure to comply with the DSCSA requirements under section 582 "Requirements", and the failure to comply with the DSCSA requirements under section 584 "National Standards For Third-Party Logistics Providers", as applicable. It appears that failure to comply with section 583 "National Standards for Prescription Drug Wholesale Distributors" is not a prohibited act. If so, then that failure may not be a finable offence.

If a drug package fails to bear the product identifier as required by section 582 "Requirements", the drug is considered "misbranded" and is therefore a violation of the FD&C.

207 Conforming Amendment, Explained

Effective January 1, 2015, Section 303(b)(1)(D) (21 U.S.C. 333(b)(1)(D)), "Prescription drug marketing violations", was amended by striking "503(e)(2)(A)" and inserting "503(e)(1)".

208 Savings Clause, Explained

Except as provided in the amendments made by the following paragraphs under "National Standards for Prescription Drug Wholesale Distributors":

- 204(1), "Requirement";
- 204(2), "Wholesale Distribution"; and
- 204(3), "Third-Party Logistics Providers";

and section 206(a), "Penalties", nothing in this title (including the amendments made by this title) shall be construed as altering any authority of the Secretary of Health and Human Services with respect to a drug subject to section 503(b)(1) of the Federal Food, Drug, and Cosmetic Act (21 U.S.C. 353(b)(1)), "Prescription by Physician", under any other provision of such Act or the Public Health Service Act (42 U.S.C. 201 et seq.).

Part 2: Selected Essays

This part contains selected essays from the RxTrace blog that have been published since the DSCSA was enacted on November 27, 2013. These essays have been edited for publication in this book. In some cases they have been updated to reflect any change in the status since the original publication.

These essays retain the first person narrative that was used in their original form on RxTrace, reflecting the author's opinions and attitudes. All essays were copyright © by Dirk Rodgers Consulting on the date of original publication.

The disclaimer from page 12 of this book also applies to these essays.

Essays About FDA Guidances Related to The DSCSA

The following FDA Guidance documents are covered in the essays in this section:

- *"The Effect of Section 585 of the FD&C Act on Drug Product Tracing and Wholesale Drug Distributor and Third-Party Logistics Provider Licensing Standards and Requirements: Questions and Answers. Guidance for Industry"*
- *"Drug Supply Chain Security Act Implementation--Annual Reporting by Prescription Drug Wholesale Distributors and Third-Party Logistics Providers"*
- *"DSCSA Implementation: Product Tracing Requirements — Compliance Policy Guidance for Industry"*
- *"DSCSA Implementation: Product Tracing Requirements for Dispensers – Compliance Policy Guidance for Industry (Revised)"*

The FDA's Draft Guidance On Data Exchange Technologies

Copyright © 2014, FDANews. Written by Dirk Rodgers.
Original text published as part of an FDANews report on the DSCSA.[69] Updated for this book on January 15, 2016.

On November 26, 2014 the FDA published draft guidance to help companies meet the January 1, 2015 requirement to exchange transaction data. The draft guidance is titled "DSCSA Standards for the Interoperable Exchange of Information for Tracing of Certain Human, Finished, Prescription Drugs: How to Exchange Product Tracing Information".[70] FDA guidance is non-binding, so companies are not required to follow approaches they contain as long as they otherwise meet the requirements contained in the

DSCSA itself.

This particular draft guidance is aimed at establishing initial standards for the interoperable exchange of the required Transaction Information, Transaction History and Transaction Statements beginning on January 1, 2015 for manufacturers, wholesale distributors and repackagers [subsequently FDA delayed enforcement until May 1, 2015], and on July 1, 2015 [subsequently FDA delayed enforcement until March 1, 2016] for dispensers as contained in Sections 582(b)(1), c(1), d(1) and e(1) for the Food, Drug and Cosmetics (FD&C) Act. Congress required the FDA publish this draft guidance before the one-year anniversary of the law in Section 582(a)(2)(A).

The draft guidance document contains five substantive pages, but only the last page contains actual guidance. The first four pages of text contain introduction, background and scope sections to help frame the actual guidance.

The draft guidance provides the FDA's current thinking, including their current working definition of the term "interoperability". The Agency believes that the term means the ability to exchange product tracing information accurately, efficiently, and consistently among trading partners. That definition is important because it is the basis for the technologies and standards that the FDA includes in their draft.

As for actual guidance, the document says that trading partners can use current paper-based or electronic-based methods for the interoperable exchange of data to provide the required product tracing information to subsequent purchasers as long as all of the information required by the DSCSA is included. The FDA lists the following methods as those that could be used but acknowledges that these are not the only methods. These include:

- Paper or electronic versions of invoices;
- Paper versions of packing lists;
- Electronic Data Interchange (EDI) standards, such as 856 Advance Ship Notice (ASN);

- EPCIS (Electronic Product Code Information Services)

The draft also indicates that Email or Web-based platforms such as Web Portals are acceptable means to transmit or access the product tracing information, as long as the information is captured, maintained, and provided in compliance with Section 582 of the FD&C Act.

By referring to these approaches in the draft, the FDA acknowledges that the standards and technologies that the industry had already been pursuing in the absence of guidance over the last year are all acceptable. But by not providing any details for applying them, FDA seemed to be ready to allow just about any application of those standards for compliance in 2015 as long as the correct data was present.

This draft guidance was very brief. It appears that the FDA chose not to step outside the tight boundaries of their DSCSA mandate for establishing initial standards for data exchange. In doing so the draft guidance left unanswered many of the data exchange-related questions raised by stakeholders during the FDA's DSCSA workshop in May of 2014.[71] Some companies were hopeful the Agency would use this draft guidance to provide answers to those questions. For example:

- Is it acceptable to abbreviate the Transaction Statement? If so, how?
- Can companies use GS1 Global Location Numbers (GLNs) or other standardized location identifiers to fulfill the "Name and address" requirements of the Transaction Information?
- Exactly what is meant by the term "container" in the Transaction Information?
- Which "name" should be used for the product in the Transaction Information?
- How should "strength" be indicated for bio-therapeutic products?
- What units should "strength" use?
- Definition of "co-licensed partner"?
- Which format of TI, TH and TS will the FDA expect in response

to requests for information?

However, the FDA indicated in the draft that they intend to issue additional guidance to facilitate the interoperable exchange of product tracing information through standardization of data and documentation practices. No target date for that additional guidance was indicated.

At the same time the new draft guidance was published, the FDA also posted a new page on their website for third-party logistics providers to use to report to the FDA annually as required by the DSCSA. The page can be found at http://www.fda.gov/Drugs/DrugSafety/DrugIntegrityandSupplyC hainSecurity/DrugSupplyChainSecurityAct/ucm423749.htm.

The same page was usable by wholesale distributors to register annually with the FDA after January 1, 2015 as required by the DSCSA. The FDA has made the reporting databases for 3PLs and wholesale distributors public.[72]

The DSCSA requires the FDA to publish regulations and additional guidance by the end of 2015, including:
- Regulations establishing standards for licensing of wholesale distributors;
- Regulations establishing standards for licensing of third-party logistics providers;
- Guidance on the processes for DSCSA waivers, exceptions and exemptions;
- Final guidance on grandfathering product;

The draft data exchange guidance from the FDA will provide some comfort to companies wondering if their chosen approach to passing the necessary transaction data after January 1, 2015 is acceptable to the FDA, but it falls short of providing a blueprint for compliance with the data exchange requirements of the new law.

Dirk.

The Draft Guidance On The Effect of Section 585 of the FD&C Imposed By The DSCSA, Explained

By Dirk Rodgers
Original essay published on RxTrace.com on October 10, 2014.[73] Updated for this book on January 1, 2016.

On October 8, 2014, the FDA published draft guidance that might seem a little confusing. The full title is *"The Effect of Section 585 of the FD&C Act on Drug Product Tracing and Wholesale Drug Distributor and Third-Party Logistics Provider Licensing Standards and Requirements: Questions and Answers. Guidance for Industry"*.[74] Because it is in "draft" form, it is published only to encourage people to submit comments about it. (See also, "The Differences Between The DSCSA, FDA Rules and Guidance".)[75]

You should not treat it as real guidance until it is published in final form sometime in the future (if ever — many draft guidances are left handing in the breeze and never finalized). As with all draft guidances, this one came with a docket, now closed, to provide the ability for people to leave comments to help the FDA figure out how to improve it before it becomes final.

The draft covers all of the topics that were contained in the Drug Supply Chain Security Act (DSCSA) Section 204 *"NATIONAL STANDARDS FOR PRESCRIPTION DRUG WHOLESALE DISTRIBUTORS"*, and Section 205, *"NATIONAL STANDARDS FOR THIRD-PARTY LOGISTICS PROVIDERS; UNIFORM NATIONAL POLICY"*. Both of these DSCSA sections resulted in updating the Food, Drug and Cosmetics Act (FD&C Act) that establishes the regulatory responsibilities of the FDA.

The draft guidance provides some Q&A aimed at industry and State legislatures and regulators around those sections, including:

- Preemption of State ePedigree, track and trace and serialization laws (see also "Preemption: What Does It Mean?")[76];
- Licensing of wholesale distributors;
- Licensing of Third-Party Logistics providers (3PLs);

The document is a little comical because so many answers to the questions posed over its five-plus pages repeat the statement from the DSCSA that *"...no state may establish or continue in effect any requirements..."* regarding the three topics listed above *"...that are inconsistent with, more stringent than, or in addition to..."*, those found in the DSCSA. There, that's the whole document summarized in three bullets and one sentence, with the word "comical" thrown in exclusively for your entertainment.

If you'd like to submit a formal comment to the FDA regarding this draft guidance document, it is too late to submit to the docket, which closed on December 7, 2014, but I am sure the FDA would be happy to receive your thoughts any time before the issue final guidance on this topic.

If you'd like to submit a comment to me regarding this essay, and my snarky use of words intended exclusively for your entertainment in describing FDA draft guidance, submit it on RxTrace.com.

Dirk.

FDA Guidance For Wholesale Distributor and 3PL Annual Reporting, Explained

By Dirk Rodgers
Original essay published on RxTrace.com on December 10, 2014.[77] Updated for this book on January 1, 2016.

On December 9, 2014, the FDA posted new draft guidance[78] for pharma wholesale distributors and third-party logistics providers to follow to meet their obligation to register their licensing information annually. The new requirement is from the Drug Supply Chain Security Act (DSCSA) that was enacted on November 27, 2013. The draft guidance explains who, what, when and how companies must report. The FDA has made the data reported available to the public through a page on their website[79].

The information the FDA collected as part of the report from both wholesale distributors and 3PLs include facility location and contact information, a unique facility identifier, license information for each State–including expiration dates–and any significant disciplinary action brought against them.

Wholesale distributors should submit their report annually between January 1 and March 31. Third-party logistics providers should submit their report annually between November 27 and March 31. Either type of entity that receives a new State license should report to the FDA within 30 days.

This new draft guidance is must-reading material for wholesale distributors and 3PLs, but is probably not that important to everyone else, except that the information is now available on the internet for use in determining which wholesale distributors are "authorized" under the DSCSA.

Being a *draft* guidance, the FDA originally provided a docket, now closed, to collect feedback from interested parties through February 9, 2015, but I am sure the FDA would be happy to receive your thoughts any time before they issue final guidance on this topic.

Dirk.

FDA Guidance Documents That Delayed Enforcement Of Certain DSCSA Provisions, Explained

By Dirk Rodgers

Based on original essays published on RxTrace.com on December 24, 2014,[80] June 30, 2015,[81] October 29, 2015,[82] and November 2, 2015[83]. Updated for this book on January 1, 2016.

MANUFACTURERS, WHOLESALE DISTRIBUTORS AND REPACKAGERS

In a direct response to concerns expressed by the Healthcare Distribution Management Association (HDMA) and others (see "HDMA Expresses Concerns About Industry Readiness for DSCSA" and "Will The DSCSA Cause Drug Shortages After January 1?"[84]), the FDA posted new guidance on December 31, 2014 that states their intention to postpone enforcement of just the requirements for manufacturers, wholesale distributors and repackagers to provide and capture Transaction Information (TI), Transaction History (TH) and Transaction Statements (TS). That requirement was to take effect on January 1, 2015 for everyone except dispensers, whose original compliance date was July 1, 2015.

This guidance document can be found on the FDA's website.

The core information is contained in the last paragraph:

> *"The product tracing requirements in sections 582(b), (c), and (e)*

of the FD&C Act take effect for manufacturers, wholesale distributors, and repackagers on January 1, 2015. However, some trading partners have expressed concern that unforeseen complications with the exchange of the required information may result in disruptions in the supply chain, and ultimately could impact patients' access to needed prescription drugs. FDA recognizes that some manufacturers, wholesale distributors, and repackagers may need additional time beyond January 1, 2015, to work with trading partners to ensure that all of the product tracing information required under section 582 of the FD&C Act is provided to and captured by the recipient trading partner. To minimize possible disruptions in the distribution of prescription drugs in the United States, FDA does not intend to take action against trading partners who do not, prior to May 1, 2015, provide or capture the product tracing information required by section 582(b)(1), (c)(1), and (e)(1) of the FD&C Act. This compliance policy is limited to the requirements that trading partners provide and capture product tracing information; it does not extend to other requirements in section 582 of the FD&C Act, such as verification related to suspect and illegitimate product (including quarantine, investigation, notification and recordkeeping) and requirements related to engaging in transactions only with authorized trading partners."

Technically, this is not a postponement of the requirement to collect and provide the transaction data, but in effect, it is, since the FDA says they will electively not enforce this requirement.

In my view, companies who are ready and able to pass the transaction data to trading partners who are able to receive it, should do so. You can consider this to be an extra four months of live testing to make sure there are no surprises in your data or the communications channel with your partners.

Companies who are not yet ready should keep moving forward as fast as they and their solution providers are able. Perhaps the new deadline will help to ensure that drug shortages do not occur as the result of the DSCSA.

This action (inaction?) by the FDA could be considered "enforcement discretion" since it does not change the law itself. Enforcement discretion is about the only option the FDA has at its disposal since only Congress can change the law (see "Will The FDA Delay The DSCSA?"[85]).

It is a holiday gift to procrastinators, but it is also a gift to those who made every attempt to be ready on time but ran into unexpected complications and delays with their trading partners and solution providers. Getting every company in the supply chain aligned with a standardized data exchange approach is harder than most people assume. Take that as a small lesson toward the 2017 and 2023 requirements and give yourself plenty of testing time in advance of those deadlines. The FDA may not be as understanding about those dates.

DISPENSERS

On June 30, 2015 the FDA posted new guidance that announced their intention to use enforcement discretion to not enforce the dispenser requirements to accept and capture Transaction Information (TI), Transaction History (TH) and a Transaction Statement (TS) until November 1, 2015, a four month delay in enforcement.

But then on October 29, 2015 they *updated* that guidance document by extending the use of enforcement discretion until March 1, 2016, an addition four months.

The original document indicates that the FDA's decision to take this action was based on the fact that *"…some dispensers have expressed concern that electronic systems used to exchange, capture, and maintain product tracing information will not be operational by this effective date."*

The core of the guidance is found in the last few paragraphs:

> *"FDA does not intend to take action against dispensers who, prior to November 1, 2015, accept ownership of product without receiving the product tracing information, as required by section*

582(d)(1)(A)(i) of the FD&C Act. This compliance policy does not extend to the requirements under section 582(b)(1), (c)(1), and (e)(1) that other trading partners (manufacturers, wholesale distributors, and repackagers) provide product tracing information to dispensers. In addition, this compliance policy does not extend to transactions in which dispensers must provide the subsequent owner with product tracing information, including transaction history, as required by section 582(d)(1)(A)(ii). If a dispenser has not received product tracing information prior to or at the time it takes ownership of a product, FDA recommends that the dispenser work with the previous owner to receive this information. FDA believes that product tracing information serves as an important tool for dispensers to meet their obligation under section 582(d)(4) to identify suspect product, quarantine the product, and investigate whether that product is illegitimate.

"Prior to November 1, 2015, FDA also does not intend to take action against dispensers who do not capture and maintain the product tracing information, as required by section 582(d)(1)(A)(iii) of the FD&C Act.

"This compliance policy does not extend to other requirements of the FD&C Act, including those in section 582, such as verification related to suspect and illegitimate product (including quarantine, investigation, notification and recordkeeping) and requirements related to engaging in transactions only with authorized trading partners."

The FDA also posted a new webinar recording entitled "DSCSA Updates and Readiness Check: Requirements for Dispensers and other Trading Partners Webinar", dated July 2015.

I guess the FDA is able to pull together an action like this and get it approved in less than two weeks (see "Dispensers Make Last Minute Appeal for Delay in DSCSA Deadline"[86]).

The revision to this guidance that pushes the date to March 1, 2016 offers the following reason for the additional delay:

> *"…because some dispensers – primarily smaller, independent pharmacies and health systems – have expressed that they need additional time. "*

However, companies should be aware of the limits to this revised guidance:

> *"This compliance policy does not extend to the requirements under section 582(b)(1), (c)(1), and (e)(1) that other trading partners (manufacturers, wholesale distributors, and repackagers) provide product tracing information to dispensers. In addition, this compliance policy does not extend to transactions in which dispensers must provide the subsequent owner with product tracing information, including transaction history, as required by section 582(d)(1)(A)(ii). If a dispenser has not received product tracing information prior to or at the time it takes ownership of a product, FDA recommends that the dispenser work with the previous owner to receive this information. FDA believes that product tracing information serves as an important tool for dispensers to meet their obligation under section 582(d)(4) to identify suspect product, quarantine the product, and investigate whether that product is illegitimate."*

In the revised guidance, FDA also warns dispensers that this delay in enforcement:

> *"…does not extend to other requirements of the FD&C Act, including those in section 582, such as verification related to suspect and illegitimate product (including quarantine, investigation, notification and recordkeeping) and requirements related to engaging in transactions only with authorized trading partners."*

What does this mean for drug manufacturers, wholesale distributors and repackagers?

IT MEANS NOTHING

You could easily make the argument that, with this new revised guidance and the delay in FDA enforcement, supply chain entities like drug manufacturers, wholesale distributors and repackagers who ship drugs to dispensers are also off the hook when it comes to providing the recipient with the DSCSA mandated Transaction Information (TI), Transaction History (TH) and a Transaction Statement (TS) documentation. It seems logical. If the FDA is not going to enforce the requirement for the dispenser to receive that documentation, then why would they enforce the requirement for the seller to provide it to them?

You could make that argument, but you would be wrong. In fact, the FDA is currently enforcing the DSCSA requirement that sellers provide buyers–including buyers who are dispensers–with TI, TH and TS. As noted above, that enforcement began on May 1, 2015.

It is clear from the wording of the newly revised guidance document that the FDA wants to be clear about this point. It says:

> "This compliance policy does not extend to the requirements under section 582(b)(1), (c)(1), and (e)(1) that other trading partners (manufacturers, wholesale distributors, and repackagers) provide product tracing information to dispensers."

But the agency goes even further in clarifying that even when a dispenser is the seller, TI, TH and TS must be provided to the buyer (except for returns or to meet a "specific patient need").

> "In addition, this compliance policy does not extend to transactions in which dispensers must provide the subsequent owner with product tracing information, including transaction history, as required by section 582(d)(1)(A)(ii)."

This will likely complicate the situations where a dispenser sells some drugs to another dispenser if the selling dispenser did not accept and save the transaction information from their supplier during this period of enforcement discretion.

The extension in enforcement of the dispenser data exchange requirement by the FDA will be a great relief for the majority of dispensers as they continue to prepare to meet the law, but drug manufacturers, wholesale distributors and repackagers should pay no attention to it.

Dirk.

Who Is Being Harmed By Four Overdue FDA DSCSA Guidances?

By Dirk Rodgers
Original essay published on RxTrace.com on January 18, 2016.[87] Updated for this book on January 1, 2016.

Congress set the calendar for many different kinds of requirements when it adopted the Drug Supply Chain Security Act, signed by the President back on November 27, 2013. One of those dates was last November 27, 2015, two years after enactment, when the FDA was required to publish four new draft guidances. So far, none of them have appeared.[88] But by the time you read this, they will probably be available on the FDA's website.

DSCSA deadlines are usually designed to ensure that things happen in a steady progression toward a kind of full track and trace in November of 2023 and FDA guidance is critical for companies to know how the FDA interprets various parts of the law. So by missing their deadline, who is being harmed, and will that harm result in their own missed deadlines in the future?

Let's take a closer look at what these missing documents are and who might need them right now.

Regulations establishing standards for licensing of third-party logistics providers [DSCSA Section 584(d)(1)]
That section reads:

> "IN GENERAL. – Not later than 2 years after the date of enactment of the Drug Supply Chain Security Act, the Secretary shall issue regulations regarding the standards for licensing under subsection (a), including the revocation and reissuance of such license, to third-party logistics providers under this section."

The sections that follow include quite a few details about how this licensing program is intended to work, plus instructions on collecting comments on the proposed regulation.

Fortunately, third-party logistics providers are not harmed by the delay in the publication of this draft guidance because their deadline for compliance with it will not be set until the final guidance is published. They will have one year after that to comply. In fact, until that time, the DSCSA considers third-party logistics providers to be "licensed". Here is Section 582(a)(7)

> "THIRD-PARTY LOGISTICS PROVIDER LICENSES. – Until the effective date of the third-party logistics provider licensing regulations under section 584, a third-party logistics provider shall be considered 'licensed' under section 581(9)(B) unless the Secretary has made a finding that the third-party logistics provider does not utilize good handling and distribution practices and publishes notice thereof."

So from a third-party logistics provider perspective, the longer the FDA takes to publish, the longer they are granted a free license to operate under the DSCSA.

Regulations establishing standards for licensing of wholesale drug distributors [DSCSA Section 583(a)]

The situation is similar for wholesale distributors regarding this missing document. Section 583(a)

> *"IN GENERAL. – The Secretary shall, not later than 2 years after the date of enactment of the Drug Supply Chain Security Act, establish by regulation standards for the licensing of persons under section 503(e)(1) (as amended by the Drug Supply Chain Security Act), including the revocation, reissuance, and renewal of such license."*

The sections that follow include even more details about how this licensing program is intended to work, plus instructions on collecting comments on the proposed regulation.

Fortunately, wholesale distributors are not harmed by the delay in the publication of this draft guidance because their deadline for compliance with it will not be set until the final guidance is published. They will have two years after that to comply. In fact, until that time, the DSCSA considers wholesale distributors to be "licensed" as long as they hold a valid state license. Here is Section 582(a)(6):

> *"WHOLESALE DISTRIBUTOR LICENSES. – Notwithstanding section 581(9)(A), until the effective date of the wholesale distributor licensing regulations under section 583, the term 'licensed' or 'authorized', as it relates to a wholesale distributor with respect to prescription drugs, shall mean a wholesale distributor with a valid license under State law. "*

Guidelines on processes for waivers, exceptions and exemptions to the DSCSA [DSCSA Section 582(a)(3)]
The meat of this section is:

> *"IN GENERAL. – Not later than 2 years after the date of enactment of the Drug Supply Chain Security Act, the Secretary shall, by guidance –*
>
>> *"(i) establish a process by which an authorized manufacturer, repackager, wholesale distributor, or*

dispenser may request a waiver from any of the requirements set forth in this section, which the Secretary may grant if the Secretary determines that such requirements would result in an undue economic hardship or for emergency medical reasons, including a public health emergency declaration pursuant to section 319 of the Public Health Service Act;

"(ii) establish a process by which the Secretary determines exceptions, and a process through which a manufacturer or repackager may request such an exception, to the requirements relating to product identifiers if a product is packaged in a container too small or otherwise unable to accommodate a label with sufficient space to bear the information required for compliance with this section; and

"(iii) establish a process by which the Secretary may determine other products or transactions that shall be exempt from the requirements of this section. ..."

The section that follows this one requires the FDA to include a process for biennial review and renewal of such waivers exceptions and exemptions.

Companies are not harmed by the delay in the publication of this guidance because, according to Section 582(a)(3)(C), the FDA will be able to provide a start date for the application process for these waivers, exceptions and exemptions that is not later than about May 27, 2017, which is about 180 days before manufacturers must begin applying the DSCSA Product Identifier on their products. From what I can tell, the DSCSA does not specifically require the FDA to first publish a draft, gather public comments, and then publish a final guidance for this program, but they probably will anyway because they have the time.

Final guidance on grandfathering product [DSCSA Section 582(a)(5)(A)]
So how about grandfathering? This section says:

> *"PRODUCT IDENTIFIER. – Not later than 2 years after the date of enactment of the Drug Supply Chain Security Act, the Secretary shall finalize guidance specifying whether and under what circumstances product that is not labeled with a product identifier and that is in the pharmaceutical distribution supply chain at the time of the effective date of the requirements of this section shall be exempted from the requirements of this section."*

Of these four overdue guidances, this is the one I am the most eager to read. There is a very interesting issue that surround whether or not the phrase "…in the pharmaceutical distribution supply chain…" includes drug packages that are sitting in the inventories of drug manufacturers and their 3PLs. For a complete explanation, see my essay from September 2015, "Will Manufacturers Be Able To Grandfather Products In Their DC And 3PL?". This guidance should tell us how the FDA interprets this phrase and that will trigger the choice of a couple different serialization strategies for manufacturers.

This could blow the lid off of the already tight schedules of some companies by moving up their effective serialization deadline, or it could relax them. For that reason, the longer this guidance is delayed, the shorter the time companies will have to react and adjust their serialization strategies. A significant delay could cause harm and could justify calls for shifting the November 2017 serialization deadline by an equal amount to give companies time to make that adjustment, depending on which way they go.

So for three out of the four overdue guidances, the delay is not really a big deal. In fact, these guidances could be pretty complex and so it makes sense that the FDA is taking the time necessary to make sure they get it right the first time. How big of a deal the delay of the fourth guidance turns out to be will depend on the FDA's interpretation of the DSCSA. I can't wait to dig into it, can you?

Dirk.

Essays About DSCSA Details

The DSCSA contains a bewildering number of new requirements that have an impact on companies in the U.S. pharma supply chain. In this section, essays cover many of those new concepts as well as some existing concepts that will need modification as the result of this new law.

DSCSA Transaction Information

By Dirk Rodgers
Original essay published on RxTrace.com on March 17, 2014.[89] Updated for this book on January 1, 2016.

In the new U.S. Drug Supply Chain Security Act (DSCSA) enacted last November as part of the Drug Quality and Security Act (DQSA), "Transaction Information" (TI) is one of three primary sets of data that supply chain sellers of drugs must provide to the buyers beginning January 1, 2015 (deferred until May 1, 2015 for manufacturers, wholesale distributors and repackagers, and at least March 1, 2016 for dispensers). I will discuss "Transaction History" (TH) and "Transaction Statements" (TS) in future essays.

On first look, TI can seem pretty simple. Here is how the DSCSA defines it:

> *"(26) TRANSACTION INFORMATION. –*
>
> *The term 'transaction information' means –*
>
> > *"(A) the proprietary or established name or names of the product;*
> > *"(B) the strength and dosage form of the product;*

> *"(C) the National Drug Code (NDC) number of the product;*
> *"(D) the container size;*
> *"(E) the number of containers;*
> *"(F) the lot number of the product;*
> *"(G) the date of the transaction;*
> *"(H) the date of the shipment, if more than 24 hours after the date of the transaction;*
> *"(I) the business name and address of the person from whom ownership is being transferred; and*
> *"(J) the business name and address of the person to whom ownership is being transferred."*

Sounds kind of like a delivery manifest or packing list.

The FDA provided additional guidance on how to represent some of these data elements in their draft guidance establishing the standards for the interoperable exchange of TI/TH/TS in paper or electronic format on November 28, 2014.[90]

I attended the Healthcare Distribution Management Association (HDMA) Distribution Management Conference (DMC) back in March of 2014. During the Distributor Traceability Updates session, representatives from the top four wholesale distribution companies in the U.S. talked about their work in a closed-door HDMA work group that was working on guidance for communicating TI/TH/TS. At that time, they expected to publish their guidance sometime in the next month or so (which they did in April of 2014[91]), which means it will not have the benefit of the FDA guidance. That means that they made their best guesses about what would be acceptable to the FDA.

WHAT MORE DO YOU NEED TO KNOW?

Just a few things. The FDA's guidance document does not explain:

- how, why and when you might want to indicate multiple "names" of a given product;

- how to format the strength and dosage form, including units and any abbreviations or standard terms/codes that should be used;
- the formatting of the NDC, including:
- whether or not a 14-digit GS1 GTIN that contains the NDC and that matches the identifier contained in the 2D barcode that will eventually be printed on the package (by November 27, 2017);
- confirmation that it is the 10-digit NDC and not the 11-digit "pseudo-NDC" used for reimbursement claims; and
- whether or not to use dashes in the number;
- confirmation that "the container size" is the package size (and not the shipping container size) and what standard terms/units and abbreviations are allowed;
- confirmation that "the number of containers" is the total number of drug packages of the given NDC that are included in the overall transaction and that this is irrespective of the number of packages in each shipping container;
- how to indicate multiple lot numbers for the same NDC in the transaction and how that relates to how "the number of containers" data is represented;
- how to properly format the date of the transaction and the date of the shipment;
- whether the business names and addresses must/may equal the exact shipping dock address (including that of a 3PL), or if they must/may be the address of the owner's headquarters;
- whether or not and how this information can be segmented in such a way that the "to" and "from" business names and addresses occur only once in a TI document that reflects a single transaction but which includes multiple NDCs and multiple lot numbers for each NDC;

Those are mostly all formatting questions—and the answers might be different for paper than they might be for the electronic version—but there are deeper questions. Some people are wondering whether or not the electronic version can make use of GS1's Global Location Number (GLN)[92], and/or perhaps a Data

Universal Numbering System (DUNS)[93] number (see "FDA Chooses DUNS For Unique Facility Identifier"[94]), in place of the business names and addresses.

When does the "transaction", or "change-of-ownership" actually take place? Is it when the buyer's purchase order is accepted by the seller, the moment the shipment takes place at the seller's (or their 3PL's) loading dock, or does it depend on the Freight On Board (FOB) terms? (See "Pedigree Will Change FOB Terms"[95].) My understanding of FOB terms is that they make it clear exactly when the product changes ownership. If the buyer and seller agree to FOB terms of "Destination", how does the seller know what date to put into the "date of transaction" field?

The DSCSA defines "transaction" to mean *"...the transfer of product between persons in which a change of ownership occurs..."*. What happens when the physical "transfer" is separated by days, weeks or even months from the "change of ownership"? This is what happens in the business practice known as Vendor Managed Inventory (VMI). In VMI, a manufacturer or wholesale distributor owns the product sitting on the inventory shelves of a dispenser and the ownership changes to the dispenser only at the moment the drug is dispensed to a patient (see "Vendor Managed Inventory Under the DSCSA").

In this case, since the product sitting on the pharmacy shelf is still owned by the manufacturer or wholesale distributor, is there any need to provide TI/TH/TS when the product is shipped (physically "transferred") from the seller's location to the eventual buyer's location? Remember, the change of ownership has not yet occurred. And when the change of ownership does occur at the time the drug is dispensed to the patient, no physical "transfer" occurs. I assume the answer is "no", but I wonder what the FDA thinks.

Up to a point, this has some parallels with the way a 3PL works and the DSCSA makes it clear that shipments into and out of a 3PL are exempt from the TI/TH/TS requirements as long as the 3PL does not take ownership.

When the sales transaction does occur in the VMI situation, what business name and address goes in the "from" and "to" fields? The names and addresses where the transaction took place, or the names and addresses of the parent companies involved? How/when must the TI/TH/TS be delivered to the dispenser?

WHAT NEXT?

Lots of questions for the FDA to answer just about TI. Maybe you can think of a few more. The deadline for submitting questions and comments to the FDA regarding the draft guidance has expired, but I am sure they would still like to hear your thoughts (see "DQSA: How Should Transaction Data Be Exchanged?"[96]).

In case you missed it, the FDA held a webinar[97] on March 12, 2014 that included an overview of the DSCSA. I thought Congress specifically prohibited the FDA from holding public meetings regarding the DSCSA until November 27, 2014 [see DSCSA section 582(i)(1)], but during the presentation Dr. Illisa Bernstein said that they would announce a public meeting soon. Apparently this one will not count as one of the five they are mandated by the DSCSA to hold. See "The 2014 FDA DSCSA Workshop".[98]

Dirk.

DSCSA Transaction History

By Dirk Rodgers
Original essay published on RxTrace.com on March 24, 2014.[99] Updated for this
book on January 1, 2016.

On the surface, Transaction History (TH) looks simple. The Drug
Supply Chain Security Act (DSCSA), which is Title II of the Drug
Quality and Security Act (DQSA), defines TH this way:

> *"(25) TRANSACTION HISTORY. –*
>
> *The term 'transaction history' means a statement in paper or
> electronic form, including the transaction information for each
> prior transaction going back to the manufacturer of the product."*

According to this simple definition, TH is the collection of the TIs
(see previous essay) from all of the prior transactions going back to
the manufacturer. By this definition, a drug sold by a secondary
wholesale distributor (a non-Authorized Distributor or Record,
ADR, for this drug), to a pharmacy, the pharmacy (the dispenser)
should receive a TH statement composed of the TI that the
manufacturer originally provided to the first wholesale distributor
(the ADR), plus the TI that the first distributor provided to the
second distributor.

By the way, an Authorized Distributor of Record (ADR) is any
wholesale distributor that the manufacturer designates, or
authorizes, to distribute their products. ADRs are expected to buy
these drugs directly from the manufacturer, or perhaps another
ADR.

The following sequence shows the TH definition above:

Transaction History (TH) Definition

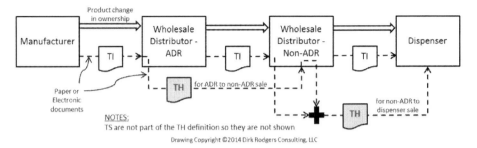

Drawing Copyright ©2014 Dirk Rodgers Consulting, LLC

But in reality, TH will be something less than this in most cases. Despite the TH definition, the DSCSA wholesale distributor requirements eliminate some of the data elements from the TH that the dispenser would receive for certain types of distributions.

For example, an ADR (as used here the ADR is the wholesale distributor who buys a drug directly from the manufacturer) is not required to include in their TI and TH statements (prior to 2023):

- the lot number of the product;
- the initial transaction date (the date they took ownership of the product); or,
- the initial shipment date from the manufacturer.

Because an ADR who only buys a drug directly does not need to include this information in their outgoing TI and TH statements, they do not need to keep careful track of the linkage between their incoming shipments from manufacturers and their outgoing shipments to their customers. Non-ADRs, on the other hand, do need to keep track of that linkage so that they can provide all of the required data fields in their TI and TH.

The non-ADR's TH can start with their purchase from the ADR so the manufacturer's TI that the ADR received will not appear in the TH statement the dispenser receives. This is because the ADR is not required to pass the exact TI document they received from the manufacturer. All the ADR needs to do is include an additional statement in their TS indicating that they bought the product directly from the manufacturer, exclusive distributor of the manufacturer or a repackager who purchased it directly from the manufacturer. The non-ADR must inform (in their TS perhaps?) their customer (the dispenser in this example) that they received a direct purchase statement in the TS they received from the ADR.

Transaction History (TH) Reality

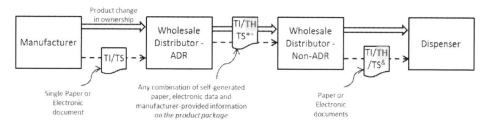

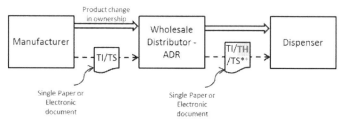

NOTES:

* These TI, TH, and TS are exempt from following the FDA guidance for formatting to be published by November 27, 2014
⁺ These TI and TH do not require lot number of the product, the initial transaction date, or the initial shipment date from the manufacturer
& This TH does not need to include the sale from the Manufacturer to the ADR and the non-ADR must inform the Dispenser that they received a direct purchase statement from the ADR

Drawing Copyright ©2014 Dirk Rodgers Consulting, LLC

ADR EXEMPTION FROM FDA FORMATTING GUIDANCE

Only wholesale distributors that do not buy drugs directly from the manufacturer must follow the formatting guidance that the FDA published on November 28, 2014.[100] The vast majority of drugs in the U.S. supply chain are distributed by wholesale distributors who buy directly from manufacturers. These distributors appear to be exempt from following the FDA's data exchange guidance.

The TI, TH and Transaction Statements (TS) (discussed in the next essay) provided in ADR-to-distributor transactions can be spread across any combination of self-generated paper, electronic or manufacturer-provided data on the product package. Whenever an ADR sells drugs to another wholesale distributor, as in the drawing above, the product package itself appears to be considered a data exchange mechanism.

The TI and TH provided to the second wholesale distributor may include the product information that the manufacturer has printed on the drug package itself. That is, any data elements called out in the definition of TI that are printed by the manufacturer on the product package—providing that package as part of the sales transaction—appears to fulfill the requirement to include those data elements in the TI and TH. Check with the FDA, but this appears to include such TI data elements as:

- The NDC;
- The lot number;
- The expiration date;
- The proprietary or established name of the product;
- The container size;
- The strength and dosage form of the product;

Whatever TI the manufacturer provides to the ADR will probably just get filed away and almost certainly will not actually be transmitted downstream as part of their TH when the drugs are sold. These special allowances for the wholesale distributors who can buy direct makes sense because these companies deal in such massive volume of product. Keeping track of it all by lot number—especially before the lot number is encoded in the machine readable barcode on each package—would be very costly and overloaded with unintended errors.

In November of 2023 the DSCSA turns into an electronic, serialization-based, one-up, one-down records retention system. At that time, supply chain parties can stop creating, passing and retaining THs.

UNANSWERED QUESTIONS ABOUT 'TH'

There are a number of unanswered questions about TH. Because TH is primarily supposed to be a collection of TIs, is it really necessary to repeat the data elements that do not change? These include most of the TI data elements (see the full list of TI data elements here). In fact, the only data elements that would actually change as the product moves from owner to owner are:

- the number of containers;
- the date of the transaction;
- the date of the shipment, if more than 24 hours after the date of the transaction;
- the business name and address of the person from whom ownership is being transferred; and
- the business name and address of the person to whom ownership is being transferred.

In addition, some people, notably those in GS1 Healthcare US, are worried about the duplication of the static data elements if they must be repeated multiple times in a single TH document. They are also worried about the need to include full business names and addresses in the "ownership change" data elements. The "from" business name and address will be repeated many, many times in their database. Most "to" business names and addresses will also be repeated many times. This could represent a huge amount of data storage and transmission space. This issue was also a concern in various preempted State pedigree laws (see "Pedigree Models and Supply Chain Master Data"[101]).

If an ADR for a given drug buys some of that drug from a non-ADR and then sells it to a customer along with some units of the same drug that they bought directly from the manufacturer, what rules apply? The larger U.S. drug distributors have voluntarily pledged not to buy drugs from anyone except the manufacture when they can, so this may not happen very often, but when it does, does the fact that they buy some units directly allow them to always follow the direct buy rules? How is the distributor supposed to know which drug packages were received from which supplier if they are the same lot number since they are not required to make use of the unit serial numbers until late 2023?

Dirk.

The DSCSA Transaction Statement

By Dirk Rodgers
Original essay published on RxTrace.com on March 31, 2014.[102] Updated for this book on January 1, 2016.

The DSCSA defines Transaction Statement (TS) this way:

> *"(27) TRANSACTION STATEMENT. –*
>
> *The 'transaction statement' is a statement, in paper or electronic form, that the entity transferring ownership in a transaction –*
>
> *(A) is authorized as required under the Drug Supply Chain Security Act;*
>
> *(B) received the product from a person that is authorized as required under the Drug Supply Chain Security Act;*
>
> *(C) received transaction information and a transaction statement from the prior owner of the product, as required under section 582;*
>
> *(D) did not knowingly ship a suspect or illegitimate product;*
>
> *(E) had systems and processes in place to comply with verification requirements under section 582;*
>
> *(F) did not knowingly provide false transaction information; and*

(G) did not knowingly alter the transaction history."

All manufacturer's, wholesale distributors and repackagers in the U.S. pharmaceutical supply chain must begin passing TI, TH and TS to the buyer whenever a change in ownership occurs, starting on January 1, 2015 [later revised to May 1, 2015]. The FDA published guidance to help you know how to format and exchange this information on November 28, 2014.[103]

The FDA is asking for comments on data exchange of this type to help them formulate their guidance but their docket has expired. To read what others have already submitted, and to submit your own thoughts and preferences, go to the FDA's submission original submission docket.[104] The FDA held a webinar on the DSCSA to provide background on the law and their action plan for the next year or so.[105]

In addition, the Healthcare Distribution Management Association (HDMA) held a webinar featuring Connie T. Jung, RPh, PhD of the FDA called "FDA Perspectives on Implementation of the Drug Supply Chain Security Act" on April 7, 2014.[106]

TRANSACTION STATEMENT, WHAT'S THE POINT?

One of the purposes of a pedigree is to provide prosecutors with evidence that they can use to bring charges and make them stick against criminals. One of the requirements for getting the most severe judgment against someone in a case like this is to establish that they intended to deceive the buyer. It's one thing to show that the transaction history for a shipment of drugs does not match the actual history, but if you can't establish that the difference was an intentional act, you might not be successful in bringing charges against the seller. Mistakes happen all the time and very few of them are intentional, criminal acts.

The Transaction Statement forces sellers of drugs to explicitly state seven different assertions regarding the transaction (the change in ownership). These are:

(A) **The seller "is authorized as required under the Drug Supply Chain Security Act"**

According to the DSCSA, an "authorized" trading partner is one that is licensed appropriately for the type of business they are, what role they are filling, and where the transaction is taking place. By making this assertion, you are stating that you are appropriately licensed at the time of the transaction;

(B) **The seller "received the product from a person that is authorized as required under the Drug Supply Chain Security Act"**

To make this assertion, you must know that the companies you originally bought this product from are also appropriately licensed as the type of role they fulfilled when you bought the product from them in the locations that the transactions took place. Keep in mind that, in some cases, your current shipment (current transaction) may include drugs received from multiple sources, including multiple sources for a given product code and lot number. In those cases, this assertion must refer to all of those suppliers. Because you must receive (and retain for 6 years) a TS from each of those suppliers in which they assert that they are "authorized" to offer the product for sale (see below), you may not need to keep track of the licensing status of each supplier in each locality you do business with them (although there may be other reasons you will want to do that). That is, your assertion that you received the product from a person that is authorized might be based on the fact that your supplier provided you with their assertion that they were authorized. The combination of these assertions results in the documentation of the chain of trust that has always existed in the U.S. pharma supply chain (see "Reliance on Trust in the U.S. Pharma Supply Chain"[107]) and turns it into evidence that can be used against criminals;

(C) **The seller "received transaction information and a transaction statement from the prior owner of the product, as required under section 582"**
to make this assertion, you must ensure that you receive proper TI and TS from all of your suppliers, starting in January, and you must keep those paper or electronic documents so you can retrieve them quickly in case of an investigation (see "DSCSA Transaction Information");

(D) **The seller "did not knowingly ship a suspect or illegitimate product"**
To make this assertion you need to have a way of identifying at shipment time (and earlier) any product for which you have receive a "suspect product" or "illegitimate product" notice from the FDA or a trading partner. Don't make this assertion without having confidence that your systems would automatically detect and stop the shipment of any product that is covered by one of these types of investigations or you will be breaking the law. It will be easy for the Justice Department to prove that you received a notification and as a result your company "knew" that the product you shipped was suspect or illegitimate at the time of the transaction. The DSCSA provides clear definitions for "illegitimate product" and "suspect product". Make sure you become familiar with those definitions. The FDA published guidance on the determination of those types of products and how to conduct investigations into them;[108]

(E) **The seller "had systems and processes in place to comply with verification requirements under section 582"**
The DSCSA includes sections that describe the verification requirements for each type of trading partner in the supply chain, including manufacturer, wholesale distributors, repackagers and

dispensers. These sections explain how each type of trading partner must detect and handle suspect and illegitimate product. These "systems and processes" must be in place by January, 2015 [subsequently enforcement was delayed] so that you can make this assertion truthfully at that time. Make sure you have updated all of your supply chain standard operating procedures (SOPs) and retrain your workers to follow them. Don't underestimate the effort this requirement takes;

(F) **The seller "did not knowingly provide false transaction information"**
To make this assertion, you must ensure that the TI you send to your customers always match the product contained in their shipments and, if you are not the manufacturer, that they reflect the information provided to you by your source(s) (see "DSCSA Transaction Information");

(G) **The seller "did not knowingly alter the transaction history"**
To make this assertion, you must ensure that the TH you send to your customers always match the product contained in the shipments and that they reflect the true histories of the products contained in the shipment. And, of course, don't modify any of the information that was provided by previous owners of the product.

As the seller, if it turns out that any one of these assertions are false, then you are committing perjury and you leave yourself open to prosecution. However, the DSCSA does not require anyone to check the validity of this information on a routine basis. The law is what I call an "after-the-fact" investigation law, which means that this transaction data will be collected from supply chain members and analyzed by the FDA, U.S. Justice Department or State regulators only in the event that something raises suspicion that there may be something illegitimate about the drugs. That is, the drugs become "suspect product", or "illegitimate product".

This should be good news for legitimate members of the supply chain, and bad news for criminals. I don't think the FDA is going to go around prosecuting people who pass a TS that has an inadvertent false statement as long as the drugs being sold are legitimate and there is nothing illegal about the current or previous transactions. But if true illegal activity is uncovered — like the sale of drugs that were illegally imported, stolen, mis-labeled, counterfeit, adulterated or any other illegitimate activity — the TI, TH and TS will be just as good as a forged pedigree to point the finger at the criminal(s) and these tools will also make the job of the prosecution easier than it was before the DSCSA.

UNANSWERED QUESTIONS ABOUT 'TS'

But there are a number of important questions about transaction statements. When a wholesale distributor sells product after January 1, 2015 which it acquired prior to that date, that company is exempt from asserting in their TS that they received TI and TH from the prior owner of the product, since that prior owner was under no obligation to provide it at that time. This is a form of "grandfathering" in product that was in supply chain inventories on the day the law goes into effect. However, the wholesale distributor in this example must provide a TS that includes the remaining assertions. The only way to respond to the other six assertions without responding to one of them is if all seven are individually answerable. So a single checkbox on an electronic or paper form may not comply.

In addition, there is at least one additional assertion that must be included in the TS under certain conditions. This occurs when a wholesale distributor is selling drugs that they acquired directly from a manufacturer, the exclusive distributor of the manufacturer, or a repackager that purchased the drugs directly from the manufacturer. In this case, the wholesale distributor must provide the subsequent owner of the product an additional assertion in their TS to indicate that they bought the drugs from one of those entities. This alerts the buyer that the wholesale distributor's TI and TH in this instance will not need to include certain data elements, including the lot numbers of the product (for more about this, see "DSCSA Transaction History").

This is a strong indication that the assertions within the TS must be individually answerable, but can they be abbreviated in some way, or must the entire text appear in every TS? Hopefully the FDA will tell us.

When a manufacturer generates a TS, should they include the assertions that they received TI and TH from the prior owner, and that they received the product from an authorized person? Clearly these do not apply to the company that makes the product, but oddly, nothing in the DSCSA appears to exempt manufacturers from these individual assertions. The FDA should make this clear in their future guidance.

Dirk.

Who Is A DSCSA Dispenser?

By Dirk Rodgers
Original essay published on RxTrace.com on September 15, 2014.[109] Updated for this book on January 1, 2016.

When the U.S. Drug Supply Chain Security Act (DSCSA) was signed into law on November 27, 2013, it introduced a new term into the supply chain lexicon: "Dispenser". It is unfortunate that the authors chose not to use a more recognizable word — like "pharmacies", or "hospitals", or "physicians" — because, if they had, more organizations in the dispensing sector might have taken more notice of the requirements they are facing. But, of course, they could not do that because they wanted to refer to all of those organizations using a single term. All of those types of organizations fall into the DSCSA definition of "dispensers" and the use of that word appears to have led to some confusion, and therefore some amount of complacency.

"Dispenser" is one of the terms the DSCSA defines so that the rest of the text does not need to repeat the full list of organizations the authors are referring to (see "Don't Skip The DQSA Definition of Terms Section"[110]). Its definition is only applicable within the text of the law and so it is one of the terms you cannot simply look up in a dictionary to figure out if it applies to you. You must apply the definition contained within the law itself. From DSCSA Section 581(3), that definition is (bullets added):

> " 'dispenser' —
>
> (A) means
>
> - a retail pharmacy,
> - hospital pharmacy,
> - a group of chain pharmacies under common ownership and control that do not act as a wholesale distributor,
> - or any other person authorized by law to dispense or administer prescription drugs,
> - and the affiliated warehouses or distribution centers of such entities under common ownership and control that do not act as a wholesale distributor; and
>
> (B) does not include a person who dispenses only products to be used in animals in accordance with section 512(a)(5)."

This definition covers a lot of companies as well as individuals in our healthcare system. In fact, it covers more companies, more locations and more people than those covered by the DSCSA definitions of "manufacturer", "wholesale distributor" and "repackager" combined. Essentially, a "DSCSA dispenser" is any company or individual that is authorized to dispense or administer prescription drugs to a patient. This not only covers the obvious companies, like CVS Health, Walgreens, Rite-Aid, Kroger, Walmart, Target, hospitals, clinics and your corner mom-and-pop pharmacy, but it also includes individual pharmacists, physicians and dentists. If there is a State or Federal law that authorizes a company or individual to dispense or administer prescription drugs to a person, that company or individual is covered in the DSCSA definition of "dispenser" and they are therefore obligated to follow the dispenser provisions of the DSCSA.

Those dispenser provisions dictate new requirements for the acquisition of drugs from suppliers in the supply chain, so if a pharmacist, physician or dentist works as an employee or contractor for a company that handles the acquisition of prescription drugs separately from their duties (and that company itself is authorized under the DSCSA and State law to do so) then that practitioner probably does not have any obligation under the DSCSA. But if the practitioner plays any role in that acquisition (including selecting the source, placing the orders, managing the inventory or even just receiving the shipments), or is an owner of a company that acquires prescription drugs, pay attention to the dispenser provisions of the DSCSA. They likely apply to you.

WHEN MUST A DISPENSER BEGIN COMPLYING?

In addition to the confusion over exactly who is a dispenser, there is a common misconception over exactly when those who fall into that category must begin to comply with the DSCSA. Ask most people who have read the DSCSA carefully and they will tell you that the date is July 1, 2015. That is where the misconception starts.

It is true that a few of the DSCSA dispenser provisions were to take effect on July 1, 2015 [enforcement by the FDA was delayed to March 1, 2016 at least], but the most important ones took effect on January 1, 2015, right along with those of manufacturers, wholesale distributors and repackagers. This includes the foundational requirement that dispensers may buy drugs only from companies that are authorized under the DSCSA to sell drugs in the U.S. supply chain. The term "Authorized" is defined by the DSCSA as holding a valid license. Most States issue licenses to wholesale distributors.

After that date, if you acquire prescription drugs from sources that do not hold a valid license in your State, you are violating Federal law. If your State is one that does not issue licenses to wholesale distributors, then your supplier must hold a valid Federal wholesale distributor license. Under the DSCSA, the buying company or person—the dispenser in this case—is responsible for knowing that the person or company they buy their prescription drugs from hold that valid license [see DSCSA Section 582(d)(3)]. That's new, and it is big, and it started back on January 1, 2015. It was *not* deferred, like the product tracing requirements.

Another provision that took effect on January 1, 2015 requires dispensers [individual healthcare practitioners are exempted, see DSCSA Section 582(d)(5)] to have in place a system for quarantining and conducting investigations into drugs in their possession or control that they, or others, suspect might be illegitimate, and drugs that have been found (by them or by others) to actually be illegitimate. There are specific actions contained in the DSCSA that dispensers must take "promptly" in these situations.

Most dispensers will probably not be touched by suspect or illegitimate product anytime soon, but be prepared to face Federal action if you are one of the few who is notified that you have acquired products that have fallen under someone's suspicion and you do not follow the procedure outlined in the DSCSA.

That notification could come from the FDA, your State Board of Pharmacy, a trading partner or the manufacturer. If it comes from the FDA and you do not follow the DSCSA steps properly, you are in violation. To avoid confusion and inaction, everyone in the supply chain—including dispensers—should now have written Standard Operating Procedures (SOPs) on file that cover these situations. For more on conducting these investigations, see "The FDA's Draft Guidance on Suspect Product"[111].

WHAT HAPPENS IN JULY 2015 AND BEYOND?

About the only thing added on July of 2015 [FDA enforcement has been deferred until at least March 1, 2016] is that dispensers [individual healthcare practitioners are exempted, see DSCSA Section 582(d)(5)] must begin receiving and providing Transaction Information (TI), Transaction History (TH), and Transaction Statements (TS) from their suppliers at the time they buy and sell prescription drugs (not including dispensing to a patient). However, dispensers may return saleable drugs to the supplier that they originally acquired them from without providing the transaction data, and they may return non-saleable drugs to the manufacturer, a returns processor, the original wholesale distributor or someone acting on behalf of any of those, without providing the transaction data. Changes of ownership from a dispenser to anyone else require the dispenser to provide the buyer with the proper transaction documentation. These documents must be stored for a period of six years and must be retrievable within two business days in the event of an investigation at any time during those six years (see "A Closer Look At The Six-Year Record-Keeping Requirement").

Dispensers may continue to buy drugs that do not contain serial numbers applied by the manufacturer or repackager as specified by the DSCSA until November of 2020. After that date dispensers must begin verifying that the lot number of suspect product corresponds to the real lot number, AND that the serial numbers (the Standardized Numerical Identifier, or SNI) on at least 3 packages, or 10% of the suspect product in their possession, whichever is greater, matches those in the suspect product notification. [See DSCSA Section 582(d)(4)(A).]

Dirk.

Who Is A DSCSA Repackager?

By Dirk Rodgers
Original essay published on RxTrace.com on November 3, 2014.[112] Updated for this book on January 1, 2016.

The DSCSA contains a lot of specific requirements for repackagers. Repackagers have most of the same requirements that manufacturers do, plus they have many of the wholesale distributor requirements. A double whammy.

Most people in the industry know what a repackager is. Typically they are companies that buy drugs from a manufacturer or a wholesale distributor and then open the packages and put the drug into a new package type. This can include putting the drug into a larger or smaller quantity package, or from bottles into blister cards or even unit dose packs for use in an automated picking machine. It can also include companies who do not buy the drugs but which offer repackaging as a service to the drug owner. It also includes companies that change the label on the manufacturer's package for whatever reason.

The one thing a repackager should never do is to change the drug itself in anyway. This includes changing the dosage form, diluting, mixing with other solutions or chemicals, etc. Otherwise the company would be considered a manufacturer.

Like manufacturers, repackagers must follow the same current Good Manufacturing Practices (cGMP) to ensure that the product is handled, packaged and labeled properly.

WHO IS A DSCSA REPACKAGER?

The DSCSA defines the term "Repackager" as:

> "...a person who owns or operates an establishment that repacks and relabels a product or package for —
>
> (A) further sale; or

(B) distribution without a further transaction."

To really understand this definition you have to apply the DSCSA definitions of the terms "distribution" and "transaction" as well as those of "product" and "package". These last two definitions are obvious enough that I won't show them, but here are the first two:

> *"The term 'distribute' or 'distribution' means the sale, purchase, trade, delivery, handling, storage, or receipt of a product, and does not include the dispensing of a product pursuant to a prescription executed in accordance with section 503(b)(1) or the dispensing of a product approved under section 512(b)."*

> *"The term 'transaction' means the transfer of product between persons in which a change of ownership occurs. ..."*

I have left out the many exemptions to "transaction" because they are not important to my analysis below. For more about those exemptions, see "Is Your Drug Exempt From The Federal Drug Supply Chain Security Act?".[113]

My interpretation of this set of definitions is that a "DSCSA Repackager" includes any company that does the typical repackaging of drugs that they buy, repackage and then sell. This is clear by clause (A) in the DSCSA definition of "repackager" where it says the repackaged drugs are for "further sale". But it also appears to include contract repackagers as well as in-house repackaging departments, such as those found in a hospital setting. This comes from the inclusion of companies that repackage drugs for "distribution without a further transaction".

As you can see, the definition of "distribution" includes receipt, handling, storage and delivery of a product and it does not require a sale, purchase or trade, although those are also part of the definition. Notice the use of the word "or" in that definition. The term "transaction" means a change of ownership. Since a repackager includes companies who repackage drugs that are for distribution without a further change of ownership, that means the term, I believe, includes contract repackaging and in-house repackaging, because ownership, or the lack thereof, does not affect the repackaging operation.

WHAT MUST A REPACKAGER DO TO MEET THE DSCSA?

Section 582 (e) of the DSCSA defines the requirements for repackagers. When accepting ownership of a DSCSA product, a repackager must receive Transaction Information (TI), Transaction History (TH) and a Transaction Statement (TS). Repackagers who do repackaging under contract and do not accept ownership of the product are apparently exempt from this requirement. In-house repackagers operating within a hospital or network under common ownership would apparently not need to receive these documents either, since the larger organization would have already received the product and they are obligated to receive these documents from their supplier (after July 1, 2015 for dispensers [FDA enforcement was delayed until at least March 1, 2016]).

Of course, any repackager whose output will be subject to additional changes of ownership must provide the next owner with TI, TH and TS.

Contract repackagers may not be exempt from the requirement to serialize the repackaged product by November 27, 2018, but in-house repackagers appear to be. That is, contract repackagers who repackage product that could be reintroduced into the supply chain with a subsequent change of ownership are required to serialize the repackaged drugs by that date. The assumption is that product processed by in-house repackagers will not be sold back into the supply chain.

In-house repackagers are also exempt from having systems in place to enable a repackager to verify suspect product. Repackagers whose output may be subject to further changes of ownership are not exempt and must have those systems by January 1, 2015.

Repackagers of all types must only deal with trading partners who are properly licensed since the beginning of 2015.

There is a lot of diversity in the repackager community but the DSCSA *seems* to address it fairly well.

Dirk.

3PL Operation Under The DSCSA

By Dirk Rodgers
Original essay published on RxTrace.com on June 1, 2015.[114] Updated for this book on January 1, 2016.

Another type of business affected by the U.S. Drug Supply Chain Security Act (DSCSA) is the third party logistics provider (3PL) business.

There are a number of important differences between wholesale distributors and 3PLs as defined in the DSCSA.

WHAT IS A 3PL?

A 3PL is a business that offers distribution services to pharmaceutical manufacturers. I know that sounds a lot like what most people think a wholesale distributor does—especially considering that wholesale distributors now charge a "fee for service" to manufacturers—but, like I said, there are important differences.

Unless products are "made-to-order" or made "just-in-time" (both rare in the pharmaceutical industry today) the pharma manufacturer must store excess production in a buffer between the manufacturing process—which usually produces in bursts known as "batches" or "lots"—and their customers—which usually have a smoother and more continuous demand curve. The product buffer needed to prevent frequent out-of-stock and back-order situations on the customer demand side is normally implemented by a distribution center (DC) that is owned by the manufacturer. Product is stored in the DC after a burst of production, and customer orders are fulfilled from the inventory of the DC, thus smoothing out the flow of goods.

The usual customers that a manufacturer's DC would ship drugs to are wholesale distributors and the larger chain pharmacies. In some cases they might also ship to governmental agencies, hospitals, clinics and other smaller entities.

But some pharma manufacturers do not want to be distracted by operational cost centers that are not directly related to their core competency: developing and (perhaps) manufacturing drugs. In these companies a drug distribution center and its operation are the kind of the services that might be outsourced to a third-party under contract. Some manufacturers might handle the distribution of their drugs that are easy to distribute but choose to outsource the distribution of drugs that have certain complexities—like cold-chain and/or controlled substances—and other companies might outsource all of their distribution operations.

The 3PL business is designed to fill this need. These companies will take over the task of receiving finished goods from the manufacturer, store them in a warehouse and fulfill customer orders on behalf of the manufacturer—all under a contract that has a pre-negotiated price associated with it. Usually these relationships do not require the 3PL to purchase the product from the manufacturer. In fact, this is the primary defining characteristic of a 3PL according to the DSCSA.

Wholesale distributors, on the other hand, always buy (take ownership of) the products that they distribute. (Be aware that some of the larger pharma wholesale distributors in the U.S. also have separate business units that are 3PLs, but don't let that confuse you—those two business units are kept separate). In most cases, wholesale distributors buy (take ownership of) drugs directly from the manufacturer. They never buy drugs directly from a 3PL, but if the manufacturer they buy from makes use of a 3PL to distribute their products, the manufacturer will instruct the 3PL to ship their product to the wholesale distributor to fulfill their order. The wholesale distributor will then pay the manufacturer's invoice for the product. So even though a 3PL was involved in the transaction to facilitate warehousing, order fulfillment and shipping, the product ownership changed only once: from the manufacturer to the wholesale distributor.

In many cases, the manufacturer's invoice is actually generated and transmitted to the wholesale distributor by the 3PL, and payment may even be made to the 3PL on behalf of the manufacturer. Even these are simply financial services rendered to the manufacturer for a fee by the 3PL.

This is an important distinction, because the DSCSA requires all changes of ownership to be documented with the passing of Transaction Information (TI), Transaction History (TH) and a Transaction Statement (TS) from the seller to the buyer. So for drugs that are sold by a manufacturer to a wholesale distributor, this transaction must result in the generation and passing of TI, TH and TS by the manufacturer and its receipt by the wholesale distributor (the law is currently in effect for manufacturers, repackagers and wholesale distributors but will be effective for dispensers on July 1, 2015 [FDA enforcement was delayed until at least March 1, 2016]).

WHAT DOES THE DSCSA SAY ABOUT 3PLs?

Not much really. Because the 3PL generally never "owns" the product, they are not obligated by the DSCSA to generate, transmit or receive the transaction documents. However, 3PLs are included in the DSCSA definition of "Trading Partners".

Beginning sometime in 2016, depending on when the FDA

publishes regulations regarding the standards for Federal and State licensing of third-party logistics providers, 3PLs must apply for and receive a license from either a third-party accreditation program approved by the FDA, or the FDA themselves. Until that time, the DSCSA created a blanket license for all existing 3PLs who currently held state licenses and who reported to the FDA by November 27, 2014 (and must continue to do so annually).

Until we see those new 3PL regulations from the FDA we will not know exactly what to expect. They were due by November 27, 2015. However, Congress provided the FDA with specific requirements for working with the states on licensing and fees. If you work for a 3PL, I suggest you familiarize yourself with those specifics in the DSCSA because the FDA's regulations will need to align with them.

The reference to "third party accreditation program" sounds suspiciously like the existing Verified-Accredited Wholesale Distributor (VAWD)[115] program offered by the National Association of Boards of Pharmacy (NABP) and which some states required for wholesale distributor licensure. I would not be surprised if the NABP announces in the coming months a new or related program that would be recognized by the FDA to fulfill the new Federal 3PL and wholesale distributor licensure requirements. I'm betting there are negotiations going on right now between the NABP and the FDA for just this sort of thing. If so, they will need to announce it as part of the FDA's mandated deadline. We'll see.

CAN A 3PL OFFER TI/TH/TS SERVICES?

The interpretation of the DSCSA 3PL regulation is pretty straightforward. I can't find any other provision in the law that would seem to block 3PLs from offering TI, TH and TS document retention, generation and transmission services as part of their overall contractual service offering. It seems like this kind of service would be a very nice extension to their menu of services because any manufacturer wishing to outsource the distribution of their drugs would also very likely want to outsource the busywork part of maintaining the DSCSA transaction documentation on their behalf.

Of course, a 3PL cannot absorb the legal responsibility that the manufacturer, repackager or wholesale distributor has to generate, provide, store and retrieve the DSCSA transaction documentation, but there are seemingly lots of things the 3PL could do to make it very easy for the manufacturer to execute their legal obligations by handling all of the technical stuff. The manufacturer would still be liable for the accuracy of the DSCSA transaction documentation and as a result, they would certainly want to create an additional liability for accuracy on the 3PL through their contract. That is, the manufacturer's contract with the 3PL should include provisions that would make the 3PL responsible for ensuring that the TI, TH and TS accurately reflect the reality of the shipments they make. That way if an error is ever detected that results in a regulatory violation, the manufacturer would be liable to the State regulators and/or the FDA and the 3PL would be liable to the manufacturer.

If you work for a 3PL, or for a manufacturer who makes use of a 3PL, I suggest that you review the 3PL provisions of the DSCSA and work with your contract partner to update your contracts to clarify the obligations and penalties under these new circumstances.

Dirk.

DSCSA "Serial Numbers"

By Dirk Rodgers
Original essay published on RxTrace.com on March 9, 2015.[116] Updated for this book on January 1, 2016.

I often write about the fact that drug manufacturers and repackagers that sell into the U.S. market must put "serial numbers", or "serialize" their drug packages and homogeneous cases before November 27, 2017, but what exactly does that mean?

Let's break it down. The Drug Supply Chain Security Act (DSCSA) defines the term "Product identifier" this way:

> *"PRODUCT IDENTIFIER. –*
>
> *The term 'product identifier' means a standardized graphic that includes, in both human-readable form and on a machine-readable data carrier that conforms to the standards developed by a widely recognized international standards development organization, the standardized numerical identifier, lot number, and expiration date of the product."* (Section 581[14])

Back in March of 2010 – 3 ½ years before Congress passed the DSCSA – the FDA published final guidance called "Guidance for Industry, Standards for Securing the Drug Supply Chain – Standardized Numerical Identification for Prescription Drug Packages"[117], which defined the term "standardized numerical identifier (SNI)" this way:

> *"The SNI for most prescription drug packages should be a serialized National Drug Code (sNDC). The sNDC is composed of the National Drug Code (NDC) (as set forth in 21 CFR Part 207) that corresponds to the specific drug product (including the particular package configuration) combined with a unique serial number, generated by the manufacturer or repackager for each individual package. Serial numbers should be numeric (numbers) or alphanumeric (include letters and/or numbers) and should have no more than 20 characters (letters and/or numbers)."* (See "FDA Aligns with GS1 SGTIN For SNDC".[118])

So the DSCSA product identifier is composed of:

- the drug's 10-digit NDC,
- a unique serial number,

- the lot number and
- the expiration date of the product.

According to the SNI guidance, the "serial number" portion of the SNI should be up to 20 characters that can be letters and/or numbers. (Notice that symbols are not allowed.)

So whenever people, including me, talk about "pharma serialization", or "putting a serial number on a drug package", or even a "serial number-based repository", it's all just shorthand for the DSCSA product identifier. The serial number is actually just one part of that identifier, but people focus in on that part because that's the part that is new and hard to implement correctly. So please don't get confused when you hear people using the terms "serial number" and "serialization" loosely.

"…A MACHINE-READABLE DATA CARRIER THAT CONFORMS TO…"

Congress did not want the FDA to go off and create their own machine-readable data carrier, but they also did not want to prescribe exactly which existing standard should be used. However, they described it in a way that there really is not any question about which standards development organization will be used: the same widely recognized international standards development organization that is used to barcode drugs in the U.S. market today: GS1. From that, we can infer that the most common implementation of the DSCSA product identifier will be a GS1 Global Trade Identification Number (GTIN) [119] (a GTIN-14 to be exact) that encodes an NDC (see "Depicting An NDC Within A GTIN" [120]) combined with a serial number that conforms to the specification that Congress provided (above) in the format of a GS1 serial number element string that is associated with that GTIN.

The only difference I can see between the serial number specification that Congress provided and the specification of a GS1 serial number is that GS1 would allow some symbols to be used (see table 7.11 of the latest GS1 General Specifications [121]), but Congress does not. That is not a big difference and is probably a good idea anyway.

In Section 582(a)(9) of the DSCSA, "PRODUCT IDENTIFIERS", includes the requirement:

> "...the applicable data —

> "(i) shall be included in a 2-dimensional data matrix barcode when affixed to, or imprinted upon, a package; and

> "(ii) shall be included in a linear or 2-dimensional data matrix barcode when affixed to, or imprinted upon, a homogeneous case..."

This means that the "machine-readable data carrier" that carries the DSCSA product identifier must be a 2-dimensional "data matrix" (otherwise known as a "GS1 DataMatrix", see "GS1 DataMatrix: An Introduction and Implementation Guideline"[122]) barcode. That is pretty specific, although they really did not say it had to be the "GS1" version of the data matrix symbology.

Also be aware that the Healthcare Distribution Management Association's (HDMA's) "HDMA Guidelines for Bar Coding in the Pharmaceutical Supply Chain"[123] (see "Updated HDMA Bar Code Guidance: A Must Read"[124]), from back in 2011 (it is a little dated and I expect an updated version sometime soon) includes the following FAQ:

> "Q: Is there a preferred length (number of characters) for the serialized number which follows AI (21)?

> "A: Yes, the preferred length is 12 digits (all numeric). This allows the same serial number to be encoded in an SGTIN-96 RFID Tag. This standard is limited to 12 digits and seems to be sufficient in length to allow for approximately 275 billion serial numbers."

They make a good point about the limitations of the early-model passive RFID tags — the 96-bit tags — that were around back then, but the DSCSA does not allow the use of RFID to carry the DSCSA product identifier so I don't think I would worry about limiting yourselves to 12 digits or all numeric just for that purpose. Of course, it is entirely possible (maybe likely, to the perennial optimists in the RFID industry) that the FDA will sanction the use of RFID tags to carry these identifiers in the future, but by then the 96-bit tags probably won't even be available. Even today, modern UHF passive RFID tags can accommodate the full 20 character alphanumeric set of characters that Congress allows.

For more details about GS1 serial numbers, see "Randomization— An Interview with Ken Traub—Part 1: GS1 Serial Number Considerations"[125].

Dirk.

Identification Of Pharma Cases In The U.S.

By Dirk Rodgers
Original essay published on RxTrace.com on April 27, 2015.[126] Updated for this book on January 1, 2016.

In an RxTrace essay I discussed controversy over the use of GS1's Serial Shipping Container Code[127] (SSCC) in the Brazil pharma supply chain to meet regulatory requirements imposed by ANVISA. But there are different controversies, or at least potential confusion, in the U.S. pharma supply chain surrounding case labels, and some of those are relate to the SSCC and its use.

A case product identification label is the label a manufacturer usually places on each homogeneous case at case-packing time to identify what is inside the corrugated box. A "homogenous case" is a case that contains units from a single NDC and all units are from a single packaging lot. The product identification label should not be confused with a shipping/logistics label, which, if it exists, is applied at the time of shipment and contains information about the destination.

Typically, cases that are shipped from a higher-volume manufacturer to a larger wholesale distributor will be placed onto a pallet. The pallet often has cases of multiple products, and even different homogeneous cases of the same product can contain different lot numbers. You can sometimes even find a Non-homogeneous case mixed in with the homogeneous cases. Further, cases on the same pallet can actually be fulfilling different purchase orders submitted by the buyer. All of these variations complicate the job of the receiving clerk.

Fortunately, the Healthcare Distribution Management Association (HDMA) has published a clear guidance document to help standardize the various labels on products, cases and pallets. It's called "HDMA Guidelines for Bar Coding in the Pharmaceutical Supply Chain (2011)[128]". Keep in mind that this document, though still helpful, has not been updated to reflect considerations introduced by the passage of the U.S. Drug Supply Chain Security Act (DSCSA). It should be updated by the HDMA soon.

BEFORE THE DSCSA

Before the DSCSA was enacted, cases were rarely serialized by the manufacturer. That is, for most products, neither the typical case product identification label nor the typical shipping/logistics label contained a serial number, unless perhaps one was applied for internal purposes by UPS, Federal Express or other courier. But a few manufacturers did apply an SSCC — which contains a serial number — to some of their shipping/logistics labels. Scheduled drugs were a likely candidate for an SSCC because the Drug Enforcement Administration (DEA) recommends not printing any kind of product identification on the outside of their shipping containers.

In the DEA's Controlled Substances Security Manual[129], under the heading "Common or Contract Carriers" it says:

> *"Although not required, precautions such as securely wrapping and sealing packages containing controlled substances and using unmarked or coded boxes or shipping containers are strongly recommended for guarding against in-transit losses."*

It's kind of hard to ship and "unmarked" box to a customer these days, but an SSCC is a nice way to keep track of which shipping case contains which product when it is referenced in an Electronic Data Interchange (EDI) Advance Ship Notice (ASN). That way, those who have access to the ASN will know what it inside, but others will not. The SSCC is composed of only a company identifier and a serial number that is unique to that company and that case.

Back in 2011, in preparation for the now preempted California Pedigree law, the HDMA updated their barcode guidance document. That document recommends the addition of a GS1 Serial Number (see "DSCSA 'Serial Numbers' ") to the barcodes they recommend on the product identification labels of homogeneous cases. See the section called "Homogenous Cases — Product Identification Labeling" on page 39 of the HDMA's 2011 barcode document. This will result in what GS1 calls a "GTIN plus Serial Number", or what a lot of other people call an "SGTIN" (for "Serialized Global Trade Item Number") placed on the case at case-packing time.

When it comes to scheduled drugs, the HDMA document sort of punts. It simply says:

> *"Drug Enforcement Administration regulations must be followed when labeling scheduled drugs. This may differ from the recommendations below."*

And

> *"(controlled substances may or may not be identified for security reasons in accordance with the labeler's policy and/or DEA*

regulations)"

The document provides no further guidance on labeling DEA scheduled drugs, but for all non-homogeneous cases of other drugs it encourages the use of an SSCC on the shipping/logistics label. See the section called "Individual Shipping Cases and Pallets — Logistics/Serial Shipping Container Code (SSCC) Label Format" on page 42 of the HDMA document.

The large wholesale distributors have included an SSCC on the shipping/logistics labels they apply, to varying degrees, for over 20 years. These labels are applied to totes and cases shipped to their customers. In some cases, their shipping/logistics label is slapped onto outgoing manufacturer's cases regardless of what labeling the manufacturer applied. That is, even if the manufacturer had included an SGTIN on their product identification label, and/or an SSCC on their shipping/logistics label, the wholesaler applies their own unique SSCC when shipping a case to a customer—again, to varying degrees. Notice that this can lead to a single case with multiple serial numbers on it—up to 3 different serial numbers, in fact. Of course, before the DSCSA, serial numbers were not really used between companies in the supply chain so this did not cause a problem.

AFTER THE DSCSA...NOVEMBER 2017

The DSCSA contains new, specific language about how manufacturers must mark cases after November 27, 2017 (2018 for Repackagers). After those dates, all homogeneous cases packed by manufacturers and repackagers in the supply chain must have a DSCSA "Product Identifier" on them. After November of 2019 wholesale distributors may not buy or sell products that do not have a DSCSA Product Identifier on them, and the same goes for dispensers after November of 2020.

A DSCSA "Product Identifier" on a homogeneous case is the NDC and serial number (together known as a Standardized Numerical Identifier, see "FDA Aligns with GS1 SGTIN For SNDC"[130]), the lot number and expiration date of the product contained inside. These data elements must be presented on the case in human readable form as well as in a 2-dimensional Datamatrix or linear barcode.

Congress made no provision in the DSCSA for the DEA's recommendation to not mark the outside of cases containing controlled substances, so after these deadlines, companies who were previously using an SSCC to provide some level of concealment of the contents of their cases may be forced to expose those contents. To continue that practice, packing one or more properly marked homogeneous case(s) inside an overpack box marked with an SSCC is probably the best solution. But with this approach you might find that wholesale distributors expect you to provide accurate aggregation data (a.k.a., serial number-based packaging hierarchy data) in your ASN so they can tell exactly what is inside before they open the overpack box.

The DSCSA does not require the seller to provide the buyer with aggregation data until maybe (probably) November of 2023 (see "When Will The DSCSA Ever Require Investments In Aggregation?"). But once every homogeneous case is serialized, wholesale distributors may feel justified in asking manufacturers and repackagers to provide them with aggregation data at the shipping container level. Technically, container-level packaging hierarchy is already being supplied by any company following HDMA's EDI ASN guidance (see "HDMA Has Updated Their EDI ASN Guidance For DSCSA, Again"[131]), but that packaging hierarchy is provided without serial numbers today. It may be logical for wholesale distributors to expect manufacturers and repackagers to include the serial numbers of each shipping container in their ASNs once every shipping container is serialized. Perhaps this could be an "intermediate" aggregation state that companies could use as a stepping stone toward full unit-level aggregation data collection.

I think the current situation where some homogenous cases can end up reaching a hospital or pharmacy with up to 3 different serial numbers on them will become more of a problem as these dispensers begin to deploy systems aimed at meeting their requirements under the DSCSA. At some point, these companies will begin to scan the serial number barcode as part of their receiving processes. When they do that, they had better find only a single serial number on each homogeneous case, and it had better be the DSCSA-mandated "product identifier" that the manufacturer or repackager applied, not an SSCC that the manufacturer or wholesale distributor applies today. Companies routinely applying an SSCC to homogeneous cases today need to figure out a new way of meeting their needs after 2017/2018.

Dirk.

The DSCSA Product Identifier On Drug Packages

By Dirk Rodgers
Original essay published on RxTrace.com on May 4, 2015.[132] Updated for this book on January 1, 2016.

According to the Drug Supply Chain Security Act (DSCSA), manufacturers must apply a new "Product Identifier" on all of their prescription drug products by November 27, 2017 (Repackagers by that date in 2018). The DSCSA Product Identifier is defined this way:

> *"PRODUCT IDENTIFIER. –*
>
> *The term 'product identifier' means a standardized graphic that includes, in both human-readable form and on a machine-readable data carrier that conforms to the standards developed by a widely recognized international standards development organization, the standardized numerical identifier, lot number, and expiration date of the product."* (Section 581[14])

In an earlier essay, "DSCSA 'Serial Numbers'" I focus on the serial number portion of the product identifier, and in my last essay "Identification Of Pharma Cases In The U.S." I focus on how the product identifiers would be placed onto cases. In this essay I want to take a look at issues surrounding the application of the product identifier on drug packages.

Section 582(a)(9) of the DSCSA, "PRODUCT IDENTIFIERS", in part says:

> "...the applicable data –
>
> "(i) shall be included in a 2-dimensional data matrix barcode when affixed to, or imprinted upon, a package; ..."

So we know that the drug's NDC and serial number (known as a Standardized Numerical Identifier, or SNI) must be presented on the label of every drug package along with its packaging lot number and expiration date in two ways:

- Encoded within a 2-dimensional (2D) Datamatrix barcode, and
- Printed in human-readable form

I find it fascinating that Congress specified the exact type of barcode that must be applied by manufacturers and repackagers rather than leaving it up to the FDA or the industry. For a long time I have held the opinion that the data carrier technology used for product identification within a given regulated market must be limited to a small set (preferably only one) of carrier technologies to ensure widespread interoperability (see "Should Regulations Dictate Technology?"[133]). But I also recognize that this approach could stifle technical progress, so I believe that the body that sets the limits must be one that is capable of recognizing when it is time to move to a better technology and has the authority to force everyone to move to it in unison. In the DSCSA, Congress identified that deciding body as the FDA.

That's good because, even though the law specifies a "data matrix" barcode as the data carrier, we do not have to go back to Congress to move to a better technology. And there are already reports of troubles with the speed of printing and verifying Datamatrix barcodes on very high-speed packaging lines (particularly in the tobacco industry but also in the drug industry). This has led people to search for faster 2D barcode technologies. The current darling is call the "DotCode". The only trouble is, the DotCode is not a GS1 standard symbology so a small group of end users, solution providers and AIDC experts is mounting a quick effort to get GS1 to consider adding it to their list of standard symbologies. A workshop was apparently held in Barcelona on May 27, 2015 to discuss it. Contact Henri Barthel of GS1 for more info. It's just the beginning of a long and winding road that will likely take years.

Fortunately, if the Datamatrix really is too slow for certain drug products, companies can petition the FDA to allow them to use the DotCode or something else. I recommend starting that process now rather than waiting until GS1 "standardizes" the DotCode. That way the two bureaucratic processes might run in parallel.

A FLAW IN RECENT GS1 US DSCSA GUIDANCE

I would like to draw your attention to the fact that the DSCSA requires the NDC to be printed on drugs in human readable form as part of the SNI portion of the Product Identifier. Unfortunately, GS1 US's recent DSCSA Guidance version 1.1[134] recommends the printing of the drug's GS1 Global Trade Item Number (GTIN)[135] for the human readable section next to the barcode. GS1 US refers to it as the "human understandable" data presentation (see page 42 of their guideline).

In fact, GS1 normally refers to the human readable data presentation as the "human readable interpretation" or "HRI". It is normally an interpretation of what is encoded in the barcode. In this case, the barcode will contain a GTIN which is based on the NDC, so it is natural for GS1 US to expect the HRI to contain a human readable GTIN. But because this is a regulated barcode, that would be wrong. In my opinion, to be compliant with the law, drug manufacturers and repackagers should *not* follow GS1 US guidance in this situation.

A GS1 GTIN — even one that is based on an NDC — is not an NDC, so the human readable form of the DSCSA Product Identifier on a drug package should never be formatted or labeled as a "GTIN" but must be formatted as a 10-digit NDC and labeled "NDC". In my interpretation, it is fine to encode the NDC within a GTIN when it is encoded within the barcode, but not in the human readable data, so technically, this should also not be referred to as the "HRI". Calling it the "human understandable" is actually a good idea.

The difference between the GTIN encoded in the barcode and the NDC in the human readable form is analogous to the difference between the expiration date encoded in the barcode and the formatting of the date in the human readable form. The format of human readable dates can be dictated by regulation, but no regulation should dictate the way a date is formatted within the barcode. That must always be left for the barcode encoding standard to dictate. This issue comes up more with the U.S. FDA Unique Device Identification (UDI) standard than it does with drugs, because the UDI rule enforced by the FDA very deliberately mandates the format of the human readable expiration date but not the barcode encoded format (see "What The UDI Date Format Says About FDA's Direction"[136]). The FDA does not seem to enforce a particular formatting of the human readable expiration date (I am not an expert on this so check with the FDA). I understand that companies should follow USP guidance for that (again, confirm this with the FDA).

My advice for the human readable presentation of the NDC and the date code goes for the label on the drug package as well as the homogenous case label since both must contain the DSCSA Product Identifier. I assume GS1 US has corrected this flaw in their next update of that guidance, which is "due any day now" (watch the GS1 US DSCSA resources page for the new guidance). [It is still not out as of January 1, 2016.]

Dirk.

'The Smallest Individual Saleable Unit' In The DSCSA

By Dirk Rodgers
Original essay published on RxTrace.com on June 8, 2015.[137] Updated for this book on January 1, 2016.

The U.S. Drug Supply Chain Security Act (DSCSA) requires manufacturers and repackagers to place DSCSA-specific "product identifiers" on all drug packages and homogeneous cases by November 27, 2017 (2018 for repackagers). These product identifiers must include a Standardized Numeric Identifier (SNI), which is composed of the drugs National Drug Code (NDC) and a unique serial number (for more on DSCSA "product identifiers", see "The DSCSA Product Identifier On Drug Packages", for more on the SNI, see "FDA Aligns with GS1 SGTIN For SNDC"[138], and for more on the NDC, see "Anatomy Of The National Drug Code"[139])
.

A common question is, what is the smallest level of packaging that must be serialized? The DSCSA text provides the answer.

This is an update to an essay I wrote back in 2013 about the same topic, but for the California pedigree law, which was subsequently preempted by the DSCSA. The California pedigree law would have required manufacturers to serialize the smallest package of drugs that will be bought by a dispenser. The DSCSA is basically the same. For some manufacturers targeting the U.S. market, that may require serialization at a lower unit of measure than they might have thought. For products that manufacturers package into multi-packs and sell to wholesalers packaged only that way, you might assume that your "smallest individual saleable unit" is the multi-pack. Think again.

For pharmaceutical manufacturers with products in this category, I strongly suggest that you poll your wholesaler customers and find out how often they break down your multi-pack today and sell the individual packages inside to their dispensing customers.

The DSCSA defines the term "Package" this way:

> *"(A) IN GENERAL. – The term 'package' means the smallest individual saleable unit of product for distribution by a manufacturer or repackager that is intended by the manufacturer for ultimate sale to the dispenser of such product.*

> *"(B) INDIVIDUAL SALEABLE UNIT. – For purposes of this paragraph, an 'individual saleable unit' is the smallest container of product introduced into commerce by the manufacturer or repackager that is intended by the manufacturer or repackager for individual sale to a dispenser.* [DSCSA Section 581(11)]

Yes, you could probably say that your multi-pack—just like today—is the level of packaging that you intend for ultimate sale to the dispenser and so that's all you will be required to serialize. And theoretically, you would be right. But, if today, before serialization is required, wholesalers routinely break your multi-pack down further as part of their friendly service to their customers; they won't be able to do that once they begin operating under the serialization requirements of the DSCSA—November 27, 2019.

After that date they will no longer be able to break any package down unless the components within are also serialized by the manufacturer or repackager.

"So what?" you say? If your product is routinely broken down by the wholesaler today, that is done to supply small pharmacies with a smaller amount of your product so they are able to dispense it before the expiration date. This has happened in the past with multi-packs of some prefilled insulin syringes, some vials and similar products.

Admittedly, not many products fall into this category, but if yours is one that does, you should think about what those small pharmacies might do if they will be forced to only buy your product in the full multi-pack. Will the pharmacies decide to start buying your multi-pack, since that's the only form available to them? Or will their wholesaler help them find some alternative drug that is serialized at a lower unit of measure instead? Poll your customers, and their customers, to find out before you establish your final serialization plan.

When you are ready to serialize the individual packages contained inside your multi-packs, make sure you consult the GS1 Healthcare GTIN Allocation Rules[140] to get the GTINs right. Then consult my essay "Anatomy Of An FDA SNI"[141] to learn how to combine a GTIN with a serial number to serialize them.

Dirk.

A Closer Look At The Six-Year Record-Keeping Requirement

By Dirk Rodgers
Original essay published on RxTrace.com on July 14, 2014.[142] Updated for this book on January 1, 2016.

The Drug Supply Chain Security Act (DSCSA) contains record-keeping requirements for drug manufacturers, wholesale distributors, repackagers and dispensers that begin on January 1, 2015 (enforcement was deferred until May 1, 2015). All companies must keep a copy of the Transaction Information (TI), Transaction

History (TH), and Transaction Statements (TS) they receive and those they send for at least six years. In addition, manufacturers and repackagers must also retain knowledge about the "product identifier" on each unit they sell into the supply chain for a period of six years after the date it was sold. Companies who perform investigations into suspect product must also keep records of their process and the outcome for six years.

There are a few implications of these record-keeping requirements. Let's take a look at some of them.

The purpose of retaining all this information is so that it can be retrieved and serve as a data source for investigations into suspect product (see "The FDA's Draft Guidance on Suspect Product"[143]) over the ensuing six years. For example, wholesale distributors must respond to requests for information from the FDA…

> *"…or other appropriate State or Federal official in the event of a recall or for the purpose of investigating a suspect product or an illegitimate product, a wholesale distributor shall, not later than 1 business day, and not to exceed 48 hours, after receiving the request or in other such reasonable time as determined by the Secretary, based on the circumstances of the request, provide the applicable transaction information, transaction history, and transaction statement for the product."* DSCSA 582(c)(1)(C).

The same type of provision exists for each type of company in the supply chain (except dispensers are given two days to respond).

Even if you are not the direct target of a particular investigation…or prosecution…you may still be called upon to contribute data about the shipments you have made over the last six years whenever you supplied product to, or received product from, someone who is the target. Their data had better match your data, where your data may be considered the basis of truth and the target company's data may be viewed with suspicion. In a case like this, you may be called upon to provide the TI, TH and TS for more than just one product or one shipment. You may need to supply all of that data for that particular supplier or customer over a period of months.

I can imagine, "…based on the circumstances…" that you might be asked for the TI, TH and TS in the following ways. Provide all transaction data involving:

1. company "XYZ" over the period "begin date" to "end date"
2. product "WXY" and lot number "ABC"
3. product "VWX" over the period "begin date" to "end date"
4. company "XYZ" and product "WXY" over the period "begin date" to "end date"
5. company "XYZ", product "XYZ" and lot number "ABC"
6. company "XYZ", product "WXY" and lot number over the period "begin date" to "end date"

You might be able to imagine other types of requests. In any case, your ability to retrieve this data within one day (two days for pharmacies) needs to include all of the forms and formats you expect to send and receive over time. That is, if you start sending or receiving paper TI, TH and TS and some Electronic Data Interchange (EDI) Advance Ship Notice (ASN) versions of that data in early 2015, and then in two years you add some exchange of EPCIS-based transaction data, you need to be able to search all of these data repositories to fulfill these requests.

Even after you stop sending or receiving a particular form of transaction data, you will need to be able to search and retrieve data from the repository of that type for another six years. See "DQSA: How Should Transaction Data Be Exchanged?"[144] and "DQSA: Getting To Electronic Transaction Data Exchange"[145].

I recently asked a person who works for a small manufacturer if they have plans for implementing this record-keeping requirement, and he said, "Oh, we already do tape backups of all our data." Hmmm. A "tape backup"?

It seems to me that this requirement is beyond the capability of a simple "tape backup" system. Because of the type of queries you might be faced with, I don't think you will want to restore data from tape and then search for the requested data, repeating until you are sure you found it all. Instead, I think you will want some way to query a database for the location of the requested data, and then perhaps restore only the one tape that contains the needed data (or open the one box of paper documents needed). This approach requires a level of intelligence that most tape backup systems do not have.

Up until now, the usefulness of EDI ASNs was fairly short. After the product reflected on a given ASN was received into inventory and matched with the supplier's invoice, the ASN wasn't really needed. Most companies probably keep them around for some period of time, but probably not for six years. Starting on January 1, 2015 (enforcement was deferred until May 1, 2015), those ASNs that are used to transmit the required TI, TH and TS fall under the six year data retention requirement of the DSCSA for both the sender and the recipient. And these are the documents you will need to retrieve based on the future "requests for information".

Don't be confused by the language "*…not later than 1 business day, and not to exceed 48 hours, after receiving the request…*". This simply covers what must happen over a weekend. For example, if the FDA (or State Board of Pharmacy, or U.S. Justice Department…) request for information arrived at 3pm on Friday, May 22, 2015, unless the requester relaxes this requirement in that specific case, you would have needed to respond by 3pm on Sunday, May 24, 2015 (48 hours later) even though it was a holiday weekend (Memorial Day). I assume they will not do something like that unless lives are in danger, but at least the law allows them to do it in any case.

If I am reading these provisions correctly, the FDA could request an even faster response time, again "…based on circumstances…". Imagine a time-critical investigation where the health of a large number of people may be at stake, perhaps.

The bottom-line implication of all this is that companies should now be ready to quickly and accurately retrieve any of the TI, TH and TS they generate and receive based on a wide range of parameters [dispensers, beginning on March 1, 2016] . And I don't think you should rely on a simple tape backup system to meet this regulatory requirement.

Dirk.

A Closer Look At Web Portals for DSCSA Transaction Data Exchange

By Dirk Rodgers
Original essay published on RxTrace.com on December 29, 2014.[146] Updated for this book on January 1, 2016.

One of the approaches that the FDA mentioned in their data exchange guidance[147], published on November 26, 2014, is the use of secure web portals. Some companies are planning to make use of web portals to pass their Transaction Information (TI), Transaction History (TH) and Transaction Statements (TS) to their customers as is now required for manufacturers, wholesale distributors and repackagers, and on July 1, 2015 for dispensers [FDA enforcement delayed at least until March 1, 2016] (see "Who Is A DSCSA Dispenser?").

So let's take a few minutes for a closer look at what they are and how they should be used, including one of the potential pitfalls that companies relying on them may face.

WHAT IS A SECURE WEB PORTAL?

Briefly, a web portal used to meet the U.S. DSCSA transaction data exchange requirements is a website provided by the seller of drugs to the supply chain company that buys from them. The website provides the buyer with access to the TI, TH and TS documents that the DSCSA requires the seller to provide to the buyer. The web portal, then, fulfills the data exchange requirements that are imposed on the seller. They can also allow the buyer to meet the DSCSA requirement that they receive the TI, TH and TS from the seller, but only if they make proper use of the sellers web portal (see below).

The term "web portal" when used to refer to the definition above is a shortened version of the true name, which is "secure web portal". That is, to be of value for meeting the data exchange requirements, a web portal offered by the seller must apply all the typical internet security features, and must allow the buyer to login and access only the transaction documents that describe their purchases from that particular seller.

A web portal is specific to a given seller's transactions so if a company in the supply chain buys from multiple companies, and if web portals are used to receive the required TI, TH and TS documents, then the buyer needs to have access to the web portals offered by each of those suppliers.

There is no standard user interface for a secure web portal and the operation of the web portals offered by each seller may be different. The only common characteristics are that the buyer needs to manually login somehow, and somehow be given access to the transaction documents for their incoming shipments from that supplier. User account management, navigation, access method, download formatting and what else the user has access to will likely all vary from supplier to supplier.

Some suppliers may offer the minimum required access to the buyer's DSCSA transaction documents, but other suppliers may integrate the web portal with their existing customer service portals which may offer features such as order entry and tracking, returns authorization and tracking, chargeback resolution and tracking, recall database, shelf label printing, etc.

THE PITFALL OF WEB PORTALS

If you plan to make use of web portals for receiving your supplier's DSCSA transaction documentation, the most important thing you must keep in mind is that, at their base, web portals are offered as a data exchange mechanism. That is, they fulfill the requirement for the seller to provide the buyer with the necessary TI, TH and TS documents at the time of the transaction.

In some cases, they may also be offered by the supplier to fulfill the buyer's DSCSA requirement to store and retrieve the transaction documents in the event of an investigation over the next six years, *but this is not always the primary purpose of the web portal.*

Do not assume that the seller will keep your DSCSA transaction documents in the web portal for six years and make them retrievable by you for that full term. The seller is not obligated to provide that level of service. As a "data exchange" mechanism, the data may only be accessible for some pre-defined duration that is significantly less than six years. It is the buyer's obligation to store and retrieve those documents for the full six years after the transaction (see "DSCSA: A Closer Look At The Six-Year Record-Keeping Requirement"). Yes, the seller has a comparable obligation to store and retrieve those documents in case of an investigation, but their obligation is separate from the buyer's obligation, even when a web portal is in use for data exchange.

All that being said, you may find that some sellers who offer web portals for data exchange may also voluntarily agree to provide that service to you for the full six years. My point is, don't assume they will all do that just because they offer a web portal for data exchange. You need to be very clear about what your supplier intends their web portal to be used for. Ask your suppliers and get it in writing.

This service is so important to you, as the drug buyer, my recommendation is that you require a firm contract that clearly establishes the seller's obligation to retain that data on your behalf for the full six year regulatory requirement. Six years is a long time to rely on the continuation of "good will" and "benevolence". If you can get a signature on a contract covering six years, then I think you can relax and assume that you will meet your DSCSA data storage and retrieval requirement…for purchases from that supplier anyway.

The only problem is, you probably won't get that for free. You may find it very difficult to get a supplier to contractually obligate themselves to provide that level of service without additional payment. The only way to find out, is to explicitly ask them if they would be willing to update an existing contract with you, or establish a new one specifically for this purpose. This is the best way to find out if the supplier intends to offer the web portal for your use as a DSCSA data storage and retrieval solution, or just a simple data exchange mechanism.

If it turns out that they are only offering the web portal as a simple data exchange mechanism, and not a full document storage and retrieval system, then you will need to make it a regular practice to download every transaction document from that portal and into your own system for long term data storage and retrieval. If you are small enough, you may be able to simply print these documents and store them physically. If you are too big to deal with all that paper, then your solution will need to be electronic and must be compatible with whatever document format the seller is offering through their portal.

Web portals sound like a simple solution to the DSCSA transaction requirements — and they are — but only for the exchange of that data. More than likely, most buyers will still need to pull those documents down into their own systems and store them for the full six year obligation.

Dirk.

Vendor Managed Inventory Under the DSCSA

By Dirk Rodgers
Original essay published on RxTrace.com on May 26, 2015.[148] Updated for this book on January 1, 2016.

One of the complexities of the modern pharmaceutical supply chain occurs when a pharmaceutical dispensing organization "outsources" the management of their on-premises inventory to their supplier, or "vendor". This is known as Vendor Managed Inventory, or VMI. There are several good reasons this might be done, including eliminating the need to deal with issues that have more to do with supply chain execution mechanics and fluctuating supply and demand than they do with the core competency of dispensing drugs.

When VMI is used in the pharma supply chain the supplier is typically a wholesale distributor whose core competency is in dealing with those exact issues. That's just what they do. The wholesaler benefits from the VMI relationship because they become the exclusive supplier to the VMI customer. VMI can be a "win-win" proposition as long as costs are kept in-check.

But what will happen to VMI relationships now that the Drug Supply Chain Security Act (DSCSA) is in effect? The DSCSA itself does not have anything to say about these business relationships so we just have to follow the logic of the law to figure it out on our own. The main thing to look for when applying the DSCSA is any change of ownership of a drug. Those are the times when a seller must provide Transaction Information (TI), Transaction History (TH) and a Transaction Statement (TS) to the buyer.

In a VMI situation, the drugs sitting in inventory at the dispensing organization's location are usually owned by the supplier. The change of ownership to the dispenser usually occurs only at the moment when a drug is administered or dispensed to a patient. The "sale" from VMI supplier to dispenser occurs on paper (or electronically anyway) as the drug is being "resold" (dispensed) to the patient. In this way the dispenser never actually carries any inventory of the VMI product. This is true even though a casual observer—or the FDA, or a state Board of Pharmacy inspector— would see lots of inventory sitting on the dispenser's shelves. The dispenser has custody of the drugs, but does not own them.

HOW DOES THE DSCSA IMPACT VMI?

Interestingly, the DSCSA does not mention any need for Third-Party Logistics (3PLs) providers to hold or provide DSCSA transaction documents. Third-Party Logistics providers also hold a large amount of inventory that they do not own and will therefore not have DSCSA documentation for. Using that as an example, I think we can assume that pharmacies that use VMI will not need to hold DSCSA transaction documents for drugs held on their shelves but are still owned by the VMI supplier.

However, at the moment of dispense, the dispenser would become the owner (momentarily) so TI, TH and TS updates will be required to show that ownership change. Presumably as a result, after July 1, 2015 [FDA enforcement has been delayed at least until March 1, 2016], the VMI supplier would have to immediately provide the dispenser with updated TI, TH and TS showing the new ownership transaction. That way the TH that the wholesaler retains, and the copy the dispenser receives, would accurately reflect the new ownership reality that has just occurred. These are just assumptions since VMI is not really discussed in the DSCSA directly.

Any dispensing organization that has decided to shed all of the pharma supply chain hassles by paying someone to manage their inventory for them probably won't want to deal with the DSCSA transaction data either. In that case they may want to rely heavily on the VMI supplier to take as much of that work off their hands as possible. The DSCSA allows third-parties – *"which can be an authorized wholesale distributor"* – to provide transaction data storage services to dispensers so it is logical that VMI suppliers would include that service.

How vendor managed inventory may be handled under the DSCSA

is subject to some speculation, as this essay shows. Companies who want to continue using that business process may want to confirm these assumptions with the FDA and/or the local Boards of Pharmacies involved.

Can you think of any other business processes in use today where a company has custody of a drug but does not own it (other than a courier/delivery company)? Do you think these same assumptions would apply to it, or would different assumptions make more sense? Let me know what you think.

Dirk.

Correction: Your Drug or Biologic Combination Product Is Probably NOT Exempt From The DSCSA

By Dirk Rodgers
Original essay published on RxTrace.com on December 16, 2013.[149] Updated for this book on January 1, 2016.

Just before the DSCSA was enacted, I published an essay that analyzed the exemption language related to combination products contained in the old California pedigree law and in H.R. 3204, which was later signed into law as the Drug Quality and Security Act (DQSA) (see "Drug-Device Combo Products Under State And Federal Pedigree Laws"[150]). In that essay I showed how these exemptions were very similar because both were based on the existing definition of a "combination product" from 21 CFR 3.2(e)[151]. My assessment of the effect of the wording in the old California pedigree law is still valid, in my opinion, but I now believe my analysis of the language in H.R. 3204 was *incorrect*. Here is why.

Of course, in the ensuing weeks the California law was preempted by the enactment of the DQSA, the official designation for what was formerly referred to as H.R. 3204 (see "Preemption: What Does It Mean?"[152]). What a difference a month can make. We are now looking at a slightly familiar but definitely different regulatory landscape.

COMBINATION PRODUCT EXEMPTION LANGUAGE. WHAT CHANGED?

The combination product exemption language *did not change* from pre-enactment version of H.R. 3204 to the final language of the DQSA, but *my interpretation of it has*. In my previous essay I focused on the language that closely matched that contained in the old California law, but in the DQSA that isn't the whole exemption clause. The full clause from Section 581(24)(B) of the DQSA is extracted here:

> *"(xii) a combination product that is not subject to approval under section 505 or licensure under section 351 of the Public Health Service Act, and that is —*
>
> > *(I) a product comprised of a device and 1 or more other regulated components (such as a drug/device, biologic/device, or drug/device/biologic) that are physically, chemically, or otherwise combined or mixed and produced as a single entity;*
> >
> > *(II) 2 or more separate products packaged together in a single package or as a unit and comprised of a drug and device or device and biological product; or*
> >
> > *(III) 2 or more finished medical devices plus one or more drug or biological products that are packaged together in what is referred to as a 'medical convenience kit' as described in clause (xiii);"*

The parts that closely match the old California law are the sub-clauses (I) through (II). But, obviously, to fully understand the meaning behind the exemption you need to analyze the full clause. Before you even get to the meaning of the sub-clauses, you first have to have a product that fits the first part of the full clause. That is, a product that meets the following:

> *"...a combination product that is not subject to approval under section 505 or licensure under section 351 of the Public Health Service Act..."*

Because of the "or" in this sentence fragment, the exemption applies to "a combination product that is *not* subject..." to one of two things:

- approval under section 505
- licensure under section 351 of the Public Health Service Act

A product that does not fit either of these two conditions might be exempt from the DQSA. To know for sure you have to continue analyzing the sub-clauses (I) through (III) — including the analysis that my earlier essay focused on exclusively.

BUT MOST OF YOU REALLY DON'T EVEN NEED TO LOOK AT THE SUB-CLAUSES

There are quite a few exemptions itemized in the Drug Supply Chain Security Act (DSCSA) that is Title II of the DQSA. Each exemption has a specific reason, I'm sure, but those reasons are not articulated in the law itself. All of them are carefully designed to exclude a small set of products from the rigorous implementation of the law. The vast majority of drugs and biologics will not fit into any of these exemption clauses. So, if you are trying to figure out if this combination product exemption definitely does NOT apply to a specific product, you may not even need to analyze those three sub-clauses, because most drugs and biologics will not even make it past these two first parts.

If a combination product is subject to *"approval under section 505"*[153], that means the FDA regulates it as a *drug*. That means the combination product's "primary mode of action[154]" or PMOA, is as a drug. If a combination product's PMOA is not a drug, then it is regulated by the FDA as either a *biologic* or a *device*, in which case it is *not* subject to *"approval under section 505"*.

If a combination product is subject to *"licensure under section 351 of the Public Health Service Act[155]"*, that means the FDA regulates it as a *biologic*. That means the combination product's "primary mode of action" or PMOA, is as a biologic. If a combination product's PMOA is *not* a biologic, then it is regulated by the FDA as either a drug or a device, in which case it is *not* subject to *"licensure under section 351 of the Public Health Service Act"*.

Putting these two together in the same form as the first part of the DQSA combination product clause, if a combination product is **not** subject to "approval under section 505" or "licensure under section 351 of the Public Health Service Act", that means the FDA does *not* regulate it as a drug or a biologic. By default, that means the combination product is regulated by the FDA as a device. Its "primary mode of action" or PMOA, is a device, even though it may also contain a drug and/or a biologic component.

By this logic, it appears that this exemption only applies to *combination products that are regulated by the FDA as devices*, or at least only those that are *not* regulated as drugs or biologics. That makes sense to me because it greatly reduces the number of products in the market that fall into this exemption category compared to the similar exemption in the old California law.

So, to be clear, my current interpretation of this whole exemption is that most combination products that have a PMOA of a "device" do not have to follow the DQSA, and thus, all combination products that have a PMOA of a drug or biologic are not exempt from the DQSA (by this particular exemption anyway).

WHY DIDN'T THEY JUST SAY THAT IN THE FIRST PLACE?

I think the reason they did not say it that way is to make it clear that, even though device PMOA combination products can contain one or more drugs and/or biologics, they are still exempt. If they didn't say it, people would wonder if those embedded drugs and/or biologics might need to comply with the DQSA. According to my interpretation of this exemption, they don't.

What's really interesting is how similar the exemptions seem between the old California pedigree law and the DQSA, but how different they turn out to be in implementation. The California law would have exempted pretty much all combination devices regardless of PMOA but it appears that the DQSA only exempts those with a PMOA of a device. In those products, the drug and/or biologic components play only a secondary role.

This is my interpretation. Make your own determination before you take action. If you aren't sure if your combination product falls into this exemption, I suggest you have a conversation with the FDA Office of Combination Products[156].

Dirk.

Aggregation –> Chargeback Accuracy –> ROI

By Dirk Rodgers
Original essay published on RxTrace.com on October 19, 2015.[157] Updated for this book on January 1, 2016.

In the fall of 2015 I attended my favorite annual conference on pharma serialization and tracing in the U.S.: The Healthcare

Distribution Management Association's (HDMA)[158] Traceability Seminar. They call it a "seminar" because the subjects of the sessions are generally the same every year, but it is better than any other third-party conference, primarily because the right people attend it: lots of people from drug manufacturers, wholesale distributors and some dispensers. With this ideal spectrum of attendees, it is very easy to get your questions answered, in the hallway between sessions if not in the sessions themselves.

Of course, every year the folks from the FDA who are directly responsible for writing regulations related to the Drug Supply Chain Security Act (DSCSA) provide an update and "answer" questions from the audience. I put the word "answer" in quotes because they really cannot provide the kind of answers that everyone would like to hear, but they do a respectable job regurgitating the language of the DSCSA instead. I understand the situation they are in and I am happy that they are willing to stand in front of such an audience when they know they cannot share the kind of details that everyone wants to know. They can only "speak" in official guidances, and they should have several new guidance documents going through the internal approval process right now. We should see them in the next few months, but they cannot give out information that will be contained in those documents until they are approved and available to everyone. Watch RxTrace for notice and analysis of those guidances once they are published.

I always look forward to the sessions when the various wholesale distributors present their current thinking about how the industry should meet different aspects of the law. I like to keep an open mind, but I also try to read between the lines by applying what I know about the internal workings of a large wholesale distributor.

This year the wholesaler session on data exchange caused me to *change my mind* about what manufacturers should do about wholesaler demands for aggregation data. Regular readers know that aggregation data is not a legal requirement until perhaps 2023, and may not even be required at that time (see "When Will The DSCSA Ever Require Investments In Aggregation?"). However, I have also been recommending that manufacturers would benefit from making investments that allow them to capture and retain aggregation data for themselves (see "The Aggregation Hoax and PIA"[159]). After I heard the wholesale distributor's current argument in favor of manufacturers providing them with aggregation data, starting by November of 2017, *I changed my mind and now agree with them*, but with one important caveat.

They "got" me with their discussion of the difficulty with handling the 2% of their shipments that are returned as "saleable" product. That is, drugs that are perfectly resellable and can be put back into stock and sold to someone else. According to the Center for Healthcare Supply Chain Research/2014-2015 HDMA Factbook[160], 94% of product returned to wholesale distributors was reported as saleable.

Wholesale distributors cannot afford to figure out which manufacturer made the product, and then request verification of that drug from that manufacturer the way I proposed in "Wholesaler Confusion Over DSCSA Aggregation Explained"[161]. This would take too much time considering the DSCSA gives the manufacturer 24 hours to respond to those requests. The DSCSA requires wholesale distributors to verify that the drug manufacturer assigned the serialized product identifier found on the returned package or homogeneous case, starting on November 27, 2019.

The alternate way is for all drug manufacturers to provide the wholesale distributor with aggregation data for all shipments. That way, when saleable returns are received by the wholesale distributor, they can simply do a look up to confirm that the manufacturer assigned that serialized product identifier without making a request outside their own network.

ROI FROM SERIALIZATION

Drug manufacturers are increasingly looking for some type of return on their investments (ROI) in serializing all drugs — something they must do in the U.S. by November 27, 2017 as the result of the DSCSA. In my view, gaining a positive ROI may not be possible, but offsetting some of the costs is certainly possible. The only problem is, extracting value from serialization beyond compliance will require the involvement of multiple departments within an organization in ways that may not be typical today. That is, the packaging, supply chain, contracts, marketing and regulatory compliance groups will need to work closely under a single plan, and corporate objectives must be adjusted, or these things are not likely to be successful. Most companies have silos that are pretty strong, and they will get in the way of the kind of changes that will be necessary to extract value beyond compliance.

But this insistence by the wholesale distributors that drug manufacturers provide them with aggregation data from the start represents one way that drug makers can capture some value beyond compliance. Some companies will be able to capture more than others, as I will explain below.

CHARGEBACKS

Chargebacks are one of the many complications of the U.S. pharma supply chain. Here is how they work. Hospitals and other drug buying organizations band together into Group Purchasing Organizations (GPOs). The primary purpose of a GPO is to negotiate a lower price for certain pharmaceuticals from the drug manufacturers on behalf of their members. Once established through a contract between a given GPO and a given manufacturer, the various wholesale distributors are notified of the terms, including the negotiated price for each NDC.

But because the wholesale distributors don't know which unit will be sold to which hospital or pharmacy, or under which contract, when they buy from the drug manufacturer, their purchases are priced at a single, "average", non-contract price. Then, whenever drugs that are the subject of one of these contracts are sold by the wholesale distributor to one of the GPO-member hospitals or pharmacies, the customer only pays the wholesale distributor the (lower) negotiated price. This leaves the wholesale distributor with a loss, which they then submit as a "chargeback claim" with the drug manufacturer for reimbursement, providing the details of the customer, the contract and the product. Once paid, everyone gets what they expected under the contract. It is intended to result in a zero-sum equation between the manufacturer and the wholesale distributor.

So you can see that wholesale distributors are not a party to the signing of these contracts, but they are an integral part of the implementation of them.

Not all drugs are candidates for the chargeback process. According to Dr. Adam Fein of The Drug Channels Institute[162], the type of drugs that are most commonly the subject of GPO contracts and therefore chargebacks are what he termed as "less differentiated brand products". Some drug companies have lots of products that are involved in GPO contracts/chargebacks and others have no products in that category. According to Dr. Fein's "2015-2016 Economic Report on Pharmaceutical Wholesalers and Specialty Distributors"[163], wholesaler chargebacks were 20.3% of net sales in 2013, growing from only 15.2% in 2009. Clearly, the importance of chargebacks is on the rise. This is partly due to the growth of hospital purchases that fall under the 340B drug program, as Dr. Fein notes in the same report.

REVERSE CHARGEBACKS

But you cannot complete a proper explanation of chargebacks without also explaining "reverse chargebacks". This is usually where people's eyes glaze over and they just start nodding, but this is where the magic happens and where the knot is that will tie all of these loose strings together. So pay attention.

A "reverse chargeback" is paid by the wholesale distributor to the drug manufacturer whenever a drug for which an earlier chargeback claim was filed and paid, is returned to the wholesale distributor. Get it? This is money that the drug manufacturer receives in order to keep the chargeback mechanism a zero-sum equation, as it is intended. It is up to the wholesale distributor to recognize whenever a drug is returned to them for which a reverse chargeback payment is consequently owed to the manufacturer.

The problem is, before serialization, it is pretty hard to figure that out in all instances. Contracts change. Drugs sit on shelves for a while before they are returned. Dispensers receive the same product lot from multiple sources and in multiple shipments. Drugs are exchanged between pharmacies and may be returned from a different address than they were originally shipped. Sometimes it is Monday. There are all kinds of things that can lead to inaccuracies in the payment of reverse chargebacks. But the unfortunate thing about these inaccuracies is that they always result in a loss for the manufacturer. Nick Basta wrote a highly readable article in Pharmaceutical Commerce magazine[164] back in 2010 about an estimate by IDC Health Insights that these losses amount to $11 billion per year[165].

But with the advent of the unit-level serialization in late 2017, it will be possible to eliminate these errors and shift that estimated $11 billion from the wholesale distributors back to its rightful owners, the drug manufacturers who participate in contracts with GPOs using the chargeback mechanism.

HERE IS ALL YOU NEED TO DO TO GET YOUR PIECE OF $11 BILLION

To get your part of that estimated $11 billion, all you need to do is negotiate with your wholesale distributors. Since they need your aggregation data to help make their processing of returns more efficient, you should give it to them. But in exchange, you must insist that they include serial numbers in their chargeback claims, and then provide you with the serial numbers of all of your drugs that they receive from their customers as returns. That way you can confirm that they are properly using that information to eliminate those errors in the chargeback and reverse chargeback process. This will not slow down their returns handling processes because the data transmission is not time-critical, as long as it gets back to you eventually. The cost to implement and operate such a solution for the wholesale distributor is a very tiny fraction of the costs to implement and operate the collection of aggregation data for drug manufacturers, especially when considering how many manufacturers there are. So your cost of collecting the aggregation data for the wholesale distributors will be repaid over time by the elimination of these errors. There is your ROI, and you don't need to wait until 2023 to start getting it!

Dirk.

Essays Answering DSCSA Questions

This section contains essays that attempt to answer important questions about applying the DSCSA. These questions usually go well beyond the contents of the DSCSA and may only truly be answered by the industry as a whole.

Is Your Drug Exempt From The Federal Drug Supply Chain Security Act?

By Dirk Rodgers
Original essay published on RxTrace.com on April 7, 2014.[166] Updated for this book on January 1, 2016.

Ever since the Drug Quality and Security Act (DQSA) was signed into law on November 27, 2013, more and more people are asking the question, "Does my drug have to follow the DQSA?". Back in 2014 I was on a monthly industry call put on by one of the Big 3 wholesale distributors to discuss the Drug Supply Chain Security Act (DSCSA), which is Title II of the DQSA.

I was surprised how many people asked the wholesaler if their specific product was covered or exempt. Of course, asking a wholesale distributor if your own product must follow a particular Federal law is not likely to get a usable response and that was true in this case, but it did not stop the next person from asking the same kind of question.

In fact, no one can answer that question for you. Even the FDA can't answer that question for you. I can't answer that question for you. Only YOU can answer that question based on your knowledge of your product's characteristics and a careful reading of certain provisions of the DSCSA. I can help you with that part.

APPLICATION OF THE DSCSA

In general, many of the provisions of the DSCSA that are related to the movement of product in the supply chain apply only to prescription drugs *"...in a finished dosage form for administration to a patient without substantial further manufacturing (such as capsules, tablets, and lyophilized products before reconstitution)"*. So if the FDA does not consider your drug to be a prescription drug ("Rx Only"), then it does not need to comply with the DSCSA.

Formally, a "prescription drug" is defined by the law to as a drug for human use that is subject to the Food, Drug and Cosmetics Act, Section 503(b)(1). This apparently exempts drugs that are strictly for use only in animals.

Further, if your drug must be sold "behind the pharmacy counter" in some States, that does not make it a prescription drug. Those are State laws and the FDA does not pay attention to State laws when regulating drugs nationally. Even if some States require your drug to be dispensed by a pharmacist only to those who have a physician-issued prescription, if the FDA has not classified it as a prescription drug, then you are off the hook when it comes to following the DSCSA. In these cases, the FDA considers your drug to be Over-The-Counter (OTC), and therefore exempt.

If your product is a device—even if the FDA requires your device to be dispensed only with a physician-issued prescription ("Rx Only")—then it is not a prescription drug and therefore it is not covered by the DSCSA.

But be careful here. Some devices are classified by the FDA as drug-device or biologic-device Combination Products (CPs). In that case, if the FDA has determined that the Primary Mode of Action (PMOA) of your product is as a drug or a biologic, then your CP is not exempt from the DSCSA (unless the FDA has already informed you that your CP must be labeled with a Unique Device Identifier,

UDI) (see "Correction: Your Drug or Biologic Combination Product Is Probably NOT Exempt From The DQSA"). If your device has a drug or biologic built into it or in combination with it, I suggest that you check with the FDA office of Combination Products[167] to make sure you understand how they would classify it before deciding to ignore the DSCSA.

OTHER EXEMPTIONS

The elimination of drugs that are only for use in animals, OTC products, and devices narrows the application of the DSCSA nicely. But we can go further. Here is a list of products that are explicitly exempt from the DSCSA. That is, they are not considered DSCSA "products" and are therefore not required to follow the DSCSA regulations:

- Blood or blood components intended for transfusion;
- Radioactive drugs or radioactive biological products that are already regulated by the Nuclear Regulatory Commission (NRC) or by a State under an agreement with the NRC;
- Imaging drugs;
- Medical gases;
- Appropriately marked homeopathic drugs;
- Compounded drugs;
- (Compounded drugs are now regulated by the Compounding Quality Act, which is Title I of the DQSA);
- Intravenous products that are intended for the replenishment of fluids and electrolytes or calories;
- Intravenous products used to maintain the equilibrium of water and minerals in the body, such as dialysis solutions;
- Products intended for irrigation, or sterile water, whether intended for such purposes or for injection.

SPECIAL CASES

On the distributor call I heard one question that the DSCSA text does not cover directly. We can use it as an example to help others who might have another unique/niche product that is regulated by the FDA but may or may not be regulated by the DSCSA. The caller's product was apparently recently licensed by the FDA as a "prescription food". I don't know what that is — perhaps a "nutraceutical" — but as long as it is recognized by the FDA as a product that requires humans to obtain a prescription before they may receive it, and as long as it is not on the list above, you can be reasonably sure it must follow the DSCSA.

In this case, you should already have a National Drug Code (NDC) assigned to your product (see "Anatomy Of The National Drug Code"[168]), which is necessary to properly identify your product under the DSCSA. If you don't have an NDC for your product, then there is a disconnect somewhere. Either you are mistaken that your product is licensed by the FDA as a drug or biologic, or you have not yet registered your product with the FDA. In either case, maybe your product is not a drug or biologic. If not, then you don't have to follow the DSCSA. Check with the FDA.

EXEMPT TRANSACTIONS

Even if your product is not exempt, you may still be exempt from following many of the provisions of the DSCSA under certain types of transactions. In most cases, these are products that would need to follow the DSCSA (not exempt) under other types of transactions, but in these transactions, they are exempt. Here is a short list of transactions that manufacturers might be involved in and that are not considered "DSCSA transactions" and are therefore exempt from following the DSCSA, but only while in these specific transactions:

- Intracompany distribution of any product between members of an affiliate or within a manufacturer;
- The distribution of product samples by a manufacturer or a licensed wholesale distributor;
- The distribution of "medical convenience kits", a collection of finished medical devices, which may include a drug product or

biological product, assembled in kit form strictly for the convenience of the purchaser or user, if:

- o the kit is assembled in an establishment that is registered by the FDA as *a device manufacturer*;
- o the kit does not contain any controlled substance; and
- o the kit manufacturer purchased the drug or biologic product contained in the kit directly from the pharmaceutical manufacturer or from a wholesale distributor that purchased it directly from the pharmaceutical manufacturer, and the primary container label of the drug or biologic product contained in the kit is not altered;
- o and the drug or biologic product contained in the kit is:
  - An intravenous solution intended for the replenishment of fluids and electrolytes;
  - A product intended to maintain the equilibrium of water and minerals in the body;
  - A product intended for irrigation or reconstitution;
  - An anesthetic;
  - An anticoagulant;
  - A vasopressor; or
  - A sympathomimetic;

As soon as you determine that your product is exempt from the DSCSA make sure you notify all trading partners who will receive that product to provide them with your rationale. Wholesale distributors, 3PLs, repackagers and dispensers will all need to decide if they agree with you, or they may expect you to provide them with the new transaction documentation when they receive your product.

If they do not agree with your determination, they may not be willing to accept it because they would feel obligated to follow the DSCSA, even if you do not, and you would not be able to give them the documentation they need to comply. That would be a disaster for you. Interpretations will vary, especially early on, and the FDA may not be willing to fill the role as an arbiter in these cases.

Only you can make the final determination if your product is exempt from the DSCSA.

Dirk.

Should You Off-Load Your DSCSA Obligations To Your Contract Partners?

By Dirk Rodgers
Original essay published on RxTrace.com on October 6, 2014.[169] Updated for this book on January 1, 2016.

Manufacturers who make use of third-party contract manufacturers, contract packagers and/or third-party logistics providers (3PLs) may wish to off-load their 2015 and 2017 obligations under the U.S. Drug Supply Chain Security Act (DSCSA) to those contract organizations. These obligations include providing Transaction Information (TI), Transaction History (TH) and Transaction Statements (TS), and collecting and holding that data in case of future investigations; and applying the necessary 2D barcode with serial numbers starting in November of 2017.

This may seem perfectly logical. After all, absorbing responsibilities is one of the big benefits that contract organizations offer their customers. But by passing on certain obligations under the law, DSCSA manufacturers may end up with higher risks in the future.

First of all, DSCSA manufacturers cannot really pass any of their obligations on to a third-party. That is, the DSCSA manufacturer has certain specific obligations that they will always be held accountable for by State and Federal regulators. The only thing a DSCSA manufacturer can do is to include specific language in their contract with the third-party to obtain additional help toward meeting those obligations. If a regulator eventually finds some deficiency in meeting one or more of those obligations, it will be the DSCSA manufacturer who will face the consequences, not the contract organization. (Of course, if there is criminal wrong-doing on the part of the contract organization, they too are certain to face consequences.)

The regulator is not going to accept a claim that it was the contract organization's fault that the law was not met. So the best you can do is to make the vendor share in those consequences through the contract you sign with them. The regulator is not likely to "recognize" your contract, but at least that contract should ensure that the contract organization will help you correct the situation and perhaps share some percentage of any fines that may be imposed by the regulator on you.

Contract language such as this is a two-way street. The DSCSA manufacturer might be able to sleep better at night knowing that their contract makes it more likely that their contract organization will correctly perform the necessary duties on their behalf, but now the price might go up. That is because the contract organization has new obligations and unknowns in their contract. How they price those obligations and unknowns will be up to each company, but odds are, the prices will go up. DSCSA compliance should be viewed as an expansion of the service that contract organizations provide and that addition should be priced accordingly.

HOW MUCH TO OFF-LOAD?

But how much of your DSCSA burden should be off-loaded to a contract packager or 3PL? During a session at the 2014 LogiPharma conference (see "Pharma Serialization: Going Totally Global Soon"[170]) , a person from a virtual manufacturer asked the members of a panel (which was composed mainly of large branded drug manufacturers) if there was anything in the DSCSA that could not be off-loaded to contract partners. The panel members couldn't think of anything, which seemed to confirm what the questioner was thinking.

Well here is what you risk if you let your contract partner perform the following duties on your behalf:

Serial Number Management

One of the great new services a contract packager can offer is to print the required 2D barcodes on each package on behalf of the DSCSA manufacturer. That barcode will need to appear on all drug packages — encoding the NDC, unique serial number, lot number and expiration date — by November 27, 2017. But who decides which unique serial number is put on which package? And how are those specific numbers chosen? This is serial number management.

If the DSCSA manufacturer lets the contract packager perform that function, their risk goes way up. Not only will their compliance be subject to the contract packager's ability to keep track of which numbers have been used and which are available, but this will also open the door to vendor lock-in. That is, it will be harder for the DSCSA manufacturer to switch to a different contract packager in the future if decisions about the management of their serial numbers on their products are left entirely up to the contract packager. Once that happens, you may be likely to see price increases just because the contract packager knows it will be hard for you to switch to a competitor. This is especially true if you let the contract packager hold the serial number and lot history on your behalf.

The way to avoid this risk is to at least get a batch-level upload of the serial numbers that have been used, and better yet, you yourself should also maintain and assign the range of potential serial numbers to be applied and provide at least a number range to the contract packager as part of the lot planning process. That way you control how your serial numbers are assigned and that will allow you to switch to a different contract vendor at any time. It will also make it easy to use two or more different contract vendors for the same product at the same time if you have capacity issues with your first vendor.

This is not as hard as it sounds. Talk to the various solution vendors to learn the costs and additional benefits. Your up-front investment should result in a lower ongoing cost from your contract packager. Watch out for contract organizations who claim there is no cost difference for serial number management. They are either just trying to lock you in, or they don't know exactly what they are doing yet so they are pricing everything high. Even at the same price, your risks will be significantly lower if you do your own number management.

Transaction Data Retention
Almost the same thing happens when you let your 3PL hold all of your shipping/transaction data on your behalf. Here I'm referring to the DSCSA TI, TH and TS data that must be held and retrievable within 48 hours starting in January 2015 (enforcement deferred until May 1, 2015) (July for DSCSA dispensers, but that was also deferred until at least March 1, 2016) (see "DSCSA: A Closer Look At The Six-Year Record-Keeping Requirement" and "Who Is A DSCSA Dispenser?"). Can your 3PL meet the six year retention requirement? What happens if/when you switch to a different 3PL at some point? Does your original contract obligate the original 3PL to continue holding your older transaction data for the full six year period and respond to verification requests related to that older data even after you have stopped using them? Or, are they going to help you move that data to your servers or your new 3PL at the end of their contract? Or, will your contract allow them to just delete all of your transaction data as soon as your contract expires? Sounds like vendor lock-in to me.

The way to avoid this is to hold that data yourself, or with a DSCSA solution provider. If you go with a DSCSA solution provider, make sure they have a clean way to export that data to you or to your next DSCSA solution provider in the event you want to switch that vendor as well. There is potential for vendor lock-in there too.

In my view, it is dangerous in the long-run for a company to off-load all of the work imposed by the DSCSA to third-parties. Companies should be actively involved in at least their own serial number management and transaction data retention and retrieval. Solution providers offer a number of ways these can be accomplished.

Dirk.

When Will The DSCSA Ever Require Investments In Aggregation?

By Dirk Rodgers
Original essay published on RxTrace.com on February 23, 2015.[171] Updated for this book on January 1, 2016.

I have been outspoken on the question of whether or not the Drug Supply Chain Security Act (DSCSA) requires companies in the supply chain to provide their customers with serial number-based aggregation data prior to 2023. In my view, it does not, but others disagree, saying that there are requirements in the law that lead to the need for aggregation data during that time. I do not agree with that either. If you would like to review those arguments and find out exactly what "aggregation data" is, here is a list of RxTrace essays you should read:

Date Published	Title
March 26th, 2012	Pharma Aggregation: How Companies Are Achieving Perfection Today[172]

November 22nd, 2013	DQSA: Will U.S. Pharma Distributors Mandate Aggregation Data In Phase 1?[173]
February 10th, 2014	Does The DQSA Require Manufacturers To Provide Aggregation Data? Survey Says...[174]
June 9th, 2014	The Aggregation Hoax and PIA[175]

BUT WHAT ABOUT AFTER 2023?

The DSCSA requires the FDA to conduct at least 5 topical public meetings between now and about 2021 to collect stakeholder input on topics that will help the FDA define how the so-called "Enhanced Drug Distribution Security" (EDDS) phase will work. That phase is to begin in November of 2023, which is quite a few years from now, but the law constrains details about how that phase is to work. One of the topics Congress instructed the FDA to collect stakeholder input on in preparation for the EDDS is the systems and processes needed to utilize the serialized product identifiers to enhance tracing at the package level, including allowing for aggregation and inference. I don't think they are likely to hold that public meeting for quite a few years (see "Interoperability And The DSCSA"[176]).

One of the few things the law says must occur as part of the EDDS is that all members of the pharma supply chain must include the unit-level serial numbers in the Transaction Information (TI) that they provide to their customers in each shipment. The EDDS will be the beginning of the fully serialized pharma supply chain in the U.S.. The DSCSA mandates very little use of serial numbers prior to that date.

But after that date, for anyone selling drugs within the supply chain, they will need to know exactly which unit-level serial numbers are contained in their shipments so they can include those serial numbers in their TIs. To do that, they will need their own serial number-based packaging hierarchy data — that is, they will need their own aggregation data—whether or not they provide that data to their customers. Anyone using a third-party logistics provider (3PL) will also need to provide that aggregation data to them as well so they can properly document the manufacturer's shipments. Odds are, customers will justifiably demand to receive that same data after 2023 to assist them with their receiving verification process, even if the FDA does not require the seller to provide it.

Given all of that, I think it is very clear that the operation of the EDDS that Congress intended will necessitate—if not mandate—the capturing and sharing of aggregation data by manufacturers, repackagers and wholesale distributors. At that time, everyone will view aggregation data as essential to the smooth operation of a secure supply chain. Fortunately, the technology to ensure the accurate capture of aggregation data has been available for several years now (see "Pharma Aggregation: How Companies Are Achieving Perfection Today" [177]).

Back when I first wrote this essay an industry friend of mine told me about a new theory going around about aggregation—this one, for the EDDS after 2023. As the theory goes, the FDA would become convinced through the public meetings that manufacturers and repackagers would not be capable of capturing "certifiably accurate" aggregation data and so errors would be inevitable, which would lead to ineffective operation of the EDDS. As a result, the theory goes, the FDA would invoke a provision in the DSCSA that allows them to establish "alternative methods" for any EDDS requirement (see DSCSA Section 582[g][2][B]), and the FDA would choose to replace the need for seller aggregation data capture by requiring the recipient to capture all of the serial numbers they receive. That's the theory anyway.

WHY THIS IS NONSENSE

If that happens, it would effectively eliminate the need for manufacturers and repackagers to capture and pass aggregation data. Problem solved, right? Not really, because it would simply push that burden onto the buyer who would now need to open all shipping containers and cases upon receipt and scan all of the unit-level barcodes. Because 87% of the drugs passing through the U.S. supply chain go through only three wholesale distributors, that means these three companies would bear the burden that was removed from many hundreds of manufacturers and repackagers. Rather than distributing the problem it would intensely concentrate it. That's not a solution.

But there are other problems with this theory. What happens when there is a cargo theft during transit between the manufacturer and the wholesale distributor? Since the manufacturer would have no idea which unit-level serial numbers were in the truck, they would not be able to update their verification database with the units that were stolen. That means stolen product would continue to be verified by the manufacturer as legitimate product. Whoops. Bad idea.

But the biggest reason this theory is nonsense, in my opinion, is that it is based on a misreading of the DSCSA itself. That section on "alternative methods" that is the basis for the theory does not apply to all participants in the supply chain. It only provides the FDA with the latitude to change provisions that impact small dispensers — defined as dispensers with 25 or fewer full-time employees — and (possibly) other dispensers where the provision results in undue economic hardship. So maybe small dispensers will not need to receive and make use of aggregation data, but that's about the only effect that provision could potentially have on aggregation. In my opinion, it just does not apply to manufacturers, repackagers or wholesale distributors.

THE ARGUMENT "IT CANNOT BE DONE" ISN'T GOING TO FLY

The 2015 RxTrace U.S. Traceability Survey Analysis, sponsored by Frequentz found that a large percentage of respondents — including a large number who work for drug manufacturers — are planning to capture aggregation data even prior to 2023. So whether or not the law requires those companies to capture and share aggregation data after 2023, they are already planning to capture it prior to that date. And they will be doing it during the time that the FDA will likely hold that public meeting to discuss aggregation and inference. This seems to make what companies will do after 2023 a moot point, at least for the manufacturers represented in this survey. But the fact that so many companies will be capturing and using aggregation data prior to 2023 is going to make it very hard for companies trying to fight aggregation as a requirement to claim that it cannot be done.

Dirk.

Is An ASN Really The Best Way to Pass Lot-Based DSCSA Transaction Data?

By Dirk Rodgers
Original essay published on RxTrace.com on February 16, 2015.[178] Updated for this book on January 1, 2016.

We are now well past the date that the DSCSA originally mandated drug manufacturers, repackagers and wholesale distributors to pass Transaction Information (TI), Transaction History (TH), and Transaction Statements (TS) to their customers in the U.S. and save a copy for six years (see "DSCSA: A Closer Look At The Six-Year Record-Keeping Requirement"). Of course, in late 2014 the FDA pushed out that part of the requirement until May 1, 2015 to ensure that the requirement did not induce or exacerbate drug shortages.

Despite that delay, many companies began passing the required data to their trading partners through Electronic Data Interchange (EDI) Advance Shipment Notices (ASNs) well before the revised date (see "HDMA Has Updated Their EDI ASN Guidance For DSCSA, Again"[179]). In fact, the vast majority of companies have

decided to use ASNs to carry the mandated information rather than GS1's Electronic Product Code Information Services[180] (EPCIS) (see "Will GS1's EPCIS Be Used Widely For DSCSA Data Exchange?"[181])
.

But are EDI ASNs the right approach to passing DSCSA transaction data? In that last essay listed above I theorized that once companies begin using ASNs to pass lot-based transaction data, they are not likely to switch from ASNs to EPCIS data exchange until sometime in 2021 or even 2022. Since posting that essay I have heard that some companies are finding it more difficult to use ASNs to carry this compliance data than they had originally thought, which leads me to wonder if the switch to EPCIS might happen sooner rather than later.

Many companies are relying on the new DSCSA-specific solutions that they purchased for the purpose of maintaining the required DSCSA transaction data to generate the ASNs that now carry that data. I have heard grumbling about DSCSA solution vendors who "don't really understand EDI", which has apparently led to difficulty solving DSCSA and non-DSCSA related problems in the ASNs that those solutions generate. Of course, not all of the vendors fall into this category, but maybe it's really just an indication that perhaps EDI is not the best way to pass that kind of information. None of these people want to go on the record with their complaints and even if they would, my intent is not to point any fingers. My point is to wonder if this initial rocky experience with ASNs for some will lead to a quicker move to the use of EPCIS than I originally predicted.

Many pharma manufacturers and wholesale distributors have historically relied on ASNs for more traditional financial purposes, and prior to the use of ASNs for carrying the DSCSA TI, TH and TS, they had a single enterprise EDI solution that generated, received and processed all EDI message types—including ASNs. But now, in some cases, those enterprise EDI solutions are being used to generate all of the EDI message types except the ASNs, which might result in some complex data issues.

I don't have enough information to be able to know for sure. Perhaps the problems will get ironed out and settle down soon into a smooth operation across the supply chain. But maybe not.

Drop me an email with your experience with your DSCSA transaction data exchange, whether ASNs, EPCIS, web portals or paper, and good or bad. If I get enough of them, I will strip all identifying information from them (including solution provider names) and post them in a future essay. If you have thoughts about the transition from EDI to EPCIS, send them to me.

Dirk.

Appendix: Full Text of The Drug Supply Chain Security Act

This appendix contains the entire original text of the Drug Supply Chain Security Act, which is Title II of the Drug Quality and Security Act of 2013, with the simple addition of selected section headings to aid in the construction of the Table of Contents.

SEC. 201. SHORT TITLE.

This title may be cited as the "Drug Supply Chain Security Act".

SEC. 202. PHARMACEUTICAL DISTRIBUTION SUPPLY CHAIN.

Chapter V (21 U.S.C. 351 et seq.) is amended by adding at the end the following:

"Subchapter H — Pharmaceutical Distribution Supply Chain

SEC. 581. DEFINITIONS

"SEC. 581. DEFINITIONS.

"In this subchapter:

581(1)AFFILIATE

"(1) AFFILIATE.—

The term 'affiliate' means a business entity that has a relationship with a second business entity if, directly or indirectly—

"(A) one business entity controls, or has the power to control, the other business entity; or

"(B) a third party controls, or has the power to control, both of the business entities.

581(2) AUTHORIZED

"(2) AUTHORIZED.—

The term 'authorized' means—

"(A) in the case of a manufacturer or repackager, having a valid registration in accordance with section 510;

"(B) in the case of a wholesale distributor, having a valid license under State law or section 583, in accordance with section 582(a)(6), and complying with the licensure reporting requirements under section 503(e), as amended by the Drug Supply Chain Security Act;

"(C) in the case of a third-party logistics provider, having a valid license under State law or section 584(a)(1), in accordance with section 582(a)(7), and complying with the licensure reporting requirements under section 584(b); and

"(D) in the case of a dispenser, having a valid license under State law.

581(3) DISPENSER

"(3) DISPENSER.—

The term 'dispenser'—

"(A) means a retail pharmacy, hospital pharmacy, a group of chain pharmacies under common ownership and control that do not act as a wholesale distributor, or any other person authorized by law to dispense or administer prescription drugs, and the affiliated warehouses or distribution centers of such entities under common ownership and control that do not act as a wholesale distributor; and

"(B) does not include a person who dispenses only products to be used in animals in accordance with section 512(a)(5).

581(4) DISPOSITION

"(4) DISPOSITION.—

The term 'disposition', with respect to a product within the possession or control of an entity, means the removal of such product from the pharmaceutical distribution supply chain, which may include disposal or return of the product for disposal or other appropriate handling and other actions, such as retaining a sample of the product for further additional physical examination or laboratory analysis of the product by a manufacturer or regulatory or law enforcement agency.

581(5) DISTRIBUTE OR DISTRIBUTION

"(5) DISTRIBUTE OR DISTRIBUTION.—

The term 'distribute' or 'distribution' means the sale, purchase, trade, delivery, handling, storage, or receipt of a product, and does not include the dispensing of a product pursuant to a prescription executed in accordance with section 503(b)(1) or the dispensing of a product approved under section 512(b).

581(6) EXCLUSIVE DISTRIBUTOR

"(6) EXCLUSIVE DISTRIBUTOR.—

The term 'exclusive distributor' means the wholesale distributor that directly purchased the product from the manufacturer and is the sole distributor of that manufacturer's product to a subsequent repackager, wholesale distributor, or dispenser.

581(7) HOMOGENEOUS CASE

"(7) HOMOGENEOUS CASE.—

The term 'homogeneous case' means a sealed case containing only product that has a single National Drug Code number belonging to a single lot.

581(8) ILLEGITIMATE PRODUCT

"(8) ILLEGITIMATE PRODUCT.—

The term 'illegitimate product' means a product for which credible evidence shows that the product—

"(A) is counterfeit, diverted, or stolen;

"(B) is intentionally adulterated such that the product would result in serious adverse health consequences or death to humans;

"(C) is the subject of a fraudulent transaction; or

"(D) appears otherwise unfit for distribution such that the product would be reasonably likely to result in serious adverse health consequences or death to humans.

581(9) LICENSED

"(9) LICENSED.—

The term 'licensed' means—

"(A) in the case of a wholesale distributor, having a valid license in accordance with section 503(e) or section 582(a)(6), as applicable;

"(B) in the case of a third-party logistics provider, having a valid license in accordance with section 584(a) or section 582(a)(7), as applicable; and

"(C) in the case of a dispenser, having a valid license under State law.

581(10) MANUFACTURER

"(10) MANUFACTURER.—

The term 'manufacturer' means, with respect to a product—

"(A) a person that holds an application approved under section 505 or a license issued under section 351 of the Public Health Service Act for such product, or if such product is not the subject of an approved application or license, the person who manufactured the product;

"(B) a co-licensed partner of the person described in subparagraph (A) that obtains the product directly from a person described in this subparagraph or subparagraph (A) or (C); or

"(C) an affiliate of a person described in subparagraph (A) or (B) that receives the product directly from a person described in this subparagraph or subparagraph (A) or (B).

581(11) PACKAGE

"(11) PACKAGE.—

"(A) IN GENERAL.—The term 'package' means the smallest individual saleable unit of product for distribution by a manufacturer or repackager that is intended by the manufacturer for ultimate sale to the dispenser of such product.

"(B) INDIVIDUAL SALEABLE UNIT.—For purposes of this paragraph, an 'individual saleable unit' is the smallest container of product introduced into commerce by the manufacturer or repackager that is intended by the manufacturer or repackager for individual sale to a dispenser.

581(12) PRESCRIPTION DRUG

"(12) PRESCRIPTION DRUG.—

The term 'prescription drug' means a drug for human use subject to section 503(b)(1).

581(13) PRODUCT

"(13) PRODUCT.—

The term 'product' means a prescription drug in a finished dosage form for administration to a patient without substantial further manufacturing (such as capsules, tablets, and lyophilized products before reconstitution), but for purposes of section 582, does not include blood or blood components intended for transfusion, radioactive drugs or radioactive biological products (as defined in section 600.3(ee) of title 21, Code of Federal Regulations) that are regulated by the Nuclear Regulatory Commission or by a State pursuant to an agreement with such Commission under section 274 of the Atomic Energy Act of 1954 (42 U.S.C. 2021), imaging drugs, an intravenous product described in clause (xiv), (xv), or (xvi) of paragraph (24)(B), any medical gas (as defined in section 575), homeopathic drugs marketed in accordance with applicable guidance under this Act, or a drug compounded in compliance with section 503A or 503B.

581(14) PRODUCT IDENTIFIER

"(14) PRODUCT IDENTIFIER.—

The term 'product identifier' means a standardized graphic that includes, in both human-readable form and on a machine-readable data carrier that conforms to the standards developed by a widely recognized international standards development organization, the standardized numerical identifier, lot number, and expiration date of the product.

581(15) QUARANTINE

"(15) QUARANTINE.—

The term 'quarantine' means the storage or identification of a product, to prevent distribution or transfer of the product, in a physically separate area clearly identified for such use or through other procedures.

581(16) REPACKAGER

"(16) REPACKAGER.—

The term 'repackager' means a person who owns or operates an establishment that repacks and relabels a product or package for—

"(A) further sale; or

"(B) distribution without a further transaction.

581(17) RETURN

"(17) RETURN.—

The term 'return' means providing product to the authorized immediate trading partner from which such product was purchased or received, or to a returns processor or reverse logistics provider for handling of such product.

581(18) RETURNS PROCESSOR OR REVERSE LOGISTICS PROVIDER

"(18) RETURNS PROCESSOR OR REVERSE LOGISTICS PROVIDER.—

The term 'returns processor' or 'reverse logistics provider' means a person who owns or operates an establishment that dispositions or otherwise processes saleable or nonsaleable product received from an authorized trading partner such that the product may be processed for credit to the purchaser, manufacturer, or seller or disposed of for no further distribution.

581(19) SPECIFIC PATIENT NEED

"(19) SPECIFIC PATIENT NEED.—

The term 'specific patient need' refers to the transfer of a product from one pharmacy to another to fill a prescription for an identified patient. Such term does not include the transfer of a product from one pharmacy to another for the purpose of increasing or replenishing stock in anticipation of a potential need.

581(20) STANDARDIZED NUMERICAL IDENTIFIER

"(20) STANDARDIZED NUMERICAL IDENTIFIER.—

The term 'standardized numerical identifier' means a set of numbers or characters used to uniquely identify each package or homogenous case that is composed of the National Drug

Code that corresponds to the specific product (including the particular package configuration) combined with a unique alphanumeric serial number of up to 20 characters.

581(21) SUSPECT PRODUCT

"(21) SUSPECT PRODUCT.—

The term 'suspect product' means a product for which there is reason to believe that such product—

"(A) is potentially counterfeit, diverted, or stolen;

"(B) is potentially intentionally adulterated such that the product would result in serious adverse health consequences or death to humans;

"(C) is potentially the subject of a fraudulent transaction; or

"(D) appears otherwise unfit for distribution such that the product would result in serious adverse health consequences or death to humans.

581(22) THIRD-PARTY LOGISTICS PROVIDER

"(22) THIRD-PARTY LOGISTICS PROVIDER.—

The term 'third-party logistics provider' means an entity that provides or coordinates warehousing, or other logistics services of a product in interstate commerce on behalf of a manufacturer, wholesale distributor, or dispenser of a product, but does not take ownership of the product, nor have responsibility to direct the sale or disposition of the product.

581(23) TRADING PARTNER

"(23) TRADING PARTNER.—

The term 'trading partner' means—

"(A) a manufacturer, repackager, wholesale distributor, or dispenser from whom a manufacturer, repackager, wholesale distributor, or dispenser accepts direct ownership of a product or to whom a manufacturer, repackager, wholesale distributor, or dispenser transfers direct ownership of a product; or

"(B) a third-party logistics provider from whom a manufacturer, repackager, wholesale distributor, or dispenser accepts direct possession of a product or to whom a manufacturer, repackager, wholesale distributor, or dispenser transfers direct possession of a product.

581(24) TRANSACTION

"(24) TRANSACTION.—

"(A) IN GENERAL.—

The term 'transaction' means the transfer of product between persons in which a change of ownership occurs.

"(B) EXEMPTIONS.—

The term 'transaction' does not include—

"(i) intracompany distribution of any product between members of an affiliate or within a manufacturer;

"(ii) the distribution of a product among hospitals or other health care entities that are under common control;

"(iii) the distribution of a product for emergency medical reasons including a public health emergency declaration pursuant to section 319 of the Public Health Service Act, except that a drug shortage not caused by a public health emergency shall not constitute an emergency medical reason;

"(iv) the dispensing of a product pursuant to a prescription executed in accordance with section 503(b)(1);

"(v) the distribution of product samples by a manufacturer or a licensed wholesale distributor in accordance with section 503(d);

"(vi) the distribution of blood or blood components intended for transfusion;

"(vii) the distribution of minimal quantities of product by a licensed retail pharmacy to a licensed practitioner for office use;

"(viii) the sale, purchase, or trade of a drug or an offer to sell, purchase, or trade a drug by a charitable organization described in section 501(c)(3) of the Internal Revenue Code of 1986 to a nonprofit affiliate of the organization to the extent otherwise permitted by law;

"(ix) the distribution of a product pursuant to the sale or merger of a pharmacy or pharmacies or a wholesale distributor or wholesale distributors, except that any records required to be maintained for the product shall be transferred to the new owner of the pharmacy or pharmacies or wholesale distributor or wholesale distributors;

"(x) the dispensing of a product approved under section 512(c);

"(xi) products transferred to or from any facility that is licensed by the Nuclear Regulatory Commission or by a State pursuant to an agreement with such Commission under section 274 of the Atomic Energy Act of 1954 (42 U.S.C. 2021);

"(xii) a combination product that is not subject to approval under section 505 or licensure under section 351 of the Public Health Service Act, and that is—

"(I) a product comprised of a device and 1 or more other regulated components (such as a drug/device, biologic/device, or drug/device/biologic) that are physically, chemically, or otherwise combined or mixed and produced as a single entity;

"(II) 2 or more separate products packaged together in a single package or as a unit and comprised of a drug and device or device and biological product; or

"(III) 2 or more finished medical devices plus one or more drug or biological products that are packaged together in what is referred to as a 'medical convenience kit' as described in clause (xiii);

"(xiii) the distribution of a collection of finished medical devices, which may include a product or biological product, assembled in kit form strictly for the convenience of the purchaser or user (referred to in this clause as a 'medical convenience kit') if—

"(I) the medical convenience kit is assembled in an establishment that is registered with the Food and Drug Administration as a device manufacturer in accordance with section 510(b)(2);

"(II) the medical convenience kit does not contain a controlled substance that appears in a schedule contained in the Comprehensive Drug Abuse Prevention and Control Act of 1970;

"(III) in the case of a medical convenience kit that includes a product, the person that manufacturers the kit—

"(aa) purchased such product directly from the pharmaceutical manufacturer or from a wholesale distributor that purchased the product directly from the pharmaceutical manufacturer; and

"(bb) does not alter the primary container or label of the product as purchased from the manufacturer or wholesale distributor; and

"(IV) in the case of a medical convenience kit that includes a product, the product is—

"(aa) an intravenous solution intended for the replenishment of fluids and electrolytes;

"(bb) a product intended to maintain the equilibrium of water and minerals in the body;

"(cc) a product intended for irrigation or reconstitution;

"(dd) an anesthetic;

"(ee) an anticoagulant;

"(ff) a vasopressor; or

"(gg) a sympathomimetic;

"(xiv) the distribution of an intravenous product that, by its formulation, is intended for the replenishment of fluids and electrolytes (such as sodium, chloride, and potassium) or calories (such as dextrose and amino acids);

"(xv) the distribution of an intravenous product used to maintain the equilibrium of water and minerals in the body, such as dialysis solutions;

"(xvi) the distribution of a product that is intended for irrigation, or sterile water, whether intended for such purposes or for injection;

"(xvii) the distribution of a medical gas (as defined in section 575); or

"(xviii) the distribution or sale of any licensed product under section 351 of the Public Health Service Act that meets the definition of a device under section 201(h).

581(25) TRANSACTION HISTORY

"(25) TRANSACTION HISTORY.—

The term 'transaction history' means a statement in paper or electronic form, including the transaction information for each prior transaction going back to the manufacturer of the product.

581(26) TRANSACTION INFORMATION

"(26) TRANSACTION INFORMATION.—

The term 'transaction information' means—

"(A) the proprietary or established name or names of the product;

"(B) the strength and dosage form of the product;

"(C) the National Drug Code number of the product;

"(D) the container size;

"(E) the number of containers;

"(F) the lot number of the product;

"(G) the date of the transaction;

"(H) the date of the shipment, if more than 24 hours after the date of the transaction;

"(I) the business name and address of the person from whom ownership is being transferred; and

"(J) the business name and address of the person to whom ownership is being transferred.

581(27) TRANSACTION STATEMENT

"(27) TRANSACTION STATEMENT.—

The 'transaction statement' is a statement, in paper or electronic form, that the entity transferring ownership in a transaction—

"(A) is authorized as required under the Drug Supply Chain Security Act;

"(B) received the product from a person that is authorized as required under the Drug Supply Chain Security Act;

"(C) received transaction information and a transaction statement from the prior owner of the product, as required under section 582;

"(D) did not knowingly ship a suspect or illegitimate product;

"(E) had systems and processes in place to comply with verification requirements under section 582;

"(F) did not knowingly provide false transaction information; and

"(G) did not knowingly alter the transaction history.

581(28) VERIFICATION OR VERIFY

"(28) VERIFICATION OR VERIFY.—

The term 'verification' or 'verify' means determining whether the product identifier affixed to, or imprinted upon, a package or homogeneous case corresponds to the standardized numerical identifier or lot number and expiration date assigned to the product by the manufacturer or the repackager, as applicable in accordance with section 582.

581(29) WHOLESALE DISTRIBUTOR

"(29) WHOLESALE DISTRIBUTOR.—

The term 'wholesale distributor' means a person (other than a manufacturer, a manufacturer's co-licensed partner, a third-party logistics provider, or repackager) engaged in wholesale distribution (as defined in section 503(e)(4), as amended by the Drug Supply Chain Security Act).

SEC. 582. REQUIREMENTS

"SEC. 582. REQUIREMENTS.

582(a) In General

"(a) In General.—

582(a)(1) OTHER ACTIVITIES

"(1) OTHER ACTIVITIES.—Each manufacturer, repackager, wholesale distributor, and dispenser shall comply with the requirements set forth in this section with respect to the role of such manufacturer, repackager, wholesale distributor, or dispenser in a transaction involving product. If an entity meets the definition of more than one of the entities listed in the preceding sentence, such entity shall comply with all applicable requirements in this section, but shall not be required to duplicate requirements.

582(a)(2) INITIAL STANDARDS

"(2) INITIAL STANDARDS.—

582(a)(2)(A) IN GENERAL

"(A) IN GENERAL.—The Secretary shall, in consultation with other appropriate Federal officials, manufacturers, repackagers, wholesale distributors, dispensers, and other pharmaceutical distribution supply chain stakeholders, issue a draft guidance document that establishes standards for the interoperable exchange of transaction information, transaction history, and transaction statements, in paper or electronic format, for compliance with this subsection and subsections (b), (c), (d), and (e). In establishing such standards, the Secretary shall consider the feasibility of establishing standardized documentation to be used by members of the pharmaceutical distribution supply chain to convey the transaction information, transaction history, and transaction statement to the subsequent purchaser of a product and to facilitate the exchange of lot level data. The standards established under this paragraph shall take into consideration the standards established under section 505D and shall comply with a form and format developed by a widely recognized international standards development organization.

582(a)(2)(B) PUBLIC INPUT

"(B) PUBLIC INPUT.—Prior to issuing the draft guidance under subparagraph (A), the Secretary shall gather comments and information from stakeholders and maintain such comments and information in a public docket for at least 60 days prior to issuing such guidance.

582(a)(2)(C) PUBLICATION

"(C) PUBLICATION.—The Secretary shall publish the standards established under subparagraph (A) not later than 1 year after the date of enactment of the Drug Supply Chain Security Act.

582(a)(3) WAIVERS, EXCEPTIONS, AND EXEMPTIONS

"(3) WAIVERS, EXCEPTIONS, AND EXEMPTIONS.—

582(a)(3)(A) IN GENERAL

"(A) IN GENERAL.—Not later than 2 years after the date of enactment of the Drug Supply Chain Security Act, the Secretary shall, by guidance—

"(i) establish a process by which an authorized manufacturer, repackager, wholesale distributor, or dispenser may request a waiver from any of the requirements set forth in this section, which the Secretary may grant if the Secretary determines that such requirements would result in an undue economic hardship or for emergency medical reasons, including a public health emergency declaration pursuant to section 319 of the Public Health Service Act;

"(ii) establish a process by which the Secretary determines exceptions, and a process through which a manufacturer or repackager may request such an exception, to the requirements relating to product identifiers if a product is packaged in a container too small or otherwise unable to accommodate a label with sufficient space to bear the information required for compliance with this section; and

"(iii) establish a process by which the Secretary may determine other products or transactions that shall be exempt from the requirements of this section.

582(a)(3)(B) CONTENT.—

"(B) CONTENT.—The guidance issued under subparagraph (A) shall include a process for the biennial review and renewal of such waivers, exceptions, and exemptions, as applicable.

582(a)(3)(C) PROCESS.—

"(C) PROCESS.—In issuing the guidance under this paragraph, the Secretary shall provide an effective date that is not later than 180 days prior to the date on which manufacturers are required to affix or imprint a product identifier to each package and homogenous case of product intended to be introduced in a transaction into commerce consistent with this section.

582(a)(4) SELF-EXECUTING REQUIREMENTS

"(4) SELF-EXECUTING REQUIREMENTS.—Except where otherwise specified, the requirements of this section may be enforced without further regulations or guidance from the Secretary.

582(a)(5) GRANDFATHERING PRODUCT

"(5) GRANDFATHERING PRODUCT.—

582(a)(5)(A) PRODUCT IDENTIFIER

"(A) PRODUCT IDENTIFIER.—Not later than 2 years after the date of enactment of the Drug Supply Chain Security Act, the Secretary shall finalize guidance specifying whether and under what circumstances product that is not labeled with a product identifier and that is in the pharmaceutical distribution supply chain at the time of the effective date of the requirements of this section shall be exempted from the requirements of this section.

582(a)(5)(B) TRACING.—

"(B) TRACING.—For a product that entered the pharmaceutical distribution supply chain prior to January 1, 2015—

"(i) authorized trading partners shall be exempt from providing transaction information as required under subsections (b)(1)(A)(i), (c)(1)(A)(ii), (d)(1)(A)(ii), and (e)(1)(A)(ii);

"(ii) transaction history required under this section shall begin with the owner of such product on such date; and

"(iii) the owners of such product on such date shall be exempt from asserting receipt of transaction information and transaction statement from the prior owner as required under this section.

582(a)(6) WHOLESALE DISTRIBUTOR LICENSES

"*(6) WHOLESALE DISTRIBUTOR LICENSES.*—Notwithstanding section 581(9)(A), until the effective date of the wholesale distributor licensing regulations under section 583, the term 'licensed' or 'authorized', as it relates to a wholesale distributor with respect to prescription drugs, shall mean a wholesale distributor with a valid license under State law.

582(a)(7) THIRD-PARTY LOGISTICS PROVIDER LICENSES

"(7) THIRD-PARTY LOGISTICS PROVIDER LICENSES.—Until the effective date of the third-party logistics provider licensing regulations under section 584, a third-party logistics provider shall be considered 'licensed' under section 581(9)(B) unless the Secretary has made a finding that the third-party logistics provider does not utilize good handling and distribution practices and publishes notice thereof.

582(a)(8) LABEL CHANGES

"*(8) LABEL CHANGES.*—Changes made to package labels solely to incorporate the product identifier may be submitted to the Secretary in the annual report of an establishment, in accordance with section 314.70(d) of chapter 21, Code of Federal Regulations (or any successor regulation).

582(a)(9) PRODUCT IDENTIFIERS

"(9) PRODUCT IDENTIFIERS.—With respect to any requirement relating to product identifiers under this subchapter—

"(A) unless the Secretary allows, through guidance, the use of other technologies for data instead of or in addition to the technologies described in clauses (i) and (ii), the applicable data—

"(i) shall be included in a 2-dimensional data matrix barcode when affixed to, or imprinted upon, a package; and

"(ii) shall be included in a linear or 2-dimensional data matrix barcode when affixed to, or imprinted upon, a homogeneous case; and

"(B) verification of the product identifier may occur by using human-readable or machine-readable methods.

582(b) Manufacturer Requirements

"(b) Manufacturer Requirements.—

582(b)(1) PRODUCT TRACING

"(1) PRODUCT TRACING.—

582(b)(1)(A) IN GENERAL

"(A) IN GENERAL.—Beginning not later than January 1, 2015, a manufacturer shall—

"(i) prior to, or at the time of, each transaction in which such manufacturer transfers ownership of a product, provide the subsequent owner with transaction history, transaction information, and a transaction statement, in a single document in an paper or electronic format; and

"(ii) capture the transaction information (including lot level information), transaction history, and transaction statement for each transaction and maintain such information, history, and statement for not less than 6 years after the date of the transaction.

582(b)(1)(B) REQUESTS FOR INFORMATION.—

"(B) REQUESTS FOR INFORMATION.—Upon a request by the Secretary or other appropriate Federal or State official, in the event of a recall or for the purpose of investigating a suspect product or an illegitimate product, a manufacturer shall, not later than 1 business day, and not to exceed 48 hours, after receiving the request, or in other such reasonable time as determined by the Secretary, based on the circumstances of the request, provide the applicable transaction information, transaction history, and transaction statement for the product.

582(b)(1)(C) ELECTRONIC FORMAT

"(C) ELECTRONIC FORMAT.—

"(i) IN GENERAL.—Beginning not later than 4 years after the date of enactment of the Drug Supply Chain Security Act, except as provided under clause (ii), a manufacturer shall provide the transaction information, transaction history, and transaction statement required under subparagraph (A)(i) in electronic format.

"(ii) EXCEPTION.—A manufacturer may continue to provide the transaction information, transaction history, and transaction statement required under subparagraph (A)(i) in a paper format to a licensed health care practitioner authorized to prescribe medication under State law or other licensed individual under the supervision or direction of such a practitioner who dispenses product in the usual course of professional practice.

582(b)(2) PRODUCT IDENTIFIER

"(2) PRODUCT IDENTIFIER.—

"(A) IN GENERAL.—Beginning not later than 4 years after the date of enactment of the Drug Supply Chain Security Act, a manufacturer shall affix or imprint a product identifier to each package and homogenous case of a product intended to be introduced in a transaction into commerce. Such manufacturer shall maintain the product identifier information for such product for not less than 6 years after the date of the transaction.

"(B) EXCEPTION.—A package that is required to have a standardized numerical identifier is not required to have a unique device identifier.

"(3) AUTHORIZED TRADING PARTNERS.—Beginning not later than January 1, 2015, the trading partners of a manufacturer may be only authorized trading partners.

"(4) VERIFICATION.—Beginning not later than January 1, 2015, a manufacturer shall have systems in place to enable the manufacturer to comply with the following requirements:

"(A) SUSPECT PRODUCT.—

"(i) IN GENERAL.—Upon making a determination that a product in the possession or control of the manufacturer is a suspect product, or upon receiving a request for verification from the Secretary that has made a determination that a product within the possession or control of a manufacturer is a suspect product, a manufacturer shall—

"(I) quarantine such product within the possession or control of the manufacturer from product intended for distribution until such product is cleared or dispositioned; and

"(II) promptly conduct an investigation in coordination with trading partners, as applicable, to determine whether the product is an illegitimate product, which shall include validating any applicable transaction history and transaction information in the possession of the manufacturer and otherwise investigating to determine whether the product is an illegitimate product, and, beginning 4 years after the date of enactment of the Drug Supply Chain Security Act, verifying the product at the package level, including the standardized numerical identifier.

"(ii) CLEARED PRODUCT.—If the manufacturer makes the determination that a suspect product is not an illegitimate product, the manufacturer shall promptly notify the Secretary, if applicable, of such determination and such product may be further distributed.

"(iii) RECORDS.—A manufacturer shall keep records of the investigation of a suspect product for not less than 6 years after the conclusion of the investigation.

582(b)(4)(B) ILLEGITIMATE PRODUCT

"(B) ILLEGITIMATE PRODUCT.—

"(i) IN GENERAL.—Upon determining that a product in the possession or control of a manufacturer is an illegitimate product, the manufacturer shall, in a manner consistent with the systems and processes of such manufacturer—

"(I) quarantine such product within the possession or control of the manufacturer from product intended for distribution until such product is dispositioned;

"(II) disposition the illegitimate product within the possession or control of the manufacturer;

"(III) take reasonable and appropriate steps to assist a trading partner to disposition an illegitimate product not in the possession or control of the manufacturer; and

"(IV) retain a sample of the product for further physical examination or laboratory analysis of the product by the manufacturer or Secretary (or other appropriate Federal or State official) upon request by the Secretary (or other appropriate Federal or State official), as necessary and appropriate.

"(ii) MAKING A NOTIFICATION.—

"(I) ILLEGITIMATE PRODUCT.—Upon determining that a product in the possession or control of the manufacturer is an illegitimate product, the manufacturer shall notify the Secretary and all immediate trading partners that the manufacturer has reason to believe may have received such illegitimate product of such determination not later than 24 hours after making such determination.

"(II) HIGH RISK OF ILLEGITIMACY.—A manufacturer shall notify the Secretary and immediate trading partners that the manufacturer has reason to believe may have in the trading partner's possession a product manufactured by, or purported to be a product manufactured by, the manufacturer not later than 24 hours after determining or being notified by the Secretary or a trading partner that there is a high risk that such product is an illegitimate product. For purposes of this subclause, a 'high risk' may include a specific high risk that could increase the likelihood that illegitimate product will enter the pharmaceutical distribution supply chain and other high risks as determined by the Secretary in guidance pursuant to subsection (h).

"(iii) RESPONDING TO A NOTIFICATION.—Upon the receipt of a notification from the Secretary or a trading partner that a determination has been made that a product is an illegitimate product, a manufacturer shall identify all illegitimate product subject to such notification that is in the possession or control of the manufacturer, including any product that is subsequently received, and shall perform the activities described in subparagraph (A).

"(iv) TERMINATING A NOTIFICATION.—Upon making a determination, in consultation with the Secretary, that a notification is no longer necessary, a manufacturer shall promptly notify immediate trading partners that the manufacturer notified pursuant to clause (ii) that such notification has been terminated.

"(v) RECORDS.—A manufacturer shall keep records of the disposition of an illegitimate product for not less than 6 years after the conclusion of the disposition.

582(b)(4)(C) REQUESTS FOR VERIFICATION

"(C) REQUESTS FOR VERIFICATION.—Beginning 4 years after the date of enactment of the Drug Supply Chain Security Act, upon receiving a request for verification from an authorized repackager, wholesale distributor, or dispenser that is in possession or control of a product such person believes to be manufactured by such manufacturer, a manufacturer shall, not later than 24 hours after receiving the request for verification or in other such reasonable time as determined by the Secretary, based on the circumstances of the request, notify the person making the request whether the product identifier, including the standardized numerical identifier, that is the subject of the request corresponds to the product identifier affixed or imprinted by the manufacturer. If a manufacturer responding to a request for verification identifies a product identifier that does not correspond to that affixed or imprinted by the manufacturer, the manufacturer shall treat such product as suspect product and conduct an investigation as described in subparagraph (A). If the manufacturer has reason to believe the product is an illegitimate product, the manufacturer shall advise the person making the request of such belief at the time such manufacturer responds to the request for verification.

582(b)(4)(D) ELECTRONIC DATABASE

"(D) ELECTRONIC DATABASE.—A manufacturer may satisfy the requirements of this paragraph by developing a secure electronic database or utilizing a secure electronic database developed or operated by another entity. The owner of such database shall establish the requirements and processes to respond to requests and may provide for data access to other members of the pharmaceutical distribution supply chain, as appropriate. The development and operation of such a database shall not relieve a manufacturer of the requirement under this paragraph to respond to a request for verification submitted by means other than a secure electronic database.

582(b)(4)(E) SALEABLE RETURNED PRODUCT

"(E) SALEABLE RETURNED PRODUCT.—Beginning 4 years after the date of enactment of the Drug Supply Chain Security Act (except as provided pursuant to subsection (a)(5)), upon receipt of a returned product that the manufacturer intends to further distribute, before further distributing such product, the manufacturer shall verify the product identifier, including the standardized numerical identifier, for each sealed homogeneous case of such product or, if such product is not in a sealed homogeneous case, verify the product identifier, including the standardized numerical identifier, on each package.

"(F) NONSALEABLE RETURNED PRODUCT.—A manufacturer may return a nonsaleable product to the manufacturer or repackager, to the wholesale distributor from whom such product was purchased, or to a person acting on behalf of such a person, including a returns processor, without providing the information described in paragraph (1)(A)(i).

582(c) Wholesale Distributor Requirements

"(c) Wholesale Distributor Requirements.—

582(c)(1) PRODUCT TRACING

"(1) PRODUCT TRACING.—

"(A) IN GENERAL.—Beginning not later than January 1, 2015, the following requirements shall apply to wholesale distributors:

"(i) A wholesale distributor shall not accept ownership of a product unless the previous owner prior to, or at the time of, the transaction provides the transaction history, transaction information, and a transaction statement for the product, as applicable under this subparagraph.

"(ii)(I)(aa) If the wholesale distributor purchased a product directly from the manufacturer, the exclusive distributor of the manufacturer, or a repackager that purchased directly from the manufacturer, then prior to, or at the time of, each transaction in which the wholesale distributor transfers ownership of a product, the wholesale distributor shall provide to the subsequent purchaser—

"(AA) a transaction statement, which shall state that such wholesale distributor, or a member of the affiliate of such wholesale distributor, purchased the product directly from the manufacturer, exclusive distributor of the manufacturer, or repackager that purchased the product directly from the manufacturer; and

"(BB) subject to subclause (II), the transaction history and transaction information.

"(bb) The wholesale distributor shall provide the transaction history, transaction information, and transaction statement under item (aa)—

"(AA) if provided to a dispenser, on a single document in a paper or electronic format; and

"(BB) if provided to a wholesale distributor, through any combination of self-generated paper, electronic data, or manufacturer-provided information on the product package.

"(II) For purposes of transactions described in subclause (I), transaction history and transaction information shall not be required to include the lot number of the product, the initial transaction date, or the initial shipment date from the manufacturer (as defined in subparagraphs (F), (G), and (H) of section 581(26)).

"(iii) If the wholesale distributor did not purchase a product directly from the manufacturer, the exclusive distributor of the manufacturer, or a repackager that purchased directly from the manufacturer, as described in clause (ii), then prior to, or at the time of, each transaction or subsequent transaction, the wholesale distributor shall provide to the subsequent purchaser a transaction statement, transaction history, and transaction information, in a paper or electronic format that complies with the guidance document issued under subsection (a)(2).

"(iv) For the purposes of clause (iii), the transaction history supplied shall begin only with the wholesale distributor described in clause (ii)(I), but the wholesale distributor described in clause (iii) shall inform the subsequent purchaser that such wholesale distributor received a direct purchase statement from a wholesale distributor described in clause (ii)(I).

"(v) A wholesale distributor shall—

"(I) capture the transaction information (including lot level information) consistent with the requirements of this section, transaction history, and transaction statement for each transaction described in clauses (i), (ii), and (iii) and maintain such information, history, and statement for not less than 6 years after the date of the transaction; and

"(II) maintain the confidentiality of the transaction information (including any lot level information consistent with the requirements of this section), transaction history, and transaction statement for a product in a manner that prohibits disclosure to any person other than the Secretary or other appropriate Federal or State official, except to comply with clauses (ii) and (iii), and, as applicable, pursuant to an agreement under subparagraph (D).

582(c)(1)(B) RETURNS

"(B) RETURNS.—

"(i) SALEABLE RETURNS.—Notwithstanding subparagraph (A)(i), the following shall apply:

"(I) REQUIREMENTS.—Until the date that is 6 years after the date of enactment of the Drug Supply Chain Security Act (except as provided pursuant to subsection (a)(5)), a wholesale distributor may accept returned product from a dispenser or repackager pursuant to the terms and conditions of any agreement between the parties, and, notwithstanding subparagraph (A)(ii), may distribute such returned product without providing the transaction history. For transactions subsequent to the return, the transaction history of such product shall begin with the wholesale distributor that accepted the returned product, consistent with the requirements of this subsection.

"(II) ENHANCED REQUIREMENTS.—Beginning 6 years after the date of enactment of the Drug Supply Chain Security Act (except as provided pursuant to subsection (a)(5)), a wholesale distributor may accept returned product from a dispenser or repackager only if the wholesale distributor can associate returned product with the transaction information and transaction statement associated with that product. For all transactions after such date, the transaction history, as applicable, of such product shall begin with the wholesale distributor that accepted and verified the returned product. For purposes of this subparagraph, the transaction information and transaction history, as applicable, need not include transaction dates if it is not reasonably practicable to obtain such dates.

"(ii) NONSALEABLE RETURNS.—A wholesale distributor may return a nonsaleable product to the manufacturer or repackager, to the wholesale distributor from whom such product was purchased, or to a person acting on behalf of such a person, including a returns processor, without providing the information required under subparagraph (A)(i).

582(c)(1)(C) REQUESTS FOR INFORMATION

"(C) REQUESTS FOR INFORMATION.—Upon a request by the Secretary or other appropriate Federal or State official, in the event of a recall or for the purpose of investigating a suspect product or an illegitimate product, a wholesale distributor shall, not later than 1 business day, and not to exceed 48 hours, after receiving the request or in other such reasonable time as determined by the Secretary, based on the circumstances of the request, provide the applicable transaction information, transaction history, and transaction statement for the product.

582(c)(1)(D) TRADING PARTNER AGREEMENTS

"(D) TRADING PARTNER AGREEMENTS.—Beginning 6 years after the date of enactment of the Drug Supply Chain Security Act, a wholesale distributor may disclose the transaction information, including lot level information, transaction history, or transaction statement of a product to the subsequent purchaser of the product, pursuant to a written agreement between such wholesale distributor and such subsequent purchaser. Nothing in this subparagraph shall be construed to limit the applicability of subparagraphs (A) through (C).

"(2) PRODUCT IDENTIFIER.—Beginning 6 years after the date of enactment of the Drug Supply Chain Security Act, a wholesale distributor may engage in transactions involving a product only if such product is encoded with a product identifier (except as provided pursuant to subsection (a)(5)).

"(3) AUTHORIZED TRADING PARTNERS.—Beginning not later than January 1, 2015, the trading partners of a wholesale distributor may be only authorized trading partners.

"(4) VERIFICATION.—Beginning not later than January 1, 2015, a wholesale distributor shall have systems in place to enable the wholesale distributor to comply with the following requirements:

582(c)(4)(A) SUSPECT PRODUCT

"(A) SUSPECT PRODUCT.—

"(i) IN GENERAL.—Upon making a determination that a product in the possession or control of a wholesale distributor is a suspect product, or upon receiving a request for verification from the Secretary that has made a determination that a product within the possession or control of a wholesale distributor is a suspect product, a wholesale distributor shall—

"(I) quarantine such product within the possession or control of the wholesale distributor from product intended for distribution until such product is cleared or dispositioned; and

"(II) promptly conduct an investigation in coordination with trading partners, as applicable, to determine whether the product is an illegitimate product, which shall include validating any applicable transaction history and transaction information in the possession of the wholesale distributor and otherwise investigating to determine whether the product is an illegitimate product, and, beginning 6 years after the date of enactment of the Drug Supply Chain Security Act (except as provided pursuant to subsection (a)(5)), verifying the product at the package level, including the standardized numerical identifier.

"(ii) CLEARED PRODUCT.—If the wholesale distributor determines that a suspect product is not an illegitimate product, the wholesale distributor shall promptly notify the Secretary, if applicable, of such determination and such product may be further distributed.

"(iii) RECORDS.—A wholesale distributor shall keep records of the investigation of a suspect product for not less than 6 years after the conclusion of the investigation.

582(c)(4)(B) ILLEGITIMATE PRODUCT

"(B) ILLEGITIMATE PRODUCT.—

"(i) IN GENERAL.—Upon determining, in coordination with the manufacturer, that a product in the possession or control of a wholesale distributor is an illegitimate product, the wholesale distributor shall, in a manner that is consistent with the systems and processes of such wholesale distributor—

"(I) quarantine such product within the possession or control of the wholesale distributor from product intended for distribution until such product is dispositioned;

"(II) disposition the illegitimate product within the possession or control of the wholesale distributor;

"(III) take reasonable and appropriate steps to assist a trading partner to disposition an illegitimate product not in the possession or control of the wholesale distributor; and

"(IV) retain a sample of the product for further physical examination or laboratory analysis of the product by the manufacturer or Secretary (or other appropriate Federal or State official) upon request by the manufacturer or Secretary (or other appropriate Federal or State official), as necessary and appropriate.

"(ii) MAKING A NOTIFICATION.—Upon determining that a product in the possession or control of the wholesale distributor is an illegitimate product, the wholesale distributor shall notify the Secretary and all immediate trading partners that the wholesale distributor has reason to believe may have received such illegitimate product of such determination not later than 24 hours after making such determination.

"(iii) RESPONDING TO A NOTIFICATION.—Upon the receipt of a notification from the Secretary or a trading partner that a determination has been made that a product is an illegitimate product, a wholesale distributor shall identify all illegitimate product subject to such notification that is in the possession or control of the wholesale distributor, including any product that is subsequently received, and shall perform the activities described in subparagraph (A).

"(iv) TERMINATING A NOTIFICATION.—Upon making a determination, in consultation with the Secretary, that a notification is no longer necessary, a wholesale distributor shall promptly notify immediate trading partners that the wholesale distributor notified pursuant to clause (ii) that such notification has been terminated.

"(v) RECORDS.—A wholesale distributor shall keep records of the disposition of an illegitimate product for not less than 6 years after the conclusion of the disposition.

582(c)(4)(C) ELECTRONIC DATABASE

"(C) ELECTRONIC DATABASE.—A wholesale distributor may satisfy the requirements of this paragraph by developing a secure electronic database or utilizing a secure electronic database developed or operated by another entity. The owner of such database shall establish the requirements and processes to respond to requests and may provide for data access to other members of the pharmaceutical distribution supply chain, as appropriate. The development and operation of such a database shall not relieve a wholesale distributor of the requirement under this paragraph to respond to a verification request submitted by means other than a secure electronic database.

582(c)(4)(D) VERIFICATION OF SALEABLE RETURNED PRODUCT

"(D) VERIFICATION OF SALEABLE RETURNED PRODUCT.—Beginning 6 years after the date of enactment of the Drug Supply Chain Security Act, upon receipt of a returned product that the wholesale distributor intends to further distribute, before further distributing such product, the wholesale distributor shall verify the product identifier, including the standardized numerical identifier, for each sealed homogeneous case of such product or, if such product is not in a sealed homogeneous case, verify the product identifier, including the standardized numerical identifier, on each package.

582(d) Dispenser Requirements

"(d) Dispenser Requirements.—

582(d)(1) PRODUCT TRACING

"(1) PRODUCT TRACING.—

582(d)(1)(A) IN GENERAL

"(A) IN GENERAL.—Beginning July 1, 2015, a dispenser—

"(i) shall not accept ownership of a product, unless the previous owner prior to, or at the time of, the transaction, provides transaction history, transaction information, and a transaction statement;

"(ii) prior to, or at the time of, each transaction in which the dispenser transfers ownership of a product (but not including dispensing to a patient or returns) shall provide the subsequent owner with transaction history, transaction information, and a transaction statement for the product, except that the requirements of this clause shall not apply to sales by a dispenser to another dispenser to fulfill a specific patient need; and "(iii) shall capture transaction information (including lot level information, if provided), transaction history, and transaction statements, as necessary to investigate a suspect product, and maintain such information, history, and statements for not less than 6 years after the transaction.

582(d)(1)(B) AGREEMENTS WITH THIRD PARTIES

"(B) AGREEMENTS WITH THIRD PARTIES.—A dispenser may enter into a written agreement with a third party, including an authorized wholesale distributor, under which the third party confidentially maintains the transaction information, transaction history, and transaction statements required to be maintained under this subsection on behalf of the dispenser. If a dispenser enters into such an agreement, the dispenser shall maintain a copy of the written agreement and shall not be relieved of the obligations of the dispenser under this subsection.

582(d)(1)(C) RETURNS

"(C) RETURNS.—

"(i) SALEABLE RETURNS.—A dispenser may return product to the trading partner from which the dispenser obtained the product without providing the information required under subparagraph (A).

"(ii) NONSALEABLE RETURNS.—A dispenser may return a nonsaleable product to the manufacturer or repackager, to the wholesale distributor from whom such product was purchased, to a returns processor, or to a person acting on behalf of such a person without providing the information required under subparagraph (A).

582(d)(1)(D) REQUESTS FOR INFORMATION

"(D) REQUESTS FOR INFORMATION.—Upon a request by the Secretary or other appropriate Federal or State official, in the event of a recall or for the purpose of investigating a suspect or an illegitimate product, a dispenser shall, not later than 2 business days after receiving the request or in another such reasonable time as determined by the Secretary, based on the circumstances of the request, provide the applicable transaction information, transaction statement, and transaction history which the dispenser received from the previous owner, which shall not include the lot number of the product, the initial transaction date, or the initial shipment date from the manufacturer unless such information was included in the transaction information, transaction statement, and transaction history provided by the manufacturer or wholesale distributor to the dispenser. The dispenser may respond to the request by providing the applicable information in either paper or electronic format. Until the date that is 4 years after the date of enactment of the Drug Supply Chain Security Act, the Secretary or other appropriate Federal or State official shall grant a dispenser additional time, as necessary, only with respect to a request to provide lot level information described in subparagraph (F) of section 581(26) that was provided to the dispenser in paper format, limit the request time period to the 6 months preceding the request or other relevant date, and, in the event of a recall, the Secretary, or other appropriate Federal or State official may request information only if such recall involves a serious adverse health consequence or death to humans.

582(d)(2) PRODUCT IDENTIFIER

"(2) PRODUCT IDENTIFIER.—Beginning not later than 7 years after the date of enactment of the Drug Supply Chain Security Act, a dispenser may engage in transactions involving a product only if such product is encoded with a product identifier (except as provided pursuant to subsection (a)(5)).

582(d)(3) AUTHORIZED TRADING PARTNERS

"(3) AUTHORIZED TRADING PARTNERS.—Beginning not later than January 1, 2015, the trading partners of a dispenser may be only authorized trading partners.

582(d)(4) VERIFICATION

"(4) VERIFICATION.—Beginning not later than January 1, 2015, a dispenser shall have systems in place to enable the dispenser to comply with the following requirements:

582(d)(4)(A) SUSPECT PRODUCT

"(A) SUSPECT PRODUCT.—

"(i) IN GENERAL.—Upon making a determination that a product in the possession or control of the dispenser is a suspect product, or upon receiving a request for verification from the Secretary that has made a determination that a product within the possession or control of a dispenser is a suspect product, a dispenser shall—

"(I) quarantine such product within the possession or control of the dispenser from product intended for distribution until such product is cleared or dispositioned; and

"(II) promptly conduct an investigation in coordination with trading partners, as applicable, to determine whether the product is an illegitimate product.

"(ii) INVESTIGATION.—An investigation conducted under clause (i)(II) shall include—

"(I) beginning 7 years after the date of enactment of the Drug Supply Chain Security Act, verifying whether the lot number of a suspect product corresponds with the lot number for such product;

"(II) beginning 7 years after the date of enactment of such Act, verifying that the product identifier, including the standardized numerical identifier, of at least 3 packages or 10 percent of such suspect product, whichever is greater, or all packages, if there are fewer than 3, corresponds with the product identifier for such product;

"(III) validating any applicable transaction history and transaction information in the possession of the dispenser; and

"(IV) otherwise investigating to determine whether the product is an illegitimate product.

"(iii) CLEARED PRODUCT.—If the dispenser makes the determination that a suspect product is not an illegitimate product, the dispenser shall promptly notify the Secretary, if applicable, of such determination and such product may be further distributed or dispensed.

"(iv) RECORDS.—A dispenser shall keep records of the investigation of a suspect product for not less than 6 years after the conclusion of the investigation.

582(d)(4)(B) ILLEGITIMATE PRODUCT

"(B) ILLEGITIMATE PRODUCT.—

"(i) IN GENERAL.—Upon determining, in coordination with the manufacturer, that a product in the possession or control of a dispenser is an illegitimate product, the dispenser shall—

"(I) disposition the illegitimate product within the possession or control of the dispenser;

"(II) take reasonable and appropriate steps to assist a trading partner to disposition an illegitimate product not in the possession or control of the dispenser; and

"(III) retain a sample of the product for further physical examination or laboratory analysis of the product by the manufacturer or Secretary (or other appropriate Federal or State official) upon request by the manufacturer or Secretary (or other appropriate Federal or State official), as necessary and appropriate.

"(ii) MAKING A NOTIFICATION.—Upon determining that a product in the possession or control of the dispenser is an illegitimate product, the dispenser shall notify the Secretary and all immediate trading partners that the dispenser has reason to believe may have received such illegitimate product of such determination not later than 24 hours after making such determination.

"(iii) RESPONDING TO A NOTIFICATION.—Upon the receipt of a notification from the Secretary or a trading partner that a determination has been made that a product is an illegitimate product, a dispenser shall identify all illegitimate product subject to such notification that is in the possession or control of the dispenser, including any product that is subsequently received, and shall perform the activities described in subparagraph (A).

"(iv) TERMINATING A NOTIFICATION.—Upon making a determination, in consultation with the Secretary, that a notification is no longer necessary, a dispenser shall promptly notify immediate trading partners that the dispenser notified pursuant to clause (ii) that such notification has been terminated.

"(v) RECORDS.—A dispenser shall keep records of the disposition of an illegitimate product for not less than 6 years after the conclusion of the disposition.

582(d)(4)(C) ELECTRONIC DATABASE

"(C) ELECTRONIC DATABASE.—A dispenser may satisfy the requirements of this paragraph by developing a secure electronic database or utilizing a secure electronic database developed or operated by another entity.

582(d)(5) EXCEPTION

"(5) EXCEPTION.—Notwithstanding any other provision of law, the requirements under paragraphs (1) and (4) shall not apply to licensed health care practitioners authorized to prescribe or administer medication under State law or other licensed individuals under the supervision or direction of such practitioners who dispense or administer product in the usual course of professional practice.

582(e) Repackager Requirements

"(e) Repackager Requirements.—

582(e)(1) PRODUCT TRACING

"(1) PRODUCT TRACING.—

582(e)(1)(A) IN GENERAL

"(A) IN GENERAL.—Beginning not later than January 1, 2015, a repackager described in section 581(16)(A) shall—

"(i) not accept ownership of a product unless the previous owner, prior to, or at the time of, the transaction, provides transaction history, transaction information, and a transaction statement for the product;

"(ii) prior to, or at the time of, each transaction in which the repackager transfers ownership of a product, provide the subsequent owner with transaction history, transaction information, and a transaction statement for the product; and

"(iii) capture the transaction information (including lot level information), transaction history, and transaction statement for each transaction described in clauses (i) and (ii) and maintain such information, history, and statement for not less than 6 years after the transaction.

"(B) RETURNS.—

"(i) NONSALEABLE PRODUCT.—A repackager described in section 581(16)(A) may return a nonsaleable product to the manufacturer or repackager, or to the wholesale distributor from whom such product was purchased, or to a person acting on behalf of such a person, including a returns processor, without providing the information required under subparagraph (A)(ii).

"(ii) SALEABLE OR NONSALEABLE PRODUCT.—A repackager described in section 581(16)(B) may return a saleable or nonsaleable product to the manufacturer, repackager, or to the wholesale distributor from whom such product was received without providing the information required under subparagraph (A)(ii) on behalf of the hospital or other health care entity that took ownership of such product pursuant to the terms and conditions of any agreement between such repackager and the entity that owns the product.

"(C) REQUESTS FOR INFORMATION.—Upon a request by the Secretary or other appropriate Federal or State official, in the event of a recall or for the purpose of investigating a suspect product or an illegitimate product, a repackager described in section 581(16)(A) shall, not later than 1 business day, and not to exceed 48 hours, after receiving the request or in other such reasonable time as determined by the Secretary, provide the applicable transaction information, transaction history, and transaction statement for the product.

582(e)(2) PRODUCT IDENTIFIER

"(2) PRODUCT IDENTIFIER.—

"(A) IN GENERAL.—Beginning not later than 5 years after the date of enactment of the Drug Supply Chain Security Act, a repackager described in section 581(16)(A)—

"(i) shall affix or imprint a product identifier to each package and homogenous case of product intended to be introduced in a transaction in commerce;

"(ii) shall maintain the product identifier information for such product for not less than 6 years after the date of the transaction;

"(iii) may engage in transactions involving a product only if such product is encoded with a product identifier (except as provided pursuant to subsection (a)(5)); and

"(iv) shall maintain records for not less than 6 years to allow the repackager to associate the product identifier the repackager affixes or imprints with the product identifier assigned by the original manufacturer of the product.

"(B) EXCEPTION.—A package that is required to have a standardized numerical identifier is not required to have a unique device identifier.

582(e)(3) AUTHORIZED TRADING PARTNERS

"(3) AUTHORIZED TRADING PARTNERS.—Beginning January 1, 2015, the trading partners of a repackager described in section 581(16) may be only authorized trading partners.

582(e)(4) VERIFICATION

"(4) VERIFICATION.—Beginning not later than January 1, 2015, a repackager described in section 581(16)(A) shall have systems in place to enable the repackager to comply with the following requirements:

"(A) SUSPECT PRODUCT.—

"(i) IN GENERAL.—Upon making a determination that a product in the possession or control of the repackager is a suspect product, or upon receiving a request for verification from the Secretary that has made a determination that a product within the possession or control of a repackager is a suspect product, a repackager shall—

"(I) quarantine such product within the possession or control of the repackager from product intended for distribution until such product is cleared or dispositioned; and

"(II) promptly conduct an investigation in coordination with trading partners, as applicable, to determine whether the product is an illegitimate product, which shall include validating any applicable transaction history and transaction information in the possession of the repackager and otherwise investigating to determine whether the product is an illegitimate product, and, beginning 5 years after the date of enactment of the Drug Supply Chain Security Act (except as provided pursuant to subsection (a)(5)), verifying the product at the package level, including the standardized numerical identifier.

"(ii) CLEARED PRODUCT.—If the repackager makes the determination that a suspect product is not an illegitimate product, the repackager shall promptly notify the Secretary, if applicable, of such determination and such product may be further distributed.

"(iii) RECORDS.—A repackager shall keep records of the investigation of a suspect product for not less than 6 years after the conclusion of the investigation.

"(B) ILLEGITIMATE PRODUCT.—

"(i) IN GENERAL.—Upon determining, in coordination with the manufacturer, that a product in the possession or control of a repackager is an illegitimate product, the repackager shall, in a manner that is consistent with the systems and processes of such repackager—

"(I) quarantine such product within the possession or control of the repackager from product intended for distribution until such product is dispositioned;

"(II) disposition the illegitimate product within the possession or control of the repackager;

"(III) take reasonable and appropriate steps to assist a trading partner to disposition an illegitimate product not in the possession or control of the repackager; and

"(IV) retain a sample of the product for further physical examination or laboratory analysis of the product by the manufacturer or Secretary (or other appropriate Federal or State official) upon request by the manufacturer or Secretary (or other appropriate Federal or State official), as necessary and appropriate.

"(ii) MAKING A NOTIFICATION.—Upon determining that a product in the possession or control of the repackager is an illegitimate product, the repackager shall notify the Secretary and all immediate trading partners that the repackager has reason to believe may have received the illegitimate product of such determination not later than 24 hours after making such determination.

"(iii) RESPONDING TO A NOTIFICATION.—Upon the receipt of a notification from the Secretary or a trading partner, a repackager shall identify all illegitimate product subject to such notification that is in the possession or control of the repackager, including any product that is subsequently received, and shall perform the activities described in subparagraph (A).

"(iv) TERMINATING A NOTIFICATION.—Upon making a determination, in consultation with the Secretary, that a notification is no longer necessary, a repackager shall promptly notify immediate trading partners that the repackager notified pursuant to clause (ii) that such notification has been terminated.

"(v) RECORDS.—A repackager shall keep records of the disposition of an illegitimate product for not less than 6 years after the conclusion of the disposition.

"(C) REQUESTS FOR VERIFICATION.—Beginning 5 years after the date of enactment of the Drug Supply Chain Security Act, upon receiving a request for verification from an authorized manufacturer, wholesale distributor, or dispenser that is in possession or control of a product they believe to be repackaged by such repackager, a repackager shall, not later than 24 hours after receiving the verification request or in other such reasonable time as determined by the Secretary, based on the circumstances of the request, notify the person making the request whether the product identifier, including the standardized numerical identifier, that is the subject of the request corresponds to the product identifier affixed or imprinted by the repackager. If a repackager responding to a verification request identifies a product identifier that does not correspond to that affixed or imprinted by the repackager, the repackager shall treat such product as suspect product and conduct an investigation as described in subparagraph (A). If the repackager has reason to believe the product is an illegitimate product, the repackager shall advise the person making the request of such belief at the time such repackager responds to the verification request.

582(e)(4)(D) ELECTRONIC DATABASE

"(D) ELECTRONIC DATABASE.—A repackager may satisfy the requirements of paragraph (4) by developing a secure electronic database or utilizing a secure electronic database developed or operated by another entity. The owner of such database shall establish the requirements and processes to respond to requests and may provide for data access to other members of the pharmaceutical distribution supply chain, as appropriate. The development and operation of such a database shall not relieve a repackager of the requirement under subparagraph (C) to respond to a verification request submitted by means other than a secure electronic database.

582(e)(4)(E) VERIFICATION OF SALEABLE RETURNED PRODUCT

"(E) VERIFICATION OF SALEABLE RETURNED PRODUCT.—Beginning 5 years after the date of enactment of the Drug Supply Chain Security Act, upon receipt of a returned product that the repackager intends to further distribute, before further distributing such product, the repackager shall verify the product identifier for each sealed homogeneous case of such product or, if such product is not in a sealed homogeneous case, verify the product identifier on each package.

582(f) Drop Shipments

"(f) Drop Shipments.—

582(f)(1) IN GENERAL

"(1) IN GENERAL.—A wholesale distributor that does not physically handle or store product shall be exempt from the provisions of this section, except the notification requirements under clauses (ii), (iii), and (iv) of subsection (c)(4)(B), provided that the manufacturer, repackager, or other wholesale distributor that distributes the product to the dispenser by means of a drop shipment for such wholesale distributor includes on the transaction information and transaction history to the dispenser the contact information of such wholesale distributor and provides the transaction information, transaction history, and transaction statement directly to the dispenser.

"(2) CLARIFICATION.—For purposes of this subsection, providing administrative services, including processing of orders and payments, shall not by itself, be construed as being involved in the handling, distribution, or storage of a product.".

SEC. 203. ENHANCED DRUG DISTRIBUTION SECURITY.

Section 582, as added by section 202, is amended by adding at the end the following:

582(g) Enhanced Drug Distribution Security

"(g) Enhanced Drug Distribution Security.—

582(g)(1) IN GENERAL

"(1) IN GENERAL.—On the date that is 10 years after the date of enactment of the Drug Supply Chain Security Act, the following interoperable, electronic tracing of product at the package level requirements shall go into effect:

582(g)(1)(A)

"(A) The transaction information and the transaction statements as required under this section shall be exchanged in a secure, interoperable, electronic manner in accordance with the standards established under the guidance issued pursuant to paragraphs (3) and (4) of subsection (h), including any revision of such guidance issued in accordance with paragraph (5) of such subsection.

582(g)(1)(B)

"(B) The transaction information required under this section shall include the product identifier at the package level for each package included in the transaction.

582(g)(1)(C)

"(C) Systems and processes for verification of product at the package level, including the standardized numerical identifier, shall be required in accordance with the standards established under the guidance issued pursuant to subsection (a)(2) and the guidances issued pursuant to paragraphs (2), (3), and (4) of subsection (h), including any revision of such guidances issued in accordance with paragraph (5) of such subsection, which may include the use of aggregation and inference as necessary.

582(g)(1)(D)

"(D) The systems and processes necessary to promptly respond with the transaction information and transaction statement for a product upon a request by the Secretary (or other appropriate Federal or State official) in the event of a recall or for the purposes of investigating a suspect product or an illegitimate product shall be required.

582(g)(1)(E)

"(E) The systems and processes necessary to promptly facilitate gathering the information necessary to produce the transaction information for each transaction going back to the manufacturer, as applicable, shall be required—

"(i) in the event of a request by the Secretary (or other appropriate Federal or State official), on account of a recall or for the purposes of investigating a suspect product or an illegitimate product; or

"(ii) in the event of a request by an authorized trading partner, in a secure manner that ensures the protection of confidential commercial information and trade secrets, for purposes of investigating a suspect product or assisting the Secretary (or other appropriate Federal or State official) with a request described in clause (i).

582(g)(1)(F)

"(F) Each person accepting a saleable return shall have systems and processes in place to allow acceptance of such product and may accept saleable returns only if such person can associate the saleable return product with the transaction information and transaction statement associated with that product.

582(g)(2) COMPLIANCE

"(2) COMPLIANCE.—

582(g)(2)(A) INFORMATION MAINTENANCE AGREEMENT

"(A) INFORMATION MAINTENANCE AGREEMENT.—A dispenser may enter into a written agreement with a third party, including an authorized wholesale distributor, under which the third party shall confidentially maintain any information and statements required to be maintained under this section. If a dispenser enters into such an agreement, the dispenser shall maintain a copy of the written agreement and shall not be relieved of the obligations of the dispenser under this subsection.

582(g)(2)(B) ALTERNATIVE METHODS

"(B) ALTERNATIVE METHODS.—The Secretary, taking into consideration the assessment conducted under paragraph (3), shall provide for alternative methods of compliance with any of the requirements set forth in paragraph (1), including—

"(i) establishing timelines for compliance by small businesses (including small business dispensers with 25 or fewer full-time employees) with such requirements, in order to ensure that such requirements do not impose undue economic hardship for small businesses, including small business dispensers for whom the criteria set forth in the assessment under paragraph (3) is not met, if the Secretary determines that such requirements under paragraph (1) would result in undue economic hardship; and

"(ii) establishing a process by which a dispenser may request a waiver from any of the requirements set forth in paragraph (1) if the Secretary determines that such requirements would result in an undue economic hardship, which shall include a process for the biennial review and renewal of any such waiver.

582(g)(3) ASSESSMENT

"(3) ASSESSMENT.—

582(g)(3)(A) IN GENERAL

"(A) IN GENERAL.—Not later than the date that is 18 months after the Secretary issues the final guidance required under subsection (h), the Secretary shall enter into a contract with a private, independent consulting firm with expertise to conduct a technology and software assessment that looks at the feasibility of dispensers with 25 or fewer full-time employees conducting interoperable, electronic tracing of products at the package level. Such assessment shall be completed not later than 8½ years after the date of enactment of the Drug Supply Chain Security Act.

582(g)(3)(B) CONDITION

"(B) CONDITION.—As a condition of the award of the contract under subparagraph (A), the private, independent consulting firm shall agree to consult with dispensers with 25 or fewer full-time employees when conducting the assessment under such subparagraph.

582(g)(3)(C) CONTENT

"(C) CONTENT.—The assessment under subparagraph (A) shall assess whether—

"(i) the necessary software and hardware is readily accessible to such dispensers;

"(ii) the necessary software and hardware is prohibitively expensive to obtain, install, and maintain for such dispensers; and

"(iii) the necessary hardware and software can be integrated into business practices, such as interoperability with wholesale distributors, for such dispensers.

"(D) PUBLICATION.—The Secretary shall—

"(i) publish the statement of work for the assessment under subparagraph (A) for public comment prior to beginning the assessment;

"(ii) publish the final assessment for public comment not later than 30 calendar days after receiving such assessment; and

"(iii) hold a public meeting not later than 180 calendar days after receiving the final assessment at which public stakeholders may present their views on the assessment.

582(g)(4) PROCEDURE

"(4) PROCEDURE.—Notwithstanding section 553 of title 5, United States Code, the Secretary, in promulgating any regulation pursuant to this section, shall—

"(A) provide appropriate flexibility by—

"(i) not requiring the adoption of specific business systems for the maintenance and transmission of data;

"(ii) prescribing alternative methods of compliance for any of the requirements set forth in paragraph (1) or set forth in regulations implementing such requirements, including—

"(I) timelines for small businesses to comply with the requirements set forth in the regulations in order to ensure that such requirements do not impose undue economic hardship for small businesses (including small business dispensers for whom the criteria set forth in the assessment under paragraph (3) is not met), if the Secretary determines that such requirements would result in undue economic hardship; and

"(II) the establishment of a process by which a dispenser may request a waiver from any of the requirements set forth in such regulations if the Secretary determines that such requirements would result in an undue economic hardship; and

"(iii) taking into consideration—

"(I) the results of pilot projects, including pilot projects pursuant to this section and private sector pilot projects, including those involving the use of aggregation and inference;

"(II) the public meetings held and related guidance documents issued under this section;

"(III) the public health benefits of any additional regulations in comparison to the cost of compliance with such requirements, including on entities of varying sizes and capabilities;

"(IV) the diversity of the pharmaceutical distribution supply chain by providing appropriate flexibility for each sector, including both large and small businesses; and

"(V) the assessment pursuant to paragraph (3) with respect to small business dispensers, including related public comment and the public meeting, and requirements under this section;

"(B) issue a notice of proposed rulemaking that includes a copy of the proposed regulation;

"(C) provide a period of not less than 60 days for comments on the proposed regulation; and

"(D) publish in the Federal Register the final regulation not less than 2 years prior to the effective date of the regulation.

582(h) Guidance Documents

"(h) Guidance Documents.—

582(h)(1) IN GENERAL

"(1) IN GENERAL.—For the purposes of facilitating the successful and efficient adoption of secure, interoperable product tracing at the package level in order to enhance drug distribution security and further protect the public health, the Secretary shall issue the guidance documents as provided for in this subsection.

582(h)(2) SUSPECT AND ILLEGITIMATE PRODUCT

"(2) SUSPECT AND ILLEGITIMATE PRODUCT.—

582(h)(2)(A) IN GENERAL

"(A) IN GENERAL.—Not later than 180 days after the date of enactment of the Drug Supply Chain Security Act, the Secretary shall issue a guidance document to aid trading partners in the identification of a suspect product and notification termination. Such guidance document shall—

"(i) identify specific scenarios that could significantly increase the risk of a suspect product entering the pharmaceutical distribution supply chain;

"(ii) provide recommendation on how trading partners may identify such product and make a determination on whether the product is a suspect product as soon as practicable; and

"(iii) set forth the process by which manufacturers, repackagers, wholesale distributors, and dispensers shall terminate notifications in consultation with the Secretary regarding illegitimate product pursuant to subsections (b)(4)(B), (c)(4)(B), (d)(4)(B), and (e)(4)(B).

582(h)(2)(B) REVISED GUIDANCE

"(B) REVISED GUIDANCE.—If the Secretary revises the guidance issued under subparagraph (A), the Secretary shall follow the procedure set forth in paragraph (5).

582(h)(3) UNIT LEVEL TRACING

"(3) UNIT LEVEL TRACING.—

582(h)(3)(A) IN GENERAL

"(A) IN GENERAL.—In order to enhance drug distribution security at the package level, not later than 18 months after conducting a public meeting on the system attributes necessary to enable secure tracing of product at the package level, including allowing for the use of verification, inference, and aggregation, as necessary, the Secretary shall issue a final guidance document that outlines and makes recommendations with respect to the system attributes necessary to enable secure tracing at the package level as required under the requirements established under subsection (g). Such guidance document shall—

"(i) define the circumstances under which the sectors within the pharmaceutical distribution supply chain may, in the most efficient manner practicable, infer the contents of a case, pallet, tote, or other aggregate of individual packages or containers of product, from a product identifier associated with the case, pallet, tote, or other aggregate, without opening each case, pallet, tote, or other aggregate or otherwise individually scanning each package;

"(ii) identify methods and processes to enhance secure tracing of product at the package level, such as secure processes to facilitate the use of inference, enhanced verification activities, the use of aggregation and inference, processes that utilize the product identifiers to enhance tracing of product at the package level, including the standardized numerical identifier, or package security features; and

"(iii) ensure the protection of confidential commercial information and trade secrets.

"(B) PROCEDURE.—In issuing the guidance under subparagraph (A), and in revising such guidance, if applicable, the Secretary shall follow the procedure set forth in paragraph (5).

582(h)(4) STANDARDS FOR INTEROPERABLE DATA EXCHANGE

"(4) STANDARDS FOR INTEROPERABLE DATA EXCHANGE.—

"(A) IN GENERAL.—In order to enhance secure tracing of a product at the package level, the Secretary, not later than 18 months after conducting a public meeting on the interoperable standards necessary to enhance the security of the pharmaceutical distribution supply chain, shall update the guidance issued pursuant to subsection (a)(2), as necessary and appropriate, and finalize such guidance document so that the guidance document—

"(i) identifies and makes recommendations with respect to the standards necessary for adoption in order to support the secure, interoperable electronic data exchange among the pharmaceutical distribution supply chain that comply with a form and format developed by a widely recognized international standards development organization;

"(ii) takes into consideration standards established pursuant to subsection (a)(2) and section 505D;

"(iii) facilitates the creation of a uniform process or methodology for product tracing; and

"(iv) ensures the protection of confidential commercial information and trade secrets.

"(B) PROCEDURE.—In issuing the guidance under subparagraph (A), and in revising such guidance, if applicable, the Secretary shall follow the procedure set forth in paragraph (5).

582(h)(5) PROCEDURE

"(5) PROCEDURE.—In issuing or revising any guidance issued pursuant to this subsection or subsection (g), except the initial guidance issued under paragraph (2)(A), the Secretary shall—

"(A) publish a notice in the Federal Register for a period not less than 30 days announcing that the draft or revised draft guidance is available;

"(B) post the draft guidance document on the Internet Web site of the Food and Drug Administration and make such draft guidance document available in hard copy;

"(C) provide an opportunity for comment and review and take into consideration any comments received;

"(D) revise the draft guidance, as appropriate;

"(E) publish a notice in the Federal Register for a period not less than 30 days announcing that the final guidance or final revised guidance is available;

"(F) post the final guidance document on the Internet Web site of the Food and Drug Administration and make such final guidance document available in hard copy; and

"(G) provide for an effective date of not earlier than 1 year after such guidance becomes final.

582(i) Public Meetings

"(i) Public Meetings.—

582(i)(1) IN GENERAL

"(1) IN GENERAL.—The Secretary shall hold not less than 5 public meetings to enhance the safety and security of the pharmaceutical distribution supply chain and provide for comment. The Secretary may hold the first such public meeting not earlier than 1 year after the date of enactment of the Drug Supply Chain Security Act. In carrying out the public meetings described in this paragraph, the Secretary shall—

"(A) prioritize topics necessary to inform the issuance of the guidance described in paragraphs (3) and (4) of subsection (h); and

"(B) take all measures reasonable and practicable to ensure the protection of confidential commercial information and trade secrets.

582(i)(2) CONTENT

"(2) CONTENT.—Each of the following topics shall be addressed in at least one of the public meetings described in paragraph (1):

"(A) An assessment of the steps taken under subsections (b) through (e) to build capacity for a unit-level system, including the impact of the requirements of such subsections on—

"(i) the ability of the health care system collectively to maintain patient access to medicines;

"(ii) the scalability of such requirements, including as it relates to product lines; and

"(iii) the capability of different sectors and subsectors, including both large and small businesses, to affix and utilize the product identifier.

"(B) The system attributes necessary to support the requirements set forth under subsection (g), including the standards necessary for adoption in order to support the secure, interoperable electronic data exchange among sectors within the pharmaceutical distribution supply chain.

"(C) Best practices in each of the different sectors within the pharmaceutical distribution supply chain to implement the requirements of this section.

"(D) The costs and benefits of the implementation of this section, including the impact on each pharmaceutical distribution supply chain sector and on public health.

"(E) Whether electronic tracing requirements, including tracing of product at the package level, are feasible, cost effective, and needed to protect the public health.

"(F) The systems and processes needed to utilize the product identifiers to enhance tracing of product at the package level, including allowing for verification, aggregation, and inference, as necessary.

"(G) The technical capabilities and legal authorities, if any, needed to establish an interoperable, electronic system that provides for tracing of product at the package level.

"(H) The impact that such additional requirements would have on patient safety, the drug supply, cost and regulatory burden, and timely patient access to prescription drugs.

"(I) Other topics, as determined appropriate by the Secretary.

582(j) Pilot Projects

"(j) Pilot Projects.—

582(j)(1) IN GENERAL

"(1) IN GENERAL.—The Secretary shall establish 1 or more pilot projects, in coordination with authorized manufacturers, repackagers, wholesale distributors, and dispensers, to explore and evaluate methods to enhance the safety and security of the pharmaceutical distribution supply chain. Such projects shall build upon efforts, in existence as of the date of enactment of the Drug Supply Chain Security Act, to enhance the safety and security of the pharmaceutical distribution supply chain, take into consideration any pilot projects conducted prior to such date of enactment, including any pilot projects that use aggregation and inference, and inform the draft and final guidance under paragraphs (3) and (4) of subsection (h).

582(j)(2) CONTENT

"(2) CONTENT.—

582(j)(2)(A) IN GENERAL

"(A) IN GENERAL.—The Secretary shall ensure that the pilot projects under paragraph (1) reflect the diversity of the pharmaceutical distribution supply chain and that the pilot projects, when taken as a whole, include participants representative of every sector, including both large and small businesses.

582(j)(2)(B) PROJECT DESIGN

"(B) PROJECT DESIGN.—The pilot projects under paragraph (1) shall be designed to—

"(i) utilize the product identifier for tracing of a product, which may include verification of the product identifier of a product, including the use of aggregation and inference;

"(ii) improve the technical capabilities of each sector and subsector to comply with systems and processes needed to utilize the product identifiers to enhance tracing of a product;

"(iii) identify system attributes that are necessary to implement the requirements established under this section; and

"(iv) complete other activities as determined by the Secretary.

582(k) Sunset

"(k) Sunset.—The following requirements shall have no force or effect beginning on the date that is 10 years after the date of enactment of the Drug Supply Chain Security Act:

"(1) The provision and receipt of transaction history under this section.

"(2) The requirements set forth for returns under subsections (b)(4)(E), (c)(1)(B)(i), (d)(1)(C)(i), and (e)(4)(E).

"(3) The requirements set forth under subparagraphs (A)(v)(II) and (D) of subsection (c)(1), as applied to lot level information only.

"(l) RULE OF CONSTRUCTION.—The requirements set forth in subsections (g)(4), (i), and (j) shall not be construed as a condition, prohibition, or precedent for precluding or delaying the provisions becoming effective pursuant to subsection (g).

"(m) REQUESTS FOR INFORMATION.—On the date that is 10 years after the date of enactment of the Drug Supply Chain Security Act, the timeline for responses to requests for information from the Secretary, or other appropriate Federal or State official, as applicable, under subsections (b)(1)(B), (c)(1)(C), and (e)(1)(C) shall be not later than 24 hours after receiving the request from the Secretary or other appropriate Federal or State official, as applicable, or in such other reasonable time as determined by the Secretary based on the circumstances of the request.".

SEC. 204. NATIONAL STANDARDS FOR PRESCRIPTION DRUG WHOLESALE DISTRIBUTORS.

(a) Amendments.—

Amendments of Section 503(e)

(1) REQUIREMENT.—Section 503(e) (21 U.S.C. 353(e)) is amended by striking paragraphs (1), (2), and (3) and inserting the following:

503(e)(1) REQUIREMENT

"(1) REQUIREMENT.—Subject to section 583:

503(e)(1)(A) IN GENERAL

"(A) IN GENERAL.—No person may engage in wholesale distribution of a drug subject to subsection (b)(1) in any State unless such person—

"(i)(I) is licensed by the State from which the drug is distributed; or

"(II) if the State from which the drug is distributed has not established a licensure requirement, is licensed by the Secretary; and

"(ii) if the drug is distributed interstate, is licensed by the State into which the drug is distributed if the State into which the drug is distributed requires the licensure of a person that distributes drugs into the State.

503(e)(1)(B) STANDARDS

"(B) STANDARDS.—Each Federal and State license described in subparagraph (A) shall meet the standards, terms, and conditions established by the Secretary under section 583.

503(e)(2) REPORTING AND DATABASE

"(2) REPORTING AND DATABASE.—

503(e)(2)(A) REPORTING

"(A) REPORTING.—Beginning January 1, 2015, any person who owns or operates an establishment that engages in wholesale distribution shall—

"(i) report to the Secretary, on an annual basis pursuant to a schedule determined by the Secretary—

"(I) each State by which the person is licensed and the appropriate identification number of each such license; and

"(II) the name, address, and contact information of each facility at which, and all trade names under which, the person conducts business; and

"(ii) report to the Secretary within a reasonable period of time and in a reasonable manner, as determined by the Secretary, any significant disciplinary actions, such as the revocation or suspension of a wholesale distributor license, taken by a State or the Federal Government during the reporting period against the wholesale distributor.

503(e)(2)(B) DATABASE

"(B) DATABASE.—Not later than January 1, 2015, the Secretary shall establish a database of authorized wholesale distributors. Such database shall—

"(i) identify each authorized wholesale distributor by name, contact information, and each State where such wholesale distributor is appropriately licensed to engage in wholesale distribution;

"(ii) be available to the public on the Internet Web site of the Food and Drug Administration; and

"(iii) be regularly updated on a schedule determined by the Secretary.

503(e)(2)(C) COORDINATION

"(C) COORDINATION.—The Secretary shall establish a format and procedure for appropriate State officials to access the information provided pursuant to subparagraph (A) in a prompt and secure manner.

503(e)(2)(D) CONFIDENTIALITY

"(D) CONFIDENTIALITY.—Nothing in this paragraph shall be construed as authorizing the Secretary to disclose any information that is a trade secret or confidential information subject to section 552(b)(4) of title 5, United States Code, or section 1905 of title 18, United States Code.

503(e)(3) COSTS

"(3) COSTS.—

503(e)(3)(A) AUTHORIZED FEES OF SECRETARY

"(A) AUTHORIZED FEES OF SECRETARY.—If a State does not establish a licensing program for persons engaged in the wholesale distribution of a drug subject to subsection (b), the Secretary shall license a person engaged in wholesale distribution located in such State and may collect a reasonable fee in such amount necessary to reimburse the Secretary for costs associated with establishing and administering the licensure program and conducting periodic inspections under this section. The Secretary shall adjust fee rates as needed on an annual basis to generate only the amount of revenue needed to perform this service. Fees authorized under this paragraph shall be collected and available for obligation only to the extent and in the amount provided in advance in appropriations Acts. Such fees are authorized to remain available until expended. Such sums as may be necessary may be transferred from the Food and Drug Administration salaries and expenses appropriation account without fiscal year limitation to such appropriation account for salaries and expenses with such fiscal year limitation.

503(e)(3)(B) STATE LICENSING FEES

"(B) STATE LICENSING FEES.—Nothing in this Act shall prohibit States from collecting fees from wholesale distributors in connection with State licensing of such distributors.".

Amendments to Section 503(e) for Wholesale Distribution

(2) WHOLESALE DISTRIBUTION.—Section 503(e) (21 U.S.C. 353(e)), as amended by paragraph (1), is further amended by adding at the end the following:

"(4) For the purposes of this subsection and subsection (d), the term 'wholesale distribution' means the distribution of a drug subject to subsection (b) to a person other than a consumer or patient, or receipt of a drug subject to subsection (b) by a person other than the consumer or patient, but does not include—

"(A) intracompany distribution of any drug between members of an affiliate or within a manufacturer;

"(B) the distribution of a drug, or an offer to distribute a drug among hospitals or other health care entities which are under common control;

"(C) the distribution of a drug or an offer to distribute a drug for emergency medical reasons, including a public health emergency declaration pursuant to section 319 of the Public Health Service Act, except that, for purposes of this paragraph, a drug shortage not caused by a public health emergency shall not constitute an emergency medical reason;

"(D) the dispensing of a drug pursuant to a prescription executed in accordance with subsection (b)(1);

"(E) the distribution of minimal quantities of drug by a licensed retail pharmacy to a licensed practitioner for office use;

"(F) the distribution of a drug or an offer to distribute a drug by a charitable organization to a nonprofit affiliate of the organization to the extent otherwise permitted by law;

"(G) the purchase or other acquisition by a dispenser, hospital, or other health care entity of a drug for use by such dispenser, hospital, or other health care entity;

"(H) the distribution of a drug by the manufacturer of such drug;

"(I) the receipt or transfer of a drug by an authorized third-party logistics provider provided that such third-party logistics provider does not take ownership of the drug;

"(J) a common carrier that transports a drug, provided that the common carrier does not take ownership of the drug;

"(K) the distribution of a drug, or an offer to distribute a drug by an authorized repackager that has taken ownership or possession of the drug and repacks it in accordance with section 582(e);

"(L) salable drug returns when conducted by a dispenser;

"(M) the distribution of a collection of finished medical devices, which may include a product or biological product, assembled in kit form strictly for the convenience of the purchaser or user (referred to in this subparagraph as a 'medical convenience kit') if—

"(i) the medical convenience kit is assembled in an establishment that is registered with the Food and Drug Administration as a device manufacturer in accordance with section 510(b)(2);

"(ii) the medical convenience kit does not contain a controlled substance that appears in a schedule contained in the Comprehensive Drug Abuse Prevention and Control Act of 1970;

"(iii) in the case of a medical convenience kit that includes a product, the person that manufacturers the kit—

"(I) purchased such product directly from the pharmaceutical manufacturer or from a wholesale distributor that purchased the product directly from the pharmaceutical manufacturer; and

"(II) does not alter the primary container or label of the product as purchased from the manufacturer or wholesale distributor; and

"(iv) in the case of a medical convenience kit that includes a product, the product is—

"(I) an intravenous solution intended for the replenishment of fluids and electrolytes;

"(II) a product intended to maintain the equilibrium of water and minerals in the body;

"(III) a product intended for irrigation or reconstitution;

"(IV) an anesthetic;

"(V) an anticoagulant;

"(VI) a vasopressor; or

"(VII) a sympathomimetic;

"(N) the distribution of an intravenous drug that, by its formulation, is intended for the replenishment of fluids and electrolytes (such as sodium, chloride, and potassium) or calories (such as dextrose and amino acids);

"(O) the distribution of an intravenous drug used to maintain the equilibrium of water and minerals in the body, such as dialysis solutions;

"(P) the distribution of a drug that is intended for irrigation, or sterile water, whether intended for such purposes or for injection;

"(Q) the distribution of medical gas, as defined in section 575;

"(R) facilitating the distribution of a product by providing solely administrative services, including processing of orders and payments; or

"(S) the transfer of a product by a hospital or other health care entity, or by a wholesale distributor or manufacturer operating at the direction of the hospital or other health care entity, to a repackager described in section 581(16)(B) and registered under section 510 for the purpose of repackaging the drug for use by that hospital, or other health care entity and other health care entities that are under common control, if ownership of the drug remains with the hospital or other health care entity at all times.".

Amendments to Section 503(e) For Third-Party Logistics Providers

(3) THIRD-PARTY LOGISTICS PROVIDERS.—Section 503(e) (21 U.S.C. 353(e)), as amended by paragraph (2), is further amended by adding at the end the following:

503(e)(5) THIRD-PARTY LOGISTICS PROVIDERS

"(5) THIRD-PARTY LOGISTICS PROVIDERS.—Notwithstanding paragraphs (1) through (4), each entity that meets the definition of a third-party logistics provider under section 581(22) shall obtain a license as a third-party logistics provider as described in section 584(a) and is not required to obtain a license as a wholesale distributor if the entity never assumes an ownership interest in the product it handles.".

Amendments to Section 503(e) Affiliate

(4) AFFILIATE.—Section 503(e) (21 U.S.C. 353(e)), as amended by paragraph (3), is further amended by adding at the end the following:

503(e)(6) AFFILIATE

"(6) AFFILIATE.—For purposes of this subsection, the term 'affiliate' means a business entity that has a relationship with a second business entity if, directly or indirectly—

"(A) one business entity controls, or has the power to control, the other business entity; or

"(B) a third party controls, or has the power to control, both of the business entities.".

(5) STANDARDS.—Subchapter H of chapter V, as added by section 202, is amended by adding at the end the following:

SEC. 583. NATIONAL STANDARDS FOR PRESCRIPTION DRUG WHOLESALE DISTRIBUTORS.

"SEC. 583. NATIONAL STANDARDS FOR PRESCRIPTION DRUG WHOLESALE DISTRIBUTORS.

583(a) In General

"(a) IN GENERAL.—The Secretary shall, not later than 2 years after the date of enactment of the Drug Supply Chain Security Act, establish by regulation standards for the licensing of persons under section 503(e)(1) (as amended by the Drug Supply Chain Security Act), including the revocation, reissuance, and renewal of such license.

583(b) Content

"(b) CONTENT.—For the purpose of ensuring uniformity with respect to standards set forth in this section, the standards established under subsection (a) shall apply to all State and Federal licenses described under section 503(e)(1) (as amended by the Drug Supply Chain Security Act) and shall include standards for the following:

"(1) The storage and handling of prescription drugs, including facility requirements.

"(2) The establishment and maintenance of records of the distributions of such drugs.

"(3) The furnishing of a bond or other equivalent means of security, as follows:

"(A)(i) For the issuance or renewal of a wholesale distributor license, an applicant that is not a government owned and operated wholesale distributor shall submit a surety bond of $100,000 or other equivalent means of security acceptable to the State.

"(ii) For purposes of clause (i), the State or other applicable authority may accept a surety bond in the amount of $25,000 if the annual gross receipts of the previous tax year for the wholesaler is $10,000,000 or less.

"(B) If a wholesale distributor can provide evidence that it possesses the required bond in a State, the requirement for a bond in another State shall be waived.

"(4) Mandatory background checks and fingerprinting of facility managers or designated representatives.

"(5) The establishment and implementation of qualifications for key personnel.

"(6) The mandatory physical inspection of any facility to be used in wholesale distribution within a reasonable time frame from the initial application of the facility and to be conducted by the licensing authority or by the State, consistent with subsection (c).

"(7) In accordance with subsection (d), the prohibition of certain persons from receiving or maintaining licensure for wholesale distribution.

583(c) Inspections

"(c) INSPECTIONS.—To satisfy the inspection requirement under subsection (b)(6), the Federal or State licensing authority may conduct the inspection or may accept an inspection by the State in which the facility is located, or by a third-party accreditation or inspection service approved by the Secretary or the State licensing such wholesale distributor.

583(d) Prohibited Persons

"(d) PROHIBITED PERSONS.—The standards established under subsection (a) shall include requirements to prohibit a person from receiving or maintaining licensure for wholesale distribution if the person—

"(1) has been convicted of any felony for conduct relating to wholesale distribution, any felony violation of subsection (i) or (k) of section 301, or any felony violation of section 1365 of title 18, United States Code, relating to product tampering; or

"(2) has engaged in a pattern of violating the requirements of this section, or State requirements for licensure, that presents a threat of serious adverse health consequences or death to humans.

583(e) Requirements

"(e) REQUIREMENTS.—The Secretary, in promulgating any regulation pursuant to this section, shall, notwithstanding section 553 of title 5, United States Code—

"(1) issue a notice of proposed rulemaking that includes a copy of the proposed regulation;

"(2) provide a period of not less than 60 days for comments on the proposed regulation; and

"(3) provide that the final regulation take effect on the date that is 2 years after the date such final regulation is published.".

(b) AUTHORIZED DISTRIBUTORS OF RECORD.—Section 503(d) (21 U.S.C. 353(d)) is amended by adding at the end the following:

503(d)(4) AUTHORIZED DISTRIBUTORS OF RECORD

"(4) In this subsection, the term 'authorized distributors of record' means those distributors with whom a manufacturer has established an ongoing relationship to distribute such manufacturer's products.".

(c) EFFECTIVE DATE.—The amendments made by subsections (a) and (b) shall take effect on January 1, 2015.

SEC. 205. NATIONAL STANDARDS FOR THIRD-PARTY LOGISTICS PROVIDERS; UNIFORM NATIONAL POLICY.

Subchapter H of chapter V, as amended by section 204, is further amended by adding at the end the following:

"SEC. 584. NATIONAL STANDARDS FOR THIRD-PARTY LOGISTICS PROVIDERS.

584(a) Requirements

"(a) REQUIREMENTS.—No third-party logistics provider in any State may conduct activities in any State unless each facility of such third-party logistics provider—

"(1)(A) is licensed by the State from which the drug is distributed by the third-party logistics provider, in accordance with the regulations promulgated under subsection (d); or

"(B) if the State from which the drug distributed by the third-party logistics provider has not established a licensure requirement, is licensed by the Secretary, in accordance with the regulations promulgated under subsection (d); and

"(2) if the drug is distributed interstate, is licensed by the State into which the drug is distributed by the third-party logistics provider if such State licenses third-party logistics providers that distribute drugs into the State and the third-party logistics provider is not licensed by the Secretary as described in paragraph (1)(B).

584(b) Reporting

"(b) REPORTING.—Beginning 1 year after the date of enactment of the Drug Supply Chain Security Act, a facility of a third-party logistics provider shall report to the Secretary, on an annual basis pursuant to a schedule determined by the Secretary—

"(1) the State by which the facility is licensed and the appropriate identification number of such license; and

"(2) the name and address of the facility and all trade names under which such facility conducts business.

584(c) Costs

"(c) COSTS.—

584(c)(1) AUTHORIZED FEES OF SECRETARY

"(1) AUTHORIZED FEES OF SECRETARY.—If a State does not establish a licensing program for a third-party logistics provider, the Secretary shall license the third-party logistics provider located in such State and may collect a reasonable fee in such amount necessary to reimburse the Secretary for costs associated with establishing and administering the licensure program and conducting periodic inspections under this section. The Secretary shall adjust fee rates as needed on an annual basis to generate only the amount of revenue needed to perform this service. Fees authorized under this paragraph shall be collected and available for obligation only to the extent and in the amount provided in advance in appropriations Acts. Such fees are authorized to remain available until expended. Such sums as may be necessary may be transferred from the Food and Drug Administration salaries and expenses appropriation account without fiscal year limitation to such appropriation account for salaries and expenses with such fiscal year limitation.

584(c)(2) STATE LICENSING FEES

"(2) STATE LICENSING FEES.—

584(c)(2)(A) STATE ESTABLISHED PROGRAM

"(A) STATE ESTABLISHED PROGRAM.—Nothing in this Act shall prohibit a State that has established a program to license a third-party logistics provider from collecting fees from a third-party logistics provider for such a license.

584(c)(2)(B) NO STATE ESTABLISHED PROGRAM

"(B) NO STATE ESTABLISHED PROGRAM.—A State that does not establish a program to license a third-party logistics provider in accordance with this section shall be prohibited from collecting a State licensing fee from a third-party logistics provider.

"(d) REGULATIONS.—

584(d)(1) IN GENERAL

"(1) IN GENERAL.—Not later than 2 years after the date of enactment of the Drug Supply Chain Security Act, the Secretary shall issue regulations regarding the standards for licensing under subsection (a), including the revocation and reissuance of such license, to third-party logistics providers under this section.

584(d)(2) CONTENT

"(2) CONTENT.—Such regulations shall—

"(A) establish a process by which a third-party accreditation program approved by the Secretary shall, upon request by a third-party logistics provider, issue a license to each third-party logistics provider that meets the requirements set forth in this section;

"(B) establish a process by which the Secretary shall issue a license to each third-party logistics provider that meets the requirements set forth in this section if the Secretary is not able to approve a third-party accreditation program because no such program meets the Secretary's requirements necessary for approval of such a third-party accreditation program;

"(C) require that the entity complies with storage practices, as determined by the Secretary for such facility, including—

"(i) maintaining access to warehouse space of suitable size to facilitate safe operations, including a suitable area to quarantine suspect product;

"(ii) maintaining adequate security; and

"(iii) having written policies and procedures to—

"(I) address receipt, security, storage, inventory, shipment, and distribution of a product;

"(II) identify, record, and report confirmed losses or thefts in the United States;

"(III) correct errors and inaccuracies in inventories;

"(IV) provide support for manufacturer recalls;

"(V) prepare for, protect against, and address any reasonably foreseeable crisis that affects security or operation at the facility, such as a strike, fire, or flood;

"(VI) ensure that any expired product is segregated from other products and returned to the manufacturer or repackager or destroyed;

"(VII) maintain the capability to trace the receipt and outbound distribution of a product, and supplies and records of inventory; and

"(VIII) quarantine or destroy a suspect product if directed to do so by the respective manufacturer, wholesale distributor, dispenser, or an authorized government agency;

"(D) provide for periodic inspection by the licensing authority, as determined by the Secretary, of such facility warehouse space to ensure compliance with this section;

"(E) prohibit a facility from having as a manager or designated representative anyone convicted of any felony violation of subsection (i) or (k) of section 301 or any violation of section 1365 of title 18, United States Code relating to product tampering;

"(F) provide for mandatory background checks of a facility manager or a designated representative of such manager;

"(G) require a third-party logistics provider to provide the applicable licensing authority, upon a request by such authority, a list of all product manufacturers, wholesale distributors, and dispensers for whom the third-party logistics provider provides services at such facility; and

"(H) include procedures under which any third-party logistics provider license—

"(i) expires on the date that is 3 years after issuance of the license; and

"(ii) may be renewed for additional 3-year periods.

584(d)(3) PROCEDURE

"(3) PROCEDURE.—In promulgating the regulations under this subsection, the Secretary shall, notwithstanding section 553 of title 5, United States Code—

"(A) issue a notice of proposed rulemaking that includes a copy of the proposed regulation;

"(B) provide a period of not less than 60 days for comments on the proposed regulation; and

"(C) provide that the final regulation takes effect upon the expiration of 1 year after the date that such final regulation is issued.

"(e) VALIDITY.—A license issued under this section shall remain valid as long as such third-party logistics provider remains licensed consistent with this section. If the Secretary finds that the third-party accreditation program demonstrates that all applicable requirements for licensure under this section are met, the Secretary shall issue a license under this section to a third-party logistics provider receiving accreditation, pursuant to subsection (d)(2)(A).

"SEC. 585. UNIFORM NATIONAL POLICY.

585(a) Product Tracing And Other Requirements

"(a) PRODUCT TRACING AND OTHER REQUIREMENTS.—Beginning on the date of enactment of the Drug Supply Chain Security Act, no State or political subdivision of a State may establish or continue in effect any requirements for tracing products through the distribution system (including any requirements with respect to statements of distribution history, transaction history, transaction information, or transaction statement of a product as such product changes ownership in the supply chain, or verification, investigation, disposition, notification, or recordkeeping relating to such systems, including paper or electronic pedigree systems or for tracking and tracing drugs throughout the distribution system) which are inconsistent with, more stringent than, or in addition to, any requirements applicable under section 503(e) (as amended by such Act) or this subchapter (or regulations issued thereunder), or which are inconsistent with—

"(1) any waiver, exception, or exemption pursuant to section 581 or 582; or

"(2) any restrictions specified in section 582.

585(b) Wholesale Distributor And Third-Party Logistics Provider Standards

"(b) WHOLESALE DISTRIBUTOR AND THIRD-PARTY LOGISTICS PROVIDER STANDARDS.—

585(b)(1) IN GENERAL

"(1) IN GENERAL.—Beginning on the date of enactment of the Drug Supply Chain Security Act, no State or political subdivision of a State may establish or continue any standards, requirements, or regulations with respect to wholesale prescription drug distributor or third-party logistics provider licensure that are inconsistent with, less stringent than, directly related to, or covered by the standards and requirements applicable under section 503(e) (as amended by such Act), in the case of a wholesale distributor, or section 584, in the case of a third-party logistics provider.

585(b)(2) STATE REGULATION OF THIRD-PARTY LOGISTICS PROVIDERS

"(2) STATE REGULATION OF THIRD-PARTY LOGISTICS PROVIDERS.—No State shall regulate third-party logistics providers as wholesale distributors.

585(b)(3) ADMINISTRATION FEES

"(3) ADMINISTRATION FEES.—Notwithstanding paragraph (1), a State may administer fee collections for effectuating the wholesale drug distributor and third-party logistics provider licensure requirements under sections 503(e) (as amended by the Drug Supply Chain Security Act), 583, and 584.

585(b)(4) ENFORCEMENT, SUSPENSION, AND REVOCATION

"(4) ENFORCEMENT, SUSPENSION, AND REVOCATION.—Notwithstanding paragraph (1), a State—

"(A) may take administrative action, including fines, to enforce a requirement promulgated by the State in accordance with section 503(e) (as amended by the Drug Supply Chain Security Act) or this subchapter;

"(B) may provide for the suspension or revocation of licenses issued by the State for violations of the laws of such State;

"(C) upon conviction of violations of Federal, State, or local drug laws or regulations, may provide for fines, imprisonment, or civil penalties; and

"(D) may regulate activities of licensed entities in a manner that is consistent with product tracing requirements under section 582.

585(c) Exception

"(c) EXCEPTION.—Nothing in this section shall be construed to preempt State requirements related to the distribution of prescription drugs if such requirements are not related to product tracing as described in subsection (a) or wholesale distributor and third-party logistics provider licensure as described in subsection (b) applicable under section 503(e) (as amended by the Drug Supply Chain Security Act) or this subchapter (or regulations issued thereunder).".

SEC. 206. PENALTIES.

Amendments of Section 301(t)

(a) PROHIBITED ACT.—Section 301(t) (21 U.S.C. 331(t)), is amended—

(1) by striking "or" after "the requirements of section 503(d),"; and

(2) by inserting ", failure to comply with the requirements under section 582, the failure to comply with the requirements under section 584, as applicable," after "in violation of section 503(e)".

(b) MISBRANDING.—Section 502 (21 U.S.C. 352), as amended by section 103, is further amended by adding at the end the following:

"(cc) If it is a drug and it fails to bear the product identifier as required by section 582.".

SEC. 207. CONFORMING AMENDMENT.

Amendments of Section 303(b)(1)(D)

(a) IN GENERAL.—Section 303(b)(1)(D) (21 U.S.C. 333(b)(1)(D)) is amended by striking "503(e)(2)(A)" and inserting "503(e)(1)".

(b) EFFECTIVE DATE.—The amendment made by subsection (a) shall take effect on January 1, 2015.

SEC. 208. SAVINGS CLAUSE.

Except as provided in the amendments made by paragraphs (1), (2), and (3) of section 204(a) and by section 206(a), nothing in this title (including the amendments made by this title) shall be construed as altering any authority of the Secretary of Health and Human Services with respect to a drug subject to section 503(b)(1) of the Federal Food, Drug, and Cosmetic Act (21 U.S.C. 353(b)(1)) under any other provision of such Act or the Public Health Service Act (42 U.S.C. 201 et seq.).

Attest:

Speaker of the House of Representatives.

Attest:

Vice President of the United States and
President of the Senate.

Concept Index

References

[1] U.S. House of Representatives, H.R. 3204, "The Drug Quality and Security Act", enacted November 27, 2013. http://www.gpo.gov/fdsys/pkg/BILLS-113hr3204enr/pdf/BILLS-113hr3204enr.pdf

[2] Rodgers, Dirk, "It's Official, President Obama Signs H.R. 3204, DQSA, Into Law", RxTrace, November 27, 2013. http://www.rxtrace.com/2013/11/its-official-president-obama-signs-h-r-3204-dqsa-into-law.html/

[3] Buyer, Stephen, "H.R. 5839 (110th): Safeguarding America's Pharmaceuticals Act of 2008", GovTrack.us, 2008, https://www.govtrack.us/congress/bills/110/hr5839

[4] Pharmaceutical Distribution Security Alliance (PDSA), see http://pdsaonline.org/

[5] PDSA slides listing members, 2013, http://www.slideshare.net/SafeMedicines/pharmaceutical-distribution-security-alliance

[6] Florida State Statutes, The Florida Pedigree Papers Law, Section 01212, http://www.flsenate.gov/Laws/statutes/2012/0499.01212

[7] Healthcare Distribution Management Association (HDMA), "2013 HDMA Map of State Pedigree Legislation/Regulations", http://www.healthcaredistribution.org/meetings/seminars/2013tnt/pdfs/statepedigreemap.pdf

[8] Rodgers, Dirk, "California Pedigree Law" tagged articles on RxTrace.com, http://www.rxtrace.com/tag/california-pedigree-law/

[9] Rodgers, Dirk, "Estimated Rise In Serialized Drugs In The U.S. Supply Chain", RxTrace, August 3, 2010, http://www.rxtrace.com/2010/08/estimated-rise-in-serialized-drugs-in-the-u-s-supply-chain.html/

[10] Rodgers, Dirk, "RFID is DEAD...at Unit-Level in Pharma", RxTrace, April, 12, 2010, http://www.rxtrace.com/2010/04/rfid-is-dead-at-unit-level-in-pharma.html/

[11] Rodgers, Dirk, "Pharma Aggregation: How Companies Are

Achieving Perfection Today", RxTrace, March 26, 2012, http://www.rxtrace.com/2012/03/pharma-aggregation-how-companies-are-achieving-perfection-today.html/

[12] Rodgers, Dirk, "Inference in the Pharmaceutical Supply Chain", RxTrace, May 24, 2010, http://www.rxtrace.com/2010/05/inference-in-the-pharmaceutical-supply-chain.html/

[13] Rodgers, Dirk, "What If RxTEC Isn't Adopted?", RxTrace, March 19, 2012. http://www.rxtrace.com/2012/03/what-if-rxtec-isnt-adopted.html/

[14] FDA, "Prescription Drug User Fee Act (PDUFA)", http://www.fda.gov/forindustry/userfees/prescriptiondruguserfee/default.htm

[15] Rodgers, Dirk, "PDUFA Will Not Include RxTEC", RxTrace, June 18, 2012, http://www.rxtrace.com/2012/06/pdufa-will-not-include-rxtec.html/

[16] Rodgers, Dirk, "The Congressional Draft Proposal to Improve Drug Distribution Security", RxTrace, October, 25, 2012, http://www.rxtrace.com/2012/10/the-congressional-draft-proposal-to-improve-drug-distribution-security.html/

[17] Rodgers, Dirk, "Congressional Legislation Development: Mad Libs Edition!", RxTrace, October, 29, 2012, http://www.rxtrace.com/2012/10/congressional-legislation-development-mad-libs-edition.html/

[18] Rodgers, Dirk, "More Thoughts On The Congressional Discussion Draft", RxTrace, November 1, 2012, http://www.rxtrace.com/2012/11/more-thoughts-on-the-congressional-discussion-draft.html/

[19] Rodgers, Dirk, "The New Pharma Track & Trace Discussion Draft In The Senate", RxTrace, April 22, 2013, http://www.rxtrace.com/2013/04/the-new-pharma-track-trace-discussion-draft-in-the-senate.html/

[20] Rodgers, Dirk, "The House Hearing on 'Securing Our Nation's Prescription Drug Supply Chain'", RxTrace, April 30, 2013, http://www.rxtrace.com/2013/04/the-house-hearing-on-securing-our-nations-prescription-drug-supply-chain.html/

[21] Rodgers, Dirk, "InBrief: A Track And Trace Bill Has Made It To The House Floor", RxTrace, May 15, 2013,

http://www.rxtrace.com/2013/05/inbrief-a-track-and-trace-bill-has-made-it-to-the-house-floor.html/

[22] Rodgers, Dirk, "InBrief: A Track & Trace bill Has Made It To The Senate Floor", RxTrace, May 22, 2013, http://www.rxtrace.com/2013/05/inbrief-a-track-trace-bill-has-made-it-to-the-senate-floor.html/

[23] Rodgers, Dirk, "InBrief: Important New Bicameral Draft Of A Pharma Supply Chain Security Bill", RxTrace, September 26, 2013, http://www.rxtrace.com/2013/09/inbrief-important-new-bicameral-draft-of-a-pharma-supply-chain-security-bill.html/

[24] Rodgers, Dirk, "Waiting For The Senate To Act On A Track & Trace Bill, Again", RxTrace, September 30, 2013, http://www.rxtrace.com/2013/09/waiting-for-the-senate-to-act-on-a-track-trace-bill-again.html/

[25] Rodgers, Dirk, "U.S. Senate Passes H.R. 3204 With A Voice Vote", RxTrace, November 18, 2013, http://www.rxtrace.com/2013/11/u-s-senate-passes-h-r-3204-with-a-voice-vote.html/

[26] FDA, "Federal Food, Drug, and Cosmetic Act (FD&C Act)", FDA.gov, accessed on 12-13-13, http://www.fda.gov/regulatoryinformation/legislation/federalfooddrugandcosmeticactFDCAct/default.htm

[27] FDA, "FD&C Act Chapter V: Drugs and Devices", FDA.gov, a cross reference of FD&C section numbers with the matching U.S. Code section numbers. http://www.fda.gov/RegulatoryInformation/Legislation/FederalFoodDrugandCosmeticActFDCAct/FDCActChapterVDrugsandDevices/default.htm#Part_A

[28] Rodgers, Dirk "Don't Skip The DQSA Definition of Terms Section", RxTrace, January 13, 2014, http://www.rxtrace.com/2014/01/dont-skip-the-dqsa-definition-of-terms-section.html/

[29] FDA, "Drug Supply Chain Security Act (DSCSA) Implementation Plan", FDA website, accessed March, 7, 2014, http://www.fda.gov/Drugs/DrugSafety/DrugIntegrityandSupplyChainSecurity/DrugSupplyChainSecurityAct/ucm382022.htm

[30] FDA, "New Drug Application (NDA)", FDA website, accessed March 7, 2014, http://www.fda.gov/drugs/developmentapprovalproces

s/howdrugsaredevelopedandapproved/approvalapplicat
ions/newdrugapplicationnda/default.htm

[31] FDA, "Abbreviated New Drug Application (ANDA): Generics", FDA website, accessed March 7, 2014, http://www.fda.gov/drugs/developmentapprovalproces s/howdrugsaredevelopedandapproved/approvalapplicat ions/abbreviatednewdrugapplicationandagenerics/defau lt.htm

[32] FDA, "Guidance for Industry, Standards for Securing the Drug Supply Chain - Standardized Numerical Identification for Prescription Drug Packages", FDA.gov, March, 2010, http://www.fda.gov/downloads/RegulatoryInformation /Guidances/UCM206075.pdf

[33] Rodgers, Dirk, "FDA Aligns with GS1 SGTIN For SNDC", RxTrace, March, 2010, http://www.rxtrace.com/2010/03/fda-aligns-with-gs1-sgtin-for-sndc.html/

[34] Rodgers, Dirk, "Anatomy Of The National Drug Code", RxTrace, January 3, 2012, http://www.rxtrace.com/2012/01/anatomy-of-the-national-drug-code.html/

[35] FDA, "Guidance for Industry, Standards for Securing the Drug Supply Chain - Standardized Numerical Identification for Prescription Drug Packages", FDA.gov, March, 2010, http://www.fda.gov/downloads/RegulatoryInformation /Guidances/UCM206075.pdf

[36] FDA, "Definition of Primary Mode of Action of a Combination Product", FDA.gov, August 25, 2005, http://www.gpo.gov/fdsys/pkg/FR-2005-08-25/pdf/05-16527.pdf

[37] Rodgers, Dirk, "Correction: Your Drug or Biologic Combination Product Is Probably NOT Exempt From The DQSA", RxTrace, December, 16, 2013, http://www.rxtrace.com/2013/12/correction-your-drug-or-biologic-combination-product-is-probably-not-exempt-from-the-dqsa.html/

[38] U.S. Congress, "Food and Drug Administration Amendments Act (FDAAA) of 2007", FDA.gov, September 27, 2007, http://www.fda.gov/regulatoryinformation/legislation/f ederalfooddrugandcosmeticactfdcact/significantamend mentstothefdcact/foodanddrugadministrationamendme

ntsactof2007/default.htm

[39] GS1 website, http://www.gs1.org/healthcare

[40] FDA, "Standards for Securing the Drug Supply Chain - Standardized Numerical Identification for Prescription Drug Packages", FDA.gov, March 2010, http://www.fda.gov/regulatoryinformation/guidances/ucm125505.htm

[41] FDA, "Changes to be described in an annual report (minor changes)", FDA.gov, Revised as of April 1, 2013, http://www.accessdata.fda.gov/scripts/cdrh/cfdocs/cfcfr/CFRSearch.cfm?fr=314.70

[42] Wikipedia, "Matrix (2D) barcodes", Wikipedia, accessed on December 18, 2013, http://en.wikipedia.org/wiki/Barcode#Matrix_.282D.29_barcodes

[43] Wikipedia, "Linear barcodes", Wikipedia, accessed on December 18, 2013, http://en.wikipedia.org/wiki/Barcode#Linear_barcodes

[44] Wikipedia, "Automatic identification and data capture", Wikipedia, accessed on March 3, 2014, http://en.wikipedia.org/wiki/Automatic_identification_and_data_capture

[45] Rodgers, Dirk, "Should Regulations Dictate Technology?", RxTrace, November 28, 2011, http://www.rxtrace.com/2011/11/should-regulations-dictate-technology.html/

[46] Rodgers, Dirk, "Updated HDMA Bar Code Guidance: A Must Read", RxTrace, January 9, 2012, http://www.rxtrace.com/2012/01/updated-hdma-bar-code-guidance-a-must-read.html/

[47] GS1 Healthcare US, "Implementation Resources" web page, accessed on December 18, 2013, http://www.gs1us.org/industries/healthcare/tools-and-resources/implementation-resources

[48] HDMA website, Healthcare Distribution Management Association, accessed on December 18, 2013, http://www.hdmanet.org/

[49] GS1 Healthcare US website, accessed December 22, 2013, http://www.gs1us.org/industries/healthcare

[50] HDMA website, accessed December 22, 2013, http://www.hdmanet.org/

[51] FDA, "Unique Device Identification System Final Rule", FDA

website, September 23, 2013,
http://www.fda.gov/medicaldevices/resourcesforyou/industry/ucm369881.htm

[52] FDA Office of Combination Products web page, accessed December 23, 2013,
http://www.fda.gov/AboutFDA/CentersOffices/OfficeofMedicalProductsandTobacco/OfficeofScienceandHealthCoordination/ucm2018184.htm

[53] GS1 Healthcare, "Healthcare Supply Chain Traceability" white paper, 2010,
http://www.gs1.org/docs/gsmp/traceability/20101025_Traceability_White_Paper_final.pdf

[54] GS1 Healthcare, "Healthcare Supply Chain Traceability" white paper, 2010,
http://www.gs1.org/docs/gsmp/traceability/20101025_Traceability_White_Paper_final.pdf

[55] FDA, "Unique Device Identification System Final Rule", FDA website, September 23, 2013,
http://www.fda.gov/medicaldevices/resourcesforyou/industry/ucm369881.htm

[56] FDA Office of Combination Products web page, accessed December 23, 2013,
http://www.fda.gov/AboutFDA/CentersOffices/OfficeofMedicalProductsandTobacco/OfficeofScienceandHealthCoordination/ucm2018184.htm

[57] GS1 Healthcare, "Healthcare Supply Chain Traceability" white paper, 2010,
http://www.gs1.org/docs/gsmp/traceability/20101025_Traceability_White_Paper_final.pdf

[58] Rodgers, Dirk, "Pharma Aggregation: How Companies Are Achieving Perfection Today", RxTrace, March 26, 2013,
https://www.rxtrace.com/2012/03/pharma-aggregation-how-companies-are-achieving-perfection-today.html/

[59] Rodgers, Dirk, "DQSA: Will U.S. Pharma Distributors Mandate Aggregation Data In Phase 1?", RxTrace, November 22, 2013,
https://www.rxtrace.com/2013/11/dqsa-will-u-s-pharma-distributors-mandate-aggregation-data-in-phase-1.html/

[60] Rodgers, Dirk, "Inference in the Pharmaceutical Supply Chain", RxTrace, May 24, 2010,

https://www.rxtrace.com/2010/05/inference-in-the-pharmaceutical-supply-chain.html/

[61] Rodgers, Dirk, "Will The Pharma Supply Chain Be Able To Use Inference? Maybe Not!", RxTrace, June 7, 2010, https://www.rxtrace.com/2010/06/will-the-pharma-supply-chain-be-able-to-use-inference-maybe-not.html/

[62] Rodgers, Dirk, "How Should Inference Work?", RxTrace, January 23, 2013, https://www.rxtrace.com/2013/01/how-should-inference-work.html/

[63] Rodgers, Dirk, California's Draft Inference Regulation", RxTrace, April 23, 2013, https://www.rxtrace.com/2013/04/californias-draft-inference-regulation.html/

[64] GS1, "EPCIS - EPC Information Services Standard", GS1 website, accessed February 10, 2014, http://www.gs1.org/gsmp/kc/epcglobal/epcis

[65] U.S. Congress, Section 505D of the Food, Drug and Cosmetics Act, Section 355e of the United Stated Code, U.S. Government Printing Office website, Accessed February 11, 2014, http://www.gpo.gov/fdsys/pkg/USCODE-2010-title21/html/USCODE-2010-title21-chap9-subchapV-partA-sec355e.htm

[66] U.S. Congress, "FDA Amendments Act of 2007", FDA website, Accessed February 11, 2014, http://www.fda.gov/regulatoryinformation/legislation/federalfooddrugandcosmeticactfdcact/significantamendmentstothefdcact/foodanddrugadministrationamendmentsactof2007/default.htm

[67] FDA, "The Prescription Drug Marketing Act, Report to Congress", FDA website, June 2001, http://www.fda.gov/downloads/regulatoryinformation/legislation/federalfooddrugandcosmeticactfdcact/significantamendmentstothefdcact/prescriptiondrugmarketingactof1987/ucm203186.pdf

[68] Department of Health and Human Services -- FDA, "Prescription Drug Marketing Act of 1987; Prescription Drug Amendments of 1992; Policies, Requirements, and Administrative Procedures—Final Rule", Federal Register, December 3, 1999, http://www.gpo.gov/fdsys/pkg/FR-1999-12-03/pdf/99-30954.pdf

[69] FDANews, contained within "Track and Trace: Understanding Requirements for Global the Drug Supply Chain Security Act", FDANews, December 2014

[70] FDA, "DSCSA Standards for the Interoperable Exchange of Information for Tracing of Certain Human, Finished, Prescription Drugs: How to Exchange Product Tracing Information, Guidance for Industry", FDA Website, November 2014, http://www.fda.gov/downloads/Drugs/GuidanceCompli anceRegulatoryInformation/Guidances/UCM424895.pdf

[71] Rodgers, Dirk, "The 2014 FDA DSCSA Workshop", RxTrace, May 12, 2014, https://www.rxtrace.com/2014/05/the-2014-fda-dscsa-workshop.html/

[72] FDA, "Wholesale Distributor and Third-Party Logistics Providers Reporting", FDA website, accessed on January 20, 2016, http://www.fda.gov/drugs/drugsafety/drugintegrityand supplychainsecurity/drugsupplychainsecurityact/ucm423 749.htm

[73] Rodgers, Dirk, "The New Draft Guidance On The Effect of Section 585 of the FD&C Imposed By The DSCSA", RxTrace, October 10, 2014, https://www.rxtrace.com/2014/10/the-new-draft-guidance-on-the-effect-of-section-585-of-the-fdc-imposed-by-the-dscsa.html/

[74] FDA, "The Effect of Section 585 of the FD&C Act on Drug Product Tracing and Wholesale Drug Distributor and Third-Party Logistics Provider Licensing Standards and Requirements: Questions and Answers", FDA Website, October 8, 2014, http://www.fda.gov/downloads/Drugs/GuidanceCompli anceRegulatoryInformation/Guidances/UCM417564.pdf

[75] Rodgers, Dirk, "The Differences Between The DSCSA, FDA Rules and Guidance", RxTrace, May 21, 2014, https://www.rxtrace.com/2014/05/the-differences-between-the-dscsa-fda-rules-and-guidance.html/

[76] Rodgers, Dirk, "Preemption: What Does It Mean?", RxTrace, December 2, 2013, https://www.rxtrace.com/2013/12/preemption-what-does-it-mean.html/

[77] Rodgers, Dirk, "FDA Posts Guidance For Wholesale Distributor and 3PL Annual Reporting", December 10,

2014, https://www.rxtrace.com/2014/12/fda-posts-guidance-for-wholesale-distributor-and-3pl-annual-reporting.html/

[78] FDA, "Drug Supply Chain Security Act Implementation--Annual Reporting by Prescription Drug Wholesale Distributors and Third-Party Logistics Providers", FDA Website, December 9, 2014, http://www.fda.gov/downloads/Drugs/GuidanceCompliance RegulatoryInformation/Guidances/UCM426126.pdf

[79] FDA, "Wholesale Distributor and Third-Party Logistics Providers Reporting", FDA website, Accessed December 29, 2015, http://www.accessdata.fda.gov/scripts/cder/wdd3plreporting/index.cfm

[80] Rodgers, Dirk, "FDA Postpones Enforcement of DSCSA Transaction Data Exchange Until May 1", RxTrace, December 26, 2014, https://www.rxtrace.com/2014/12/fda-postpones-enforcement-of-dscsa-transaction-data-exchange-until-may-1.html/

[81] Rodgers, Dirk, "FDA Publishes New Guidance Delaying Dispenser 3T Requirements Until November 1, 2015", RxTrace, June 30, 2015, https://www.rxtrace.com/2015/06/fda-publishes-new-guidance-delaying-dispenser-3t-requirements-until-november-1-2015.html/

[82] Rodgers, Dirk, "FDA Extends Dispenser Delay in DSCSA Enforcement", RxTrace, June 30, 2015, https://www.rxtrace.com/2015/10/fda-extends-dispenser-delay-in-dscsa-enforcement.html/

[83] Rodgers, Dirk, "Pay No Attention To The Enforcement Delay Unless You Are A Dispenser", RxTrace, November 2, 2015, https://www.rxtrace.com/2015/11/pay-no-attention-to-the-enforcement-delay-unless-you-are-a-dispenser.html/

[84] Rodgers, Dirk, "Will The DSCSA Cause Drug Shortages After January 1?", RxTrace, November 17, 2014, https://www.rxtrace.com/2014/11/will-the-dscsa-cause-drug-shortages-after-january-1.html/

[85] Rodgers, Dirk, "Will The FDA Delay The DSCSA?", RxTrace, September 29, 2014, https://www.rxtrace.com/2014/09/will-the-fda-delay-the-dscsa.html/

[86] Rodgers, Dirk, "Dispensers Make Last Minute Appeal for Delay in DSCSA Deadline", RxTrace, June 29, 2015, https://www.rxtrace.com/2015/06/dispensers-make-last-minute-appeal-for-delay-in-dscsa-deadline.html/

[87] Rodgers, Dirk, "Who Is Being Harmed By Four Overdue FDA DSCSA Guidances?", RxTrace, January 18, 2016, https://www.rxtrace.com/2016/01/who-is-being-harmed-by-four-overdue-fda-dscsa-guidances.html/

[88] Rodgers, Dirk, "FDA DSCSA Deadline Passes Quietly", RxTrace, November 30, 2015, https://www.rxtrace.com/2015/11/fda-dscsa-deadline-passes-quietly.html/

[89] Rodgers, Dirk, "DSCSA: Transaction Information", RxTrace, March 17, 2014, https://www.rxtrace.com/2014/03/dscsa-transaction-information.html/

[90] FDA, "DSCSA Standards for the Interoperable Exchange of Information for Tracing of Certain Human, Finished, Prescription Drugs: How to Exchange Product Tracing Information, Guidance for Industry", FDA Website, November 2014, http://www.fda.gov/downloads/Drugs/GuidanceCompliananceRegulatoryInformation/Guidances/UCM424895.pdf

[91] HDMA, "EDI Guideline For 856 Advance Ship Notice to Support Implementation of DSCSA (July2014)", HDMA website, revised July 2014, http://www.hdmanet.org/publications/edi-guidelines-for-856-advance-ship-notice

[92] GS1, "Global Location Number (GLN)", GS1 website, accessed December 30, 2015, http://www.gs1.org/gln

[93] Dun & Bradstreet, "The D-U-N-S® Number", Dun & Bradstreet website, accessed December 30, 2015, http://www.dnb.com/get-a-duns-number.html

[94] Rodgers, Dirk, "FDA Chooses DUNS For Unique Facility Identifier", RxTrace, September 9, 2013, https://www.rxtrace.com/2013/09/fda-chooses-duns-for-unique-facility-identifier.html/

[95] Rodgers, Dirk, "Pedigree Will Change FOB Terms", RxTrace, October 19, 2010, https://www.rxtrace.com/2010/10/pedigree-changes-fob.html/

[96] Rodgers, Dirk, "DQSA: How Should Transaction Data Be

Exchanged?", RxTrace, February 20, 2014,
https://www.rxtrace.com/2014/02/dqsa-how-should-transaction-data-be-exchanged.html/

[97] FDA, Webinar: "CDER Small Business and Industry Assistance (CDER SBIA) Webinar on The Drug Supply Chain Security Act (Title II of the Drug Quality and Security Act): Overview & Implementation", FDA website, March 12, 2014,
http://www.fda.gov/Drugs/DevelopmentApprovalProcess/SmallBusinessAssistance/ucm388150.htm

[98] Rodgers, Dirk, "The 2014 FDA DSCSA Workshop", RxTrace, May 12, 2014, https://www.rxtrace.com/2014/05/the-2014-fda-dscsa-workshop.html/

[99] Rodgers, Dirk, "DSCSA: Transaction History", RxTrace, March 24, 2024,
https://www.rxtrace.com/2014/03/dscsa-transaction-history.html/

[100] FDA, "DSCSA Standards for the Interoperable Exchange of Information for Tracing of Certain Human, Finished, Prescription Drugs: How to Exchange Product Tracing Information, Guidance for Industry", FDA Website, November 2014,
http://www.fda.gov/downloads/Drugs/GuidanceComplianceRegulatoryInformation/Guidances/UCM424895.pdf

[101] Rodgers, Dirk, "Pedigree Models and Supply Chain Master Data", RxTrace, October 19, 2009,
https://www.rxtrace.com/2009/10/pedigree-models-and-supply-chain-master-data.html/

[102] Rodgers, Dirk, "DSCSA: Transaction Statement", RxTrace, March 31, 2014,
https://www.rxtrace.com/2014/03/dscsa-transaction-statement.html/

[103] FDA, "DSCSA Standards for the Interoperable Exchange of Information for Tracing of Certain Human, Finished, Prescription Drugs: How to Exchange Product Tracing Information, Guidance for Industry", FDA Website, November 2014,
http://www.fda.gov/downloads/Drugs/GuidanceComplianceRegulatoryInformation/Guidances/UCM424895.pdf

[104] FDA, Docket for "DSCSA Standards for the Interoperable Exchange of Information for Tracing of Certain Human, Finished, Prescription Drugs: How to Exchange Product

Tracing Information", Regulations.gov website, Accessed December 30, 2015, The docket is closed but you can view the comments submitted by others.
http://www.regulations.gov/#!docketDetail;rpp=100;so=DESC;sb=docId;po=0;D=FDA-2014-D-1981

[105] FDA, Webinar: "CDER Small Business and Industry Assistance (CDER SBIA) Webinar on The Drug Supply Chain Security Act (Title II of the Drug Quality and Security Act): Overview & Implementation", FDA website, March 12, 2014,
http://www.fda.gov/Drugs/DevelopmentApprovalProcess/SmallBusinessAssistance/ucm388150.htm

[106] HDMA, Webinar: "FDA Perspectives on Implementation of the Drug Supply Chain Security Act", HDMA website, April 7, 2014,
https://www.healthcaredistribution.org/publications/webinar-fda-perspectives-on-implmentation-of-the-dscsa

[107] Rodgers, Dirk, "Reliance on Trust in the U.S. Pharma Supply Chain", RxTrace, April 26, 2011,
https://www.rxtrace.com/2011/04/reliance-on-trust-in-the-u-s-pharma-supply-chain.html/

[108] FDA, "Drug Supply Chain Security Act Implementation: Identification of Suspect Product and Notification", FDA website, June 6, 2014,
http://www.fda.gov/downloads/Drugs/GuidanceComplianceRegulatoryInformation/Guidances/UCM400470.pdf

[109] Rodgers, Dirk, "Who Is A DSCSA Dispenser?", RxTrace, September 15, 2014,
https://www.rxtrace.com/2014/09/who-is-a-dscsa-dispenser.html/

[110] Rodgers, Dirk, "Don't Skip The DQSA Definition of Terms Section", RxTrace, January 13, 2014,
https://www.rxtrace.com/2014/01/dont-skip-the-dqsa-definition-of-terms-section.html/

[111] Rodgers, Dirk, "The FDA's Draft Guidance on Suspect Product, and Farewell Columbus", RxTrace, June 23, 2014,
https://www.rxtrace.com/2014/06/the-fdas-draft-guidance-on-suspect-product-and-farewell-columbus.html/

[112] Rodgers, Dirk, "Who Is A DSCSA Repackager?", RxTrace, November 3, 2014,
https://www.rxtrace.com/2014/11/who-is-a-dscsa-

repackager.html/
[113] Rodgers, Dirk, "Is Your Drug Exempt From The Federal Drug Supply Chain Security Act?", RxTrace, April 7, 2014, https://www.rxtrace.com/2014/04/is-your-drug-exempt-from-the-federal-drug-supply-chain-security-act.html/
[114] Rodgers, Dirk, "3PL Operation Under The DSCSA", RxTrace, June 1, 2015, https://www.rxtrace.com/2015/06/3pl-operation-under-the-dscsa.html/
[115] NABP, "VAWD", NABP website, accessed December 30, 2015, http://www.nabp.net/programs/accreditation/vawd
[116] Rodgers, Dirk, "DSCSA 'Serial Numbers'", RxTrace, March 9, 2015, https://www.rxtrace.com/2015/03/dscsa-serial-numbers.html/
[117] FDA, "Guidance for Industry Standards for Securing the Drug Supply Chain – Standardized Numerical Identification for
Prescription Drug Packages", FDA website, accessed December 30, 2015, http://www.fda.gov/downloads/RegulatoryInformation/Guidances/UCM206075.pdf
[118] Rodgers, Dirk, "FDA Aligns with GS1 SGTIN For SNDC", RxTrace, March 29, 2010, https://www.rxtrace.com/2010/03/fda-aligns-with-gs1-sgtin-for-sndc.html/
[119] GS1, "Global Trade Item Number (GTIN)", GS1 website, accessed December 30, 2015, http://www.gs1.org/gtin
[120] Rodgers, Dirk, "Depicting An NDC Within A GTIN", RxTrace, January 23, 2012, https://www.rxtrace.com/2012/01/depicting-an-ndc-within-a-gtin.html/
[121] GS1, "GS1 General Specifications", GS1 website, accessed December 30, 2015, http://www.gs1.org/barcodes-epcrfid-id-keys/gs1-general-specifications
[122] GS1, "GS1 DataMatrix Guideline", GS1, July 2015, http://www.gs1.org/docs/barcodes/GS1_DataMatrix_Guideline.pdf
[123] HDMA, "HDMA Guidelines for Bar Coding in the Pharmaceutical Supply Chain", HDMA, 2011, http://www.hdmanet.org/publications/hdma-guidelines-for-bar-coding-in-the-pharmaceutical-supply-

chain

124 Rodgers, Dirk, "Updated HDMA Bar Code Guidance: A Must Read", RxTrace, January 9, 2012, https://www.rxtrace.com/2012/01/updated-hdma-bar-code-guidance-a-must-read.html/

125 Traub, Ken, "Randomization—An Interview with Ken Traub—Part 1: GS1 Serial Number Considerations", RxTrace, April 21, 2014, https://www.rxtrace.com/2014/04/randomization-an-interview-with-ken-traub-part-1-gs1-serial-number-considerations.html/

126 Rodgers, Dirk, "Identification Of Pharma Cases In The U.S.", RxTrace, April 27, 2015, https://www.rxtrace.com/2015/04/u-s-pharma-case-identification.html/

127 GS1 US, "An Introduction to the Serial Shipping Container Code (SSCC)", GS1 US website, accessed December 30, 2015, http://www.gs1us.org/DesktopModules/Bring2mind/DMX/Download.aspx?command=core_download&entryid=364&language=en-US&PortalId=0&TabId=785

128 HDMA, "HDMA Guidelines for Bar Coding in the Pharmaceutical Supply Chain", HDMA, 2011, http://www.hdmanet.org/publications/hdma-guidelines-for-bar-coding-in-the-pharmaceutical-supply-chain

129 DEA, "Controlled Substances Security Manual", DEA website, accessed December 30, 2015, http://deadiversion.usdoj.gov/pubs/manuals/sec/index.html

130 Rodgers, Dirk, "FDA Aligns with GS1 SGTIN For SNDC", RxTrace, March 29, 2010, https://www.rxtrace.com/2010/03/fda-aligns-with-gs1-sgtin-for-sndc.html/

131 Rodgers, Dirk, "HDMA Has Updated Their EDI ASN Guidance For DSCSA, Again", RxTrace, July 22, 2014, https://www.rxtrace.com/2014/07/hdma-has-updated-their-edi-asn-guidance-for-dscsa-again.html/

132 Rodgers, Dirk, "The DSCSA Product Identifier On Drug Packages", RxTrace, May 4, 2015, https://www.rxtrace.com/2015/05/the-dscsa-product-identifier-on-drug-packages.html/

[133] Rodgers, Dirk, "Should Regulations Dictate Technology?", RxTrace, November 28, 2011, https://www.rxtrace.com/2011/11/should-regulations-dictate-technology.html/

[134] GS1 US, "Implementation Guideline - Applying GS1 Standards to U.S. Pharmaceutical Supply Chain Business Processes to support DSCSA, vsn 1.1", GS1 US website, accessed December 30, 2015, http://www.gs1us.org/industries/healthcare/gs1-healthcare-us-initiative/dscsa/implementation-guide

[135] GS1, "Global Trade Item Number (GTIN)", GS1 website, accessed December 30, 2015, http://www.gs1.org/gtin

[136] Rodgers, Dirk, "What The UDI Date Format Says About FDA's Direction", RxTrace, September 16, 2013, https://www.rxtrace.com/2013/09/what-the-udi-date-format-says-about-fdas-direction.html/

[137] Rodgers, Dirk, "InBrief: 'The Smallest Individual Saleable Unit' In The DSCSA", RxTrace, June 8, 2015, https://www.rxtrace.com/2015/06/inbrief-the-smallest-individual-saleable-unit-in-the-dscsa.html/

[138] Rodgers, Dirk, "FDA Aligns with GS1 SGTIN For SNDC", RxTrace, March 29, 2010, https://www.rxtrace.com/2010/03/fda-aligns-with-gs1-sgtin-for-sndc.html/

[139] Rodgers, Dirk, "Anatomy Of The National Drug Code", RxTrace, January 3, 2012, https://www.rxtrace.com/2012/01/anatomy-of-the-national-drug-code.html/

[140] GS1, "Healthcare GTIN Allocation Rules", GS1 website, accessed December 30, 2015, http://www.gs1.org/1/gtinrules/index.php/p=static/t=healthcare

[141] Rodgers, Dirk, "Anatomy Of An FDA SNI", RxTrace, January 30, 2012, https://www.rxtrace.com/2012/01/anatomy-of-an-fda-sni.html/

[142] Rodgers, Dirk, "DSCSA: A Closer Look At The Six-Year Record-Keeping Requirement", RxTrace, July 14, 2014, https://www.rxtrace.com/2014/07/dscsa-a-closer-look-at-the-six-year-record-keeping-requirement.html/

[143] Rodgers, Dirk, "The FDA's Draft Guidance on Suspect Product, and Farewell Columbus", RxTrace, June 23, 2014, https://www.rxtrace.com/2014/06/the-fdas-draft-

guidance-on-suspect-product-and-farewell-columbus.html/

[144] Rodgers, Dirk, "DQSA: How Should Transaction Data Be Exchanged?", RxTrace, February 20, 2014, https://www.rxtrace.com/2014/02/dqsa-how-should-transaction-data-be-exchanged.html/

[145] Rodgers, Dirk, "DQSA: Getting To Electronic Transaction Data Exchange", RxTrace, November 21, 2013, https://www.rxtrace.com/2013/11/dqsa-getting-to-electronic-transaction-data-exchange.html/

[146] Rodgers, Dirk, "A Closer Look At Web Portals for DSCSA Transaction Data Exchange", RxTrace, December 29, 2014, https://www.rxtrace.com/2014/12/a-closer-look-at-web-portals-for-dscsa-transaction-data-exchange.html/

[147] FDA, "DSCSA Standards for the Interoperable Exchange of Information for Tracing of Certain Human, Finished, Prescription Drugs: How to Exchange Product Tracing Information", FDA website, accessed December 30, 2015, http://www.fda.gov/downloads/Drugs/GuidanceCompli anceRegulatoryInformation/Guidances/UCM424895.pdf

[148] Rodgers, Dirk, "Vendor Managed Inventory Under the DSCSA", RxTrace, May 26, 2015, https://www.rxtrace.com/2015/05/vendor-managed-inventory-under-the-dscsa.html/

[149] Rodgers, Dirk, "Correction: Your Drug or Biologic Combination Product Is Probably NOT Exempt From The DQSA", RxTrace, December 16, 2013, https://www.rxtrace.com/2013/12/correction-your-drug-or-biologic-combination-product-is-probably-not-exempt-from-the-dqsa.html/

[150] Rodgers, Dirk, "Drug-Device Combo Products Under State And Federal Pedigree Laws", RxTrace, November 11, 2013, https://www.rxtrace.com/2013/11/drug-device-combo-products-under-state-and-federal-pedigree-laws.html/

[151] FDA, "CFR - Code of Federal Regulations Title 21", FDA website, accessed December 31, 2015, http://www.accessdata.fda.gov/scripts/cdrh/cfdocs/cfcf r/CFRSearch.cfm?fr=3.2

[152] Rodgers, Dirk, "Preemption: What Does It Mean?", RxTrace, December 3, 2013, https://www.rxtrace.com/2013/12/preemption-what-does-it-mean.html/

[153] FDA, "FD&C Act Chapter V: Drugs and Devices", FDA website, accessed December 31, 2015, http://www.fda.gov/RegulatoryInformation/Legislation/FederalFoodDrugandCosmeticActFDCAct/FDCActChapterVDrugsandDevices/

[154] FDA, "Definition of Primary Mode of Action of a Combination Product", FDA website, accessed December 31, 2015, http://www.fda.gov/ohrms/dockets/98fr/05-16527.htm

[155] U.S. Congress, "PUBLIC HEALTH SERVICE ACT", U.S. House of Representatives website, accessed December 31, 2015, https://legcounsel.house.gov/Comps/PHSA-merged.pdf

[156] FDA, "Combination Products", FDA website, accessed December 31, 2015, http://www.fda.gov/CombinationProducts/

[157] Rodgers, Dirk, "Aggregation –> Chargeback Accuracy –> ROI", RxTrace, October 19, 2015, https://www.rxtrace.com/2015/10/aggregation-chargeback-accuracy-roi.html/

[158] HDMA, HDMA website, accessed December 31, 2015, http://www.hdmanet.org/

[159] Rodgers, Dirk, "The Aggregation Hoax and PIA", RxTrace, June 9, 2014, https://www.rxtrace.com/2014/06/the-aggregation-hoax-and-pia.html/

[160] HDMA, "86th Edition HDMA Factbook: The Facts, Figures and Trends in Healthcare (2015-2016)", HDMA website, accessed December 31, 2015, http://www.hdmanet.org/publications/86th-edition-hdma-factbook

[161] Rodgers, Dirk, "Wholesaler Confusion Over DSCSA Aggregation Explained", RxTrace, August 17, 2015, https://www.rxtrace.com/2015/08/wholesaler-confusion-over-dscsa-aggregation-explained.html/

[162] The Drug Channels Institute, website, accessed December 31, 2015, http://drugchannelsinstitute.com/

[163] Fein, Adam J., "2015-16 ECONOMIC REPORT ON PHARMACEUTICAL WHOLESALERS AND SPECIALTY DISTRIBUTORS", The Drug Channels Institute, September, 2015, http://drugchannelsinstitute.com/products/industry_report/wholesale/

[164] Basta, Nick, "Revenue Leakage in Biopharma Distribution

Channels Is $11 Billion Annually, Says IDC Health Insights",
Pharmaceutical Commerce, February 25, 2010,
http://pharmaceuticalcommerce.com/information_tech
nology?articleid=1924

[165] Newmark, Eric, "Pharmaceutical Revenue Leakage: Live
Chat Replay", IDC Insights website, accessed December
31, 2015, https://idc-community.com/health/life-
sciences/pharmaceutical-revenue-leakage-live-chat-
replay

[166] Rodgers, Dirk, "Is Your Drug Exempt From The Federal
Drug Supply Chain Security Act?", RxTrace, April 7, 2014,
https://www.rxtrace.com/2014/04/is-your-drug-
exempt-from-the-federal-drug-supply-chain-security-
act.html/

[167] FDA, "Combination Products", FDA website, accessed
December 31, 2015,
http://www.fda.gov/CombinationProducts/

[168] Rodgers, Dirk, "Anatomy Of The National Drug Code",
RxTrace, January 3, 2012,
https://www.rxtrace.com/2012/01/anatomy-of-the-
national-drug-code.html/

[169] Rodgers, Dirk, "Should You Off-Load Your DSCSA
Obligations To Your Contract Partners?", RxTrace, October
6, 2014, https://www.rxtrace.com/2014/10/should-you-
off-load-your-dscsa-obligations-to-your-contract-
partners.html/

[170] Rodgers, Dirk, "Pharma Serialization: Going Totally Global
Soon", RxTrace, September 22, 2014,
https://www.rxtrace.com/2014/09/pharma-
serialization-going-totally-global-soon.html/

[171] Rodgers, Dirk, "When Will The DSCSA Ever Require
Investments In Aggregation?", RxTrace, February 23, 2015,
https://www.rxtrace.com/2015/02/when-will-the-dscsa-
ever-require-investments-in-aggregation.html/

[172] Rodgers, Dirk, "Pharma Aggregation: How Companies Are
Achieving Perfection Today", RxTrace, March 26, 2012,
https://www.rxtrace.com/2012/03/pharma-
aggregation-how-companies-are-achieving-perfection-
today.html/

[173] Rodgers, Dirk, "DQSA: Will U.S. Pharma Distributors
Mandate Aggregation Data In Phase 1?", RxTrace,
November 22, 2013,

https://www.rxtrace.com/2013/11/dqsa-will-u-s-pharma-distributors-mandate-aggregation-data-in-phase-1.html/

[174] Rodgers, Dirk, "Does The DQSA Require Manufacturers To Provide Aggregation Data? Survey Says…", RxTrace, February 10, 2014, https://www.rxtrace.com/2014/02/does-the-dqsa-require-manufacturers-to-provide-aggregation-data-survey-says.html/

[175] Rodgers, Dirk, "The Aggregation Hoax and PIA", RxTrace, June 9, 2014, https://www.rxtrace.com/2014/06/the-aggregation-hoax-and-pia.html/

[176] Rodgers, Dirk, "Interoperability And The DSCSA", RxTrace, February 9, 2015, https://www.rxtrace.com/2015/02/interoperability-and-the-dscsa.html/

[177] Rodgers, Dirk, "Pharma Aggregation: How Companies Are Achieving Perfection Today", RxTrace, March 26, 2012, https://www.rxtrace.com/2012/03/pharma-aggregation-how-companies-are-achieving-perfection-today.html/

[178] Rodgers, Dirk, "Is An ASN Really The Best Way to Pass Lot-Based DSCSA Transaction Data?", RxTrace, February 16, 2015, https://www.rxtrace.com/2015/02/is-an-asn-really-the-best-way-to-pass-lot-based-dscsa-transaction-data.html/

[179] Rodgers, Dirk, "HDMA Has Updated Their EDI ASN Guidance For DSCSA, Again", RxTrace, July 22, 2014, https://www.rxtrace.com/2014/07/hdma-has-updated-their-edi-asn-guidance-for-dscsa-again.html/

[180] GS1, "EPCIS", GS1 website, accessed December 30, 2015, http://www.gs1.org/epcis/epcis/latest

[181] Rodgers, Dirk, "Will GS1's EPCIS Be Used Widely For DSCSA Data Exchange?", RxTrace, October 13, 2014, https://www.rxtrace.com/2014/10/will-gs1s-epcis-be-used-widely-for-dscsa-data-exchange.html/

COUPON

Get a FREE three month ALL ACCESS subscription to RxTrace, where you will find much more content related to the DSCSA and all pharma serialization and tracing regulations around the world!

Simply send an email to **dirk@dirkrodgers.com** and ask for instructions.

Offer valid only where not prohibited by law. Offer valid only for new subscribers and only when available. RxTrace is a registered trademark of Dirk Rodgers Consulting, LLC, an Ohio corporation.

Made in the USA
San Bernardino, CA
15 March 2016